Heirloom Knitting

Happy Knitting!

Sharon Miller

Heirloom Knitting

Sharon Miller

The Shetland Times Ltd.,
Lerwick.
2002

Heirloom Knitting

ISBN 978 1 898852 75 9

First published by The Shetland Times Ltd., 2002.
Reprinted 2004, 2007, 2008.

British Library Cataloguing-in-Publication Data
A catalogue record for this book
is available from the British Library.

Printed and published by
The Shetland Times Ltd.,
Gremista, Lerwick,
Shetland, ZE1 OPX.

For Michael, with love and thanks.

Contents

Foreword

Knitting is a personal thing. Every knitter has a different tension, style and preference, but common to all who knit for pleasure is the satisfaction that can be taken from a beautiful hand-knitted piece. Few things present this more than Shetland lace knitting, widely regarded as one of the best forms of the craft to have evolved. Once mastered, the hum-drum pick up and put down sessions of knitting, together with the careful selection and working of patterns, have an almost miraculous ending; never fully apparent until the knitting is completely finished by a process called *dressing**. Then comes the reward. The first, proper view of the gossamer-like structure of geometric lacy design gives such a sense of achievement, it makes Shetland lace knitting almost addictive. Deservedly, the finest examples of Shetland lace are in museums, and pieces like the Ring Shawls, rightly command prices in hundreds of pounds, a reflection of the time and skill needed to make them.

With the patterns in this book, any moderately experienced knitter can learn to create heirlooms, which if properly cared for, will last through generations. Don't be daunted by the apparent complexity of Shetland lace knitting, the majority of the patterns aren't too involved when looked at row by row. Simple mathematics and patient chart following are all that's necessary – anyone who has done counted cross-stitch sewing and who has basic knitting skills can knit Shetland lace.

The knitting charts present the lace patterns in an easy to read and do form. They eliminate the mistakes that occur in written patterns due to typographical errors. Many of these charts record patterns no longer available in books, or which have never been recorded. I have graded the patterns and sample projects according to levels of experience to help; otherwise the possible combinations are entirely the knitter's choice.

This is the book I wanted when I started Shetland lace knitting. It is intended as a resource. It gives a brief history, useful help and a comprehensive collection of patterns – many for the first time. There is endless scope for variation and I explain how any of the patterns can be experimented with to produce something more valued because of its uniqueness. This continues another tradition in Shetland lace knitting, where knitters developed their own ways of working patterns.

Finally, although Shetland lace is traditionally made using the finest ply wools which best display its airy grace; these patterns could be made in almost any yarn, so I hope that they will inspire anyone who enjoys lace knitting.

*Single words or phrases in italics in the text are explained in the "Glossary".

A Shetland Lace Sampler showing some of the easier patterns.

Acknowledgments

The author dedicates this book to her family especially, whose unfailing support and enthusiasm made this book possible.

She would also like particularly to thank her friends for their encouragement and the following for their help with research:

Museum and Archives Section, Department of Education & Community Services, Lerwick, Shetland.
Shetland Textile Museum.
American Museum in Bath.
National Museums of Scotland.
Jamieson and Smith, Shetland Wool Brokers Ltd.
Okehampton Library.

The Shetland Times Ltd and the author also wish to thank the following for permission to reproduce the following:

Photographs on pages 181 and 185: Mr Oliver Henry.
Sketch on page 25: Jamieson and Smith, Shetland Wool Brokers Ltd., Lerwick.
Museum prints on pages 3, 9, 11, 12, Knitting Advice, 109, 187 and 217: Museum and Archives Section, Department of Education & Community Services, Lerwick, Shetland.

Heirloom Knitting

Section One – Introduction

What is Shetland Lace?

Knitting, which can be simply defined as the construction of a fabric by using needles to loop yarn through loops of yarn, has traditionally been altered in three broadly distinct ways:

1. Changing the **texture** of the stitches – e.g. Aran knitting;
2. Changing the **colour** of the stitches – e.g. Fair Isle knitting;
3. Changing the **structure** or 'openness' of the stitches – e.g. Shetland lace knitting.

As a working definition for today, Shetland lace is hand-knitted lace which uses the traditional, "open" lace patterns and yarn of the Shetland Islands. Predominantly, the development of Shetland lace depended on the strength and quality of the finer wool of the Shetland sheep. This was hand plucked from around the neck, and its exceptionally soft and long *staple* meant that it could be spun into one of the very best and finest woollen yarns available – perfectly suited for the delicate lace knitting that developed in Shetland in the nineteenth century.

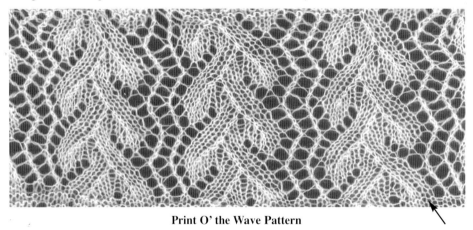

Print O' the Wave Pattern

The typical knitting actions for Shetland lace couldn't be simpler: cast on and off, slip 1, make 1 or 2, knit 1, knit 2 or 3 together. Generally, there's no knitting into the backs of stitches or making stitch clusters, as the yarn used is normally so fine that these would not display well. The very plainness of the garter stitch background that the lace patterns are usually worked on doesn't mar their beauty. Indeed, using garter stitch gives an essential degree of rigidity to some patterns worked with fine yarns – the fabric is less inclined to "roll in", or "pull together", which it would if it were entirely stocking stitched. (Although stocking stitch is used – e.g. with the Print O' the Wave pattern shown above – it has a tendency to overstretch lengthways unless it is carefully dressed*.)

The lace patterns themselves are mathematically simple, nearly always involving pairs of *increases* and *decreases*. This doesn't affect the overall number of stitches in a row, for every time you make 1, you decrease by 1; usually with the next stitch action. But pretty effects are obtained by delaying decreases, as can be seen in the Print O' the Wave pattern, where most of the knit stitches are slanted (see arrow). This effect, for example, is caused by first making each of the pattern row increases but then delaying its paired decrease for two stitches – causing the knit stitches in between to "lean".

---

*When using yarns thicker than a classic 4 ply – Shetland Lace-weight 2 ply, it might well be advisable to use stocking stitch to best display the pattern – see "Stitch Advice".

Compare Chequered Acre and Shetland Fir Cone. These share the same underlying placing of the increases (holes, or properly, *eyelets*) in the pattern; but in Chequered Acre, the decreases are worked immediately, in Shetland Fir Cone they are delayed, arching stitches in that pattern.

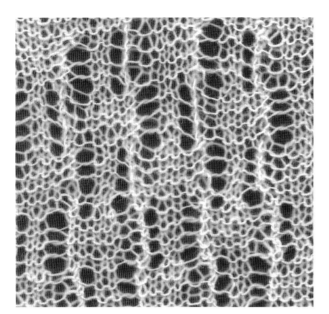

Chequered Acre Pattern

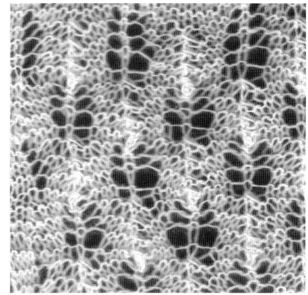

Shetland Fir Cone Pattern

Apart from patterns like Shetland Fir Cone and the famous Old Shell which are formed using these *delayed decreases*, the patterns in Shetland lace are chiefly made by consecutively worked pairs of increases and decreases in *plain knitting*. In Shetland lace, these create characteristically regular geometric shapes, e.g. isosceles triangles, kites (diamond shapes) and hexagons.

Now in the Shetland Museum, Lerwick, this triangular shawl is a very early example of Shetland lace and is thought to have been made as a christening shawl for John Bruce of Sumburgh in June, 1837. The vertical bars placed on the border mark a panel of repeating pattern.

Shetland lace today usually means very finely knitted shawls, stoles and extra special baby wear such as christening dresses, which are still customarily made in the traditional way; using three main design elements – centres, borders and edgings. These are explained more fully later in the book* but it's useful to consider how the border – the most intricate part from a design point of view – is constructed. As can be seen from John Bruce's christening shawl, the border is made up of recurring vertical panels of pattern, laid side by side. This is typical in Shetland lace patterns. Once you have composed the panel layout for c.30 – 60 stitches, you simply repeat the groups of stitches for a row, then work outwards (or inwards) on them, row by row. As easily demonstrated by this shawl, the individual lace patterns spring out symmetrically from a point in the panel to make "V" based triangular shapes, before again returning to that point with inverted "V" shapes. Even in the later and most elaborately patterned Shetland lace shawls, this working from or to fixed points is a constant.

While considering design, it is interesting to note that one of the most admired forms of Shetland lace, the Ring Shawl, seems to bear a direct relationship to the typical Indian or "Paisley" woven shawl of the time, also then highly fashionable. Both customarily have plainer centres, intricate borders of larger pattern elements, fancy fringes/edgings; and some of the shapes and names are common – the Tree of Life, its "Sprouting Seed" and feathery shapes (see the shawl's borders shown on pages 164 and 187).

Now, a word about terminology, which could prove useful in identifying how patterns are made. There is a subtle distinction between **lace knitting** and **knitted lace**. When looking at a piece of knitting, if the threads in the open work (holes) are in pairs twisted round each other, the design has been knitted with alternating *pattern and plain* rows – **lace knitting**. If, on the other hand, the single threads are straight and untwisted, then the design is pattern every row – **knitted lace**. For example, compare Rose Lace with Rose Diamond Lace. The only difference between the two patterns is that Rose Lace is *plain knitted* every other row. This not only makes it twice as big, but the angles on the triangles become more acute as well.

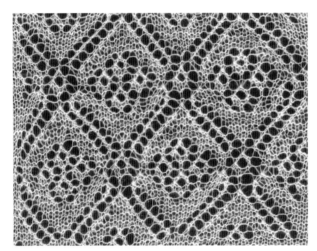

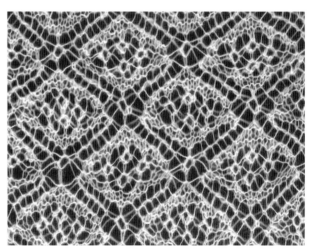

Rose Lace – lace knitting   **Rose Diamond Lace – knitted lace**

I must mention that there is a question about whether the term "Shetland lace" is accurate or not. It is held by some authorities that lace cannot be made by knitting – that technically this type of knitting is "open-work"; but I accept an early and long standing definition of lace that co-dates with the sixteenth century initial flowering of this craft: "A delicate, open-work fabric of linen, cotton, silk, woollen, or metal threads, usually with inwrought or applied patterns" (Oxford English Dictionary). This encompasses Shetland lace because generally, it has openwork patterns made by "yarn over" eyelets of paired increases and decreases on a plain knitted, solid *ground*. Shetland lace knitting in its simpler forms could be seen as a photographic negative, or "black-on-white" version of lace. More archetypal laces have the (usually white) threads contrasting against a (black) background. Even using this stricter white-on-black definition, there are very complex knitted lace patterns, such as Rose Diamond Lace pictured above, or the fine *Unst laces* where this applies – the delicate patterns are made by solid threads against an open background. This for me, shows how Shetland lace can be classed a true lace.

*See "A Note on the Patterns," and "Shetland Shawls and Stoles".

It could well be argued that there are actually very few Shetland lace patterns at all – most of the patterns were worked in other countries e.g. Russia, The Azores and Spain, in their own traditions of fine white lace knitting – I do not intend to explore this, though I would tentatively propose that a characteristic that distinguishes the best Shetland lace from others is the high degree of geometric planning in the use of motifs in the lace pattern composition. Without a doubt, there was a large cross-cultural practice of patterns and techniques, especially in Europe, and it would be very hard for a community such as Shetland placed at one of the main thoroughfares of trade from earliest times on, not to reflect this. What must be celebrated without question is the artistic status the Shetlanders achieved with this knitting. So much so, that whenever Shetland lace is commonly referred to, it is the highly evolved, gossamer-fine knitting of intricate design that comes to mind. I therefore shall use the term Shetland lace for this book.

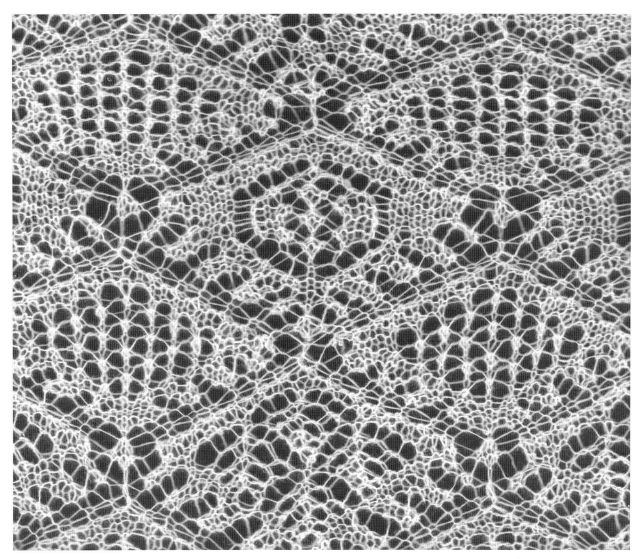

One of the complex border designs thought to have been initially worked on the northern-most of the Shetland Islands, Unst; home of some of the most delicate lace knitting in the nineteenth century.

The Shetland Islands (other names are Zetland, Ultima Thule ancient, or Hjaltland) are off the North East coast of Scotland, and lie in the path of the warming North Atlantic Current, which gives them relatively milder but very windy weather. The islands are between latitudes 59°30' and 61 degrees North and so are subject to short winter days of roughly six hours light; but in summer have almost continuous daylight – the "simmer dim".

There are around a hundred separate islands, only about a dozen of which are inhabited today. The islands are treeless and rocky and have boggy, poorish soil. This has led Shetlanders to depend on fishing, farming and trade. Lerwick is the capital and was the main centre for the Shetland lace trade.

Extract from *A Guide To Shetland* 1871, by Robert Cowie:

The open lace knitting, for which the islands are now famed, was never heard of until a very recent period; and I have much pleasure in giving an account of its origin, kindly furnished by an accomplished lady of Lerwick, who is personally acquainted with all the circumstances.

The late Samuel Laing, Esq., of Papdale, when a candidate for the representation of the County in 1833, was while in Lerwick the guest of the late Mrs Charles Ogilvy, to whose infant son Miss Laing afterwards sent a present of a beautiful christening cap, knitted by herself of thread such as is used in the manufacture of the celebrated Lille stockings. This cap was much admired, and a lady related to the family succeeded in making an exact copy of it. While doing so, it occurred to her that fine woollen mitts knitted in a similar style would look well; and she accordingly made a pair, and subsequently a very handsome invalid cap for a gentleman. This was in 1837, when the late Mr Frederick Dundas first became MP for the county. Having received the cap as a present, the honourable gentleman showed it to his landlady in Lerwick, requesting her to try to induce some of her young acquaintances to imitate it in shawls. This she did, but with little result.

In 1839 Mr Edward Standen of Oxford, while travelling through the islands, saw a shawl which the above-mentioned lady was knitting, and on his return to Lerwick he also mentioned the subject to the person with whom he lodged, urging her to advise young women to knit shawls of that description. Mr Standen, who was extensively engaged in the hosiery trade himself, now succeeded in giving fresh impetus to the fine knitting of Shetland, and, by introducing the goods into the London market, was the means of creating what had been for a few years previously followed as a pastime for a few amateurs into an important branch of industry, affording employment to a large proportion of the female population of the islands.

The articles first sent to market appear to have been somewhat rudely executed, having been knitted on wooden pins. However, steel wires were soon introduced and year by year the manufacture gradually improved, until it reached its present perfection. Many of the peasant girls display great artistic talent in the invention and arrangement of patterns, which are formed, as they express it, 'out of their own heads'.

The manufacture of fine Shetland shawls thus became common about 1840, but it was not till five years afterwards that the demand for them became very great. About 1850 the shawls were to some extent superseded in the markets by veils, in which a large trade was soon carried on. More recently neckties and various other fancy articles have been produced by the neat-fingered knitters of Zetland. The amount sold is said to yield £10,000 to £12,000 yearly. Wool from the native sheep has of late years become rather scarce, and therefore the importation of Pyrenean wool, mohair, etc., has been found necessary.

Historical Background

As this is primarily a pattern collection and explanatory workbook, I shall only give an outline of the main known facts regarding the history of Shetland lace; for those interested in learning more, I indicate the reference books that give more information in the Bibliography.

Shetland lace is inseparably linked to the history of the Shetlanders' crofting lifestyle and native sheep. The unprotected position of the Shetland Islands, on the North Western reaches of Europe, has led to the natural selection and breeding of some of the hardiest of sheep, providing an invaluable resource of wool, meat and leather. By circa 800 AD when the Vikings arrived, the sheep were so numerous the Vikings called one of the islands, "Fair Isle" – Isle of Sheep.

The economy of Shetland always depended on three broadly entwined activities – fishing, trade and farming (or crofting[1] from the 1700s onwards), and the variable income gained from these needed to be supplemented by as many sources as possible. Knitting everyday items of clothing became a source of income, from perhaps as early as the 1300s. By the end of the nineteenth century, the womenfolk knitted whenever possible as they went about their daily chores and two distinct traditions of local knitting developed, the coloured, mosaic-like patterns such as Fair Isle knitting and the delicate lacy knitting – usually in one colour, now known as Shetland lace.

Knitting is an activity that can be done by one person, from fleece to finished article, and has been an important means of clothing production for centuries. The craft's very portability was a significant advantage, as knitting is something that can be done alongside other duties.

In Shetland, knitting equipment was simply needles or "wires" (an old term still used there) and spun wool. It was a source of pride that the patterns, learnt at a mother's knee* or worked out from an example, were retained in the knitter's head. The knitting itself could be rolled and secured by safety pins or hooks to the knitter's belt. The belt also usually housed a *knitting sheath* or *whisk*; an attachment that by freeing up one of the hands, greatly improved knitting speed. Once equipped, knitting could be done whilst walking, tending livestock or supervising children.

By the 1500s, there was a thriving Shetland industry of knitted hose, caps and gloves produced for trade – usually with the Dutch and Hansiatic fishing fleets. Here, the indigenous fineness and softness of the local wool was a decided advantage and one that quickly attracted an economic premium. By the 1800s, fine Unst stockings were more expensive than others, selling for as much as 30 shillings as against 5d for the cheapest hose. Throughout the 1700s, knitted hose was one of the main items for trade and barter, but as noted by Arthur Edmondston of Unst in 1809, this trade was badly affected by the Napoleonic Wars.

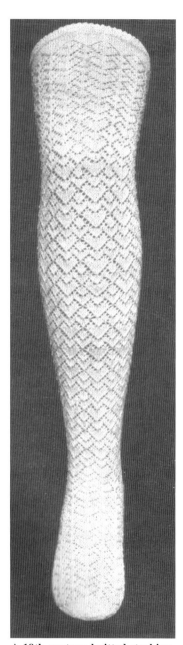

A 19th century knitted stocking, similar to those knitted in Shetland.

---

*girls started to learn to knit patterns by knitting the alternate plain rows between the patterned ones their mothers worked.

[1] Crofting - The farming of a small enclosed area of arable rented land, together with shared farming of the more productive strips – "riggs" of land, each croft taking a turn to grow crops.

The Napoleonic wars and their disastrous effects on the knitting trade coincided with a period of improvements in frame-knitting that meant that English centres such as Leicester, were able to fill their local markets with cheaper knitted everyday items. To compound the problem, a period of bad harvests and poor returns from fishing was experienced during the 1820s to1840s; this led many of the local gentry to be genuinely concerned as to how the Shetland economy could be sustained. Although there is debate about whom and when, there seems no doubt that some encouragement towards the knitting of fashionable lace was given by visitors and traders in the early 1830s, (see extract from Robert Cowie). Certainly, other kindly intentioned people such as Mrs Ogilvy of Lerwick and Eliza Edmondson of Unst, helped spur the development of Shetland lace. At this time, knitting as a pastime for ladies was in vogue and the first knitting manuals were produced with aristocratic patronage, additionally feeding the demand for novel knitting designs. Among the middle classes "the new knitting stitches" (Mrs Gaskell, "Cranford" 1851-53, but writing of a slightly earlier period) were much discussed, and it seems more than probable that similar exchanges of pattern could have taken place in Shetland. If the crofter knitters couldn't read, they were so practised that they could soon copy a pattern, and were so skilled, they were quick to develop on any patterns they saw. Local merchants and traders were equally fast in seeing business possibilities in this exquisite, novel knitwear and promoted it in London and on trade-stands abroad. Although knitters continued knitting when out and about, the very finest Shetland lace knitting was more suited as an indoor winter activity, when harsh weather and the lack of daylight at that latitude precluded much outside work. A knitter might customarily have two pieces of knitting on the go, an everyday item – say, family socks for "outside" knitting when walking home with a kishie (a basket carried on the back) of peat; and an "indoors" lace piece intended for sale or trade, knitted by the light from an oil lamp and the open fire.

Dressing shawls in a courtyard at Clairmont Place, Lerwick in the 1900s. It appears that several shawls are being stretched at a time on each frame. In the background Hap and shaded Crepe shawls are being dressed. White and coloured lace shawls are in the foreground. After being washed, shawls were threaded onto cotton through their edgings' points and stretched onto a pegged frame. This was skilled work and the dressers offered purchasers an expert laundry service by return of post.

In Queen Victoria's reign (1837 – 1901) the lace knitting of the Shetland Isles, particularly from the northern-most Isle of Unst where the wool was finest, was at its zenith. Coupled to the development of regular steamer transport to and from Shetland in 1836 and the development of a national postal service in 1840, the popularity and demand for Shetland lace was additionally encouraged by two important factors.

The first was the acclaim of presents of lace hosiery and shawls to the Royal Family that resulted in regular orders from Royalty and the nobility. (Victoria herself was a knitter who could appreciate the skill required for the lace.) Secondly, the much admired displays at competitions and stands arranged by entrepreneurial merchants; notably at the enormously influential Great Exhibition of 1851. This was held at The Crystal Palace, London, as a showcase for the best of everything the world could produce. Edward Standen (the merchant referred to in Cowie's extract) exhibited an ivory and madder striped Shetland wedding veil on his stand. Frocks, socks, kneecaps, stockings, leggings, nightcaps, wigs (!) were also offered in "machine spun wool and silk". Additionally, Shetland shawls in three categories: **"hap"**, an everyday 2 ply colour banded shawl with a plain knitted centre and usually Old Shell patterned borders (and one of few articles that was knitted for the Shetlanders' own use); **"crepe"**, a 1 ply single colour luxury version of the Hap; and **"lace"** the intricately lacy 1 ply shawl. One of the most prized of Shetland exports was to become known as the "Ring Shawl", a finely spun, elaborately patterned lace shawl up to 72 inches square yet weighing only 2 or 3 ounces*, so fine that it could be pulled through a wedding ring.

For approximately the next fifty years, high fashion had an honoured place for Shetland lace. Shawls, veils, *clouds*, neck-scarves, gloves, handkerchiefs, stoles, cloaks, trains and stockings were exported as well as everyday items such as underclothing and tray cloths. This had a substantial economic effect on the local population; many crofts in times of hardship relied almost entirely on the knitted lace trade for their family's survival and did their best to increase the poor financial return from even this type of knitting by selling direct to visitors instead of through agents. Today, a fine hand spun Ring Shawl can be valued at £2,500 – having taken well over 600 hours to knit and many more to have spun. It is certain that the original Shetland lace knitters were never adequately rewarded for their work – a very industrious lace knitter could hope for only 6 shillings per week in 1872.

Shetland Lace

> "...but no Knitting exceeds in beauty of texture that made in Shetland at Unst. The wool from which this is made is obtained from sheep which resemble those in the mountains of Thibet, and is of three kinds, that from the "Mourat" a brown coloured sheep, being the most valued, that from the "Shulah," a grey sheep, ranking next, and the white and black varieties being the least esteemed. The finest wool is taken from the neck of the living animal, and it is spun and prepared by the natives, and Knitted in warm shawls two yards square, and yet so light and fine, that they are easily passed through a wedding ring...The sheep producing it are of small size, and run wild all the year over the hills until – the ground being covered with snow – they descend to the sea shore and feed on weed. The staple of these sheep is longer than that of the Merino, and their skins are much employed as Furs. The breed goes by the name of Beaver Sheep, and the wool produced is of various colours, viz., black, brown, grey, and white."

The Dictionary of Needlework, 1882.

* approx. 180cm weighing 80g.

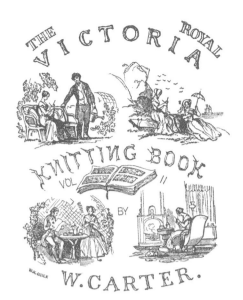

The above Frontispiece is from an early knitting book for "the approbation of Ladies", 1840, named in honour of the new Queen.

The illustration shows two comforters (scarves), gaiters(leg wear) and a cut fringe. Knitting was at this point, an elegant and genteel pastime for the leisured classes.

Right up until the Second World War, it was still comparatively common for a Shetland knitter to produce, spin and knit her own wool, both for the hap shawls where fractions of ounces of contrasting shades of wool were matched and spun; and for the finest "gossamer" lace – the yarn then made was much finer than that commercially available now, see Section Four.

The knitter typically had cared for the sheep since birth and in summer time, her work included "caa-ing" the sheep into the "krø" (rounding up the sheep into an enclosure) where she hand plucked or "rooed" their silkiest wool from behind their ears and from around the neck. This was slower than shearing but ensured the maximum length of staple (fibre of wool) because it was pulled or drawn out, not cut. Rooing was a summer activity, when the fleece is naturally being shed and is hanging off the sheep, so the process is painless but time-consuming.

A visitor, writing in the late 1930s, recorded that from the collected fleece, the spinner picked out the twigs, dirt and so on, before lightly dressing the wool mass in seal oil before a large fire. In this warm atmosphere, wool and oil were thoroughly mixed before spinning could begin.

To prepare for spinning into lace *worsted*, the wool was placed on *hand cards* and the hairs gently teased and separated (or the wool mass was combed – again by hand or with a metal comb), until the finished rourers (rolls of wool – "rolags" English) were ready to be spun. Once two pirns (bobbins) had been separately spun, these were doubled together (plied) to form an ultra-fine 2 ply that was wound into *hanks* on a wool winder called a reel ("niddy-noddy"). This fine yarn was measured in "cuts". Each full turn of the reel wound about 2 *yards* of wool, termed a "thread"; a hundred turns or threads made a "cut". Only then was the oil washed out, – or, if destined for the finest gossamer knitting, still left in and the yarn knitted up (the oil giving essential extra strength). This was work only for expert spinners, usually the older women, who had acquired the necessary skill over years of practice. Even so, Mrs Edmondston wrote in 1861, that only a few were capable of spinning 9,000 yards from an ounce of wool – this being made into a 3 ply of 3,000 yards. As the century drew to a close, handspinning slowly began to decline, as silk, black mohair and commercially produced Scotch worsted were more regularly imported for lace knitting, as fashion and economics demanded.

Rooing at the Lee krø, near Setter, in the 1890s. The man with a kishie (basket) of food for the women is Charles Ratter of Pund, Setter.

Three of the Sutherland family (probably photographed at the end of the 19ᵗʰ century – or early 20ᵗʰ century) who were renowned for making and knitting some of the finest Shetland yarn and knitted lace, including some for Royal presentations. From left to right, they are pictured carding rolls of wool with hand cards, spinning wool (with what appears to be an upright Highland spinning wheel) and knitting fine Shetland lace.

Popularity for anything fashionable seems to last at most two generations – about fifty years; and by the 1900s, the fashion for ladies recreational knitting and for the knitted lace-wear itself was increasingly replaced by one for crochet and filet crochet, as popularised by contemporary ladies magazines. The demise of the crinoline and the bustle saw the relegation of the use of shawls to invalid and baby wear. Then, this diminishing market for hand knitted lace was further badly affected by the necessary economies of the First World War.

By the 1920s, Shetland lace knitting as a widespread practice began to die out, and Fair Isle knitting – again, with royal patronage triggered by initial Shetland presentations – went on the upswing. The young and dashing Prince of Wales (later the Duke of Windsor) was informally portrayed by Sir Henry Lander wearing a Fair Isle pullover in the early 1920s. Soon, Fair Isle was the mainstay of the Shetland hand knitting trade, as it became the fashion for casual dress, particularly suited for the latest pastimes of golf and hiking.

By the 1950s, Shetland lace was recognised as an expert craft form much admired, but little practiced and less recorded. James Norbury (an influential post-war knitter designer who had his own television programme) was one of the first to record some Shetland lace patterns and he too, saw the advantages in presenting them in charted form. Others, using the more established conventions of writing knitting patterns, have published books and pattern pamphlets, which both have satisfied and perplexed the enthusiast knitter. When one has waded

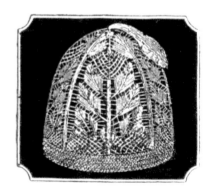

A Victorian nightcap.

through the pages of printed line-by-line instructions and been nonplussed by the growing pattern's inaccuracies due to first losing one's place and then by printing errors that seem to have unavoidably crept in, it is easy to see why so many good knitters have been discouraged from lace knitting as "too difficult". However and despite this, Shetland lace today continues to be highly regarded as a classic form of knitting and has a dedicated world-wide interest. Shetland lace shawls are especially appreciated and have always remained in demand; in 1999, the Queen commissioned one to be presented to the Empress of Japan and they are widely treasured for christening and weddings. Now, with the adoption of much-simpler-to-use knitting charts, Shetland lace is experiencing something of a revival.

A knitted hood "worn as a Bedouin", from *The Young Ladies Journal*, Vol. 3, 1873. This is representative of other two colour striped Shetland lace. I have seen a madder and white striped wedding veil similar to this. I believe these to be knitted horizontally, in pattern bands of alternating colour; judging from the undulations in the stripe. Note the fancy fringed edging then fashionable.

Baby's Open Knit Spencer.

"This exquisite little spencer is knitted in shell and feather pattern, with white Shetland wool, of which 2 ozs. will be required and a pair of No. 13 bone knitting needles. The spencer is not shaped, but being fine work and an open stitch, it fits any figure to perfection."

An 1880s knitting pattern for a spencer – a short overcoat named after the Spencer family.

Pattern Names

It is generally held by those who collect knitting patterns that the linking of names to patterns is a nightmare. Commonly, there are local names for patterns made around the world, and so the same pattern can easily turn up with at least two different names. Throughout the work for this book I have found a similar degree of confusion over the naming of Shetland lace knitting patterns. One reference calls Spider Lace by the name Bird's Eye; another calls it Lace Holes; yet another source gives the Lace Holes pattern the name Dewdrops. Similarly, Old Spanish Lace is the name I have found given to two different patterns – Madeira Wave and Madeira Cascade. The fern motif has also been variously named as Small Tree, Madeira, Leaf and Fan. A Fern Stitch pattern didn't result in the fern motif expected but in a pattern well known in collections as Candlelight.

Although it seems generally agreed among knitting experts that Shetland lace pattern names originate from naturally occurring forms there is still confusion here. One evocatively describes Old Shell as Old Shale, deriving from the tracks left by the sea on a pebbled shore; others affirm the name to be Old Shell – the native dialect being misunderstood by the other expert as Old Shale.

These problems probably arise from the oral based culture of Shetland and the skill of the knitters themselves, who easily learnt patterns from watching others or by working them out from knitted pieces – as well as freely creating patterns themselves. There was no need to have the patterns in written form and so unfortunately for us, the certainty of original names, if there ever were any, seems not to exist from this source. The earliest knitting manuals from the 1830s (e.g. Mrs Gaugain, Mrs Beeton), gave directions and "receipts" for knitting Shetland shawls but again, as common at that time, no actual pattern names were recorded.

A visitor at the end of the 1800s stayed with the Sutherland* family and was probably one of the first to note down some of the Shetland lace patterns that she saw being knitted and she did record names for them. Interestingly, these reflect the romantic names of knitting patterns of the time – Queen's Lace, Irish Lace, Coburg Lace – rather than names from nature. This could indicate the continuing cross-fertilisation of European patterns with the Shetland Islands, which was always an important link in the chain of Western mercantile trade.

As far as possible, I have given the most consistently used names of the patterns. I note in the text accompanying the pattern, the alternatives that I have found. Where patterns had no names recorded at the time of their collection, I have tried to identify the main known motifs in their design and named them accordingly – simply for the sake of expediency. Where I believe I have made a new pattern (such as Field of Flowers) or created a variation, I will say so in the text. All patterns have arisen from experiment. Feather and Fan is derived from Old Shell; Leaf Pattern from Horseshoe Pattern; and as a final thought, it's interesting to wonder at what point a variation becomes an accepted new pattern in its own right.

* The Shetland Museum has an example of a Mrs Sutherland's Lace Edging, which I have re-created on page 172. She may be one of the ladies shown on page 12.

Knitting & Knitting Charts

Knitting charts have been off-putting to most British and American knitters. They have not been in our tradition and so we have come to think of them as alien or "too difficult to follow". A confession, as recently as about a year ago, I felt the same. When faced by a dauntingly long British knitting pattern of row-by-row written instructions, I would take a deep breath and convert it to a personal version of abbreviations, e.g. T = K2 tog., 3 = K.3., O = M.1., in an effort to make them manageable. Then, while looking at an old European book of charted knitting patterns, all fell into place. It's so much easier to follow a chart and once having the experience, I re-examined foreign charts – German and Japanese – and I found that I could now follow those. So, regardless of language, knitting designs from around the world were readily available.

As an amazing bonus, lace knitting, particularly Shetland lace knitting – my long time enthusiasm, became about ten times easier. To start with, I converted existing published pages of instructions into chart form and found they were very representational. They had visual clarity. No more wondering where I was in a long paragraph of "k.2 tog., m.1, k.3, m.1, k.2 tog…" there it was –＼O ●●● O／ I still write them this way off-grid (in pattern notes to myself) but charting them on a ten square grid with one square usually equalling a stitch – as with the patterns in this book – gives bearings. Better still, each pattern row's information now has a visible relationship to pattern rows above and below and the knitting in hand. No need for row counters or paper clips marking the page; a quick glance from chart to knitting shows where I am.

Charting lace knitting patterns makes their original construction much more understandable, so opening up endless possibilities of variation. When you see a charted motif such as the Tree of Life, you can see how it could also be moved, enlarged, substituted or modified. This could never be apparent from the written pattern – even if you are certain it was correctly presented. Another bonus from using symbols is that a charted pattern is much less likely to contain mistakes. No more the stark horror of finding out that five intricate rows of four hundred stitches before, there had been a mistake in the text – and then you had to try to figure out where that applied to your knitting. Despite extensive checking, I can't say there are no mistakes (I apologise just in case), but charting makes mistakes both less likely and more obvious. If I have given a seven in a chart line when there are only six squares, without any accompanying text saying why, get suspicious!

All these advantages are there for any knitter willing to try. Thanks to the recent success of counted cross-stitch sewing, many people are accustomed to reading needlework charts. It's only a small step to translate this skill on to knitting charts. I have tried to keep my chart symbols very simple and representational. As far as possible, they are current knitting chart symbols used world-wide today, though I have favoured symbols that represent the final stitch result: e.g. O (large circle) = "make a stitch" – which gives a hole in the knitting;＼ or ／(back or forward slash) = "knit two stitches together" – which creates a slant in the knitting – the direction of the slash indicates the direction the slanted stitches will lie.

If you really can't work from a chart, it is possible to convert these charts back into conventionally written patterns. But have a look at the easier level charts first if you are not already a confident chart knitter; read the knitting advice and the pattern notes through from the beginning. I've tried to make this book as user friendly as possible and hope that it will help you to appreciate Shetland lace knitting and encourage you to create your own heirlooms. If nothing else, you will find a new insight and respect for lace knitters when next you look at their exhibits in museums.

Heirloom Knitting

Section Two – Knitting Advice

Mrs Petrie and her daughters knitting. The first and second knitters are knitting lace – the first, a stole with a Madeira and Diamond patterned centre – I know this from another photograph taken at exactly the same time, which shows the knitting better. The third knitter is making a coloured Hap shawl and the last is knitting a Fair Isle garment. This photograph is from the 1900s and is now in the Shetland Museum's collection.

Knitting Experience

Although this is not a manual for absolute beginners to knitting, primarily being a collection of Shetland lace knitting patterns, it is designed to be a guide for those who wish to develop or refine their basic knitting skills. If you are a novice knitter with a good knitting reference book to hand, you should be able to work through this book. Obviously, knitters with more experience can select any pattern and should find the "Projects Section" an inspiration for their own work. More skilled knitters will find the collected patterns a resource, and will be interested in seeing how I have dealt with some common design problems in the "Projects", etc.

So, to give new knitters a structure to work through I have categorised the patterns into approximate levels of experience and some of the patterns – up to level * * * * – I have called teaching patterns, because I have used these to explain things it's necessary to understand before progressing with that level. As well as outlining the classified experience levels, I will also give a suggested plan – "Working Through this Book" – to help those who may need it.

Level * * knitters are the starters in knitting and must be able to do these basics:

knit and purl; slip stitch; cast on; cast off; make an *"over"* – an extra stitch by bringing the wool forward; knit two stitches together; be able to knit garter stitch and stocking stitch.

Ideally, they would have previously followed an uncomplicated, standard knitting pattern (with written directions) in a classic double knitting yarn with appropriate needles. The patterns for this level alternate *patterned rows* (the odd rows) with *plain rows* (the even rows).

Take some time and read all of the "Knitting Advice" section right through. **The teaching patterns for this level are given in "How to Read a Chart" and the Brand Iron Edging. Additional advice is with the Field of Flowers and Old Shell Patterns.**

Level * * * knitters should know the above, they should also be able to do the following:

slip 1, knit 2 together, pass slipped stitch over, ("s.1, k.2 tog., p.s.s.o.") – this is termed a *double decrease* because it disposes of two stitches. The pattern rows are still pattern-every-other-row but are slightly larger and more complex.

These knitters should have tried knitting with classic 4 ply (which broadly equates to a Shetland Lace-weight 2 ply) using needles ranging from 3 – 3.50mm (British 11 – 9, American 2 – 4). **The teaching patterns are Cat's Paw and Rippled Diamond Edging.**

Level * * * * knitters should be familiar with all the above and used to pattern-every-row patterns. Ideally, they should be confident knitting with classic 3 ply and 2 ply yarn (equating with Shetland 1 ply), on the finer size needles 3 – 2mm (British 11 – 14, American 2 – 00).

They would also have begun to understand how knitted lace is constructed and be reasonably happy to begin to experiment with the motifs in the "Design Library" by changing their size, spacing or creating half-motifs, Section Four helps with these points.

The teaching patterns for level * * * * are Cyprus Edging where *double increases* are explained **and Wave Edging** where the *Lacy Edge Stitch* is explained. By this stage, the patterns have become quite sizeable and complex. **Additionally, Shetland Bead Lace and Bead Diamond introduce the designs with patterned stitches on every row and are transitional teaching patterns between level * * * and level * * * *.**

Level * * * * * knitters are very confident and experienced, understand knitted lace construction and are willing to freely adapt and combine motifs from the "Design Library" and elsewhere for their own work.

Nowhere do I stress speed of knitting – I am not a fast knitter myself and anyway, the best lace knitting depends on accuracy of stitch formation and consistency of tension.

Conclusion

All knitting for pleasure should be pleasurable. One of the most pleasing things about knitting Shetland lace is its versatility; it can be adapted to suit your mood and experience. If you want an uncomplicated pastime while watching television, there is an appropriate pattern. If you are feeling creative and inspired, Shetland lace designing rises to the challenge and becomes as intriguing as a mystery, as you combine motifs and piece together the pattern elements to best effect. As an interesting aside, knitting has many benefits not immediately apparent. Many prisoners of war claimed that knitting kept them sane and surgeons and generals have knitted to improve both their concentration and their fine dexterity. You will certainly keep your maths up to scratch! Finally, whatever skill level of knitter you identify yourself as, we all may share a similar fascination with this relaxing craft.

N.B. Unfamiliar terms or words that are in italics will be explained in the "Glossary" at the end of this book. When I refer to **experienced knitters** in the book, I mean level * * * * knitters and above.

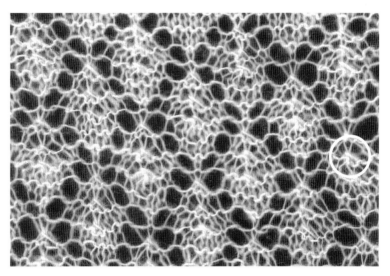

Tip: "Front" view of Leaf Lace – the double decrease's "lock stitch" (circled) slope upwards from right to left.

Compare with the photograph of Leaf Lace Pattern, page 65 (which is shown from the "back"). Although technically there is no "right" or "wrong" side with Shetland lace knitting when it is garter stitched every row, it can be helpful to be able to identify a front from a back when piecing together items of knitting. Generally speaking, odd rows are "front" rows.

Working Through this Book

Reserved Stitches
(Used Up As Edging Is Knitted)

Lace Pattern Panel

Direction of Knitting

Invisible Cast On

This page is for knitters who want a plan to work through the book to develop their experience. **I suggest buying in about 10 – 16 hanks of white Shetland Lace-weight 2 ply and 8 – 10 hanks of white Shetland Cobweb 1 ply; I can't be exact about quantities, because you have to have a stock in hand to work from.** Always have plenty of the same batch to knit large projects from – order in extra; any left over yarn can be used up in sample swatches, baby coats, scarves and so on.

Level * * Knitters

Read through the "Knitting Advice". Knit the scarf demonstrated in "How to Read a Chart" and then look at the patterns for this level to see if you understand them. Try the first project now. You might want to knit at least two of the baby jackets, one plain and one patterned.

Look at a knitting reference book for how to do the *double decrease* (▲) or ask a knitter friend to show you. Read through the patterns for level * * *. If you understand them, try "Project 2", you could just knit this in one colour if you prefer – it would be easier.

Level * * * Knitters

Check through the above first, then choose a centre pattern from this level to make a simple lace scarf – see diagram* left. Cast on enough stitches with the Knitting Cast On; this would be in the range of c. 70 – 85 stitches, using a Shetland Lace-weight 2 ply and British size 8/9 (3.5 – 4.0 mm) needles.

For example, working from the information with the **Trellis Diamond Pattern** you could cast on either 73 or 85 stitches. After casting on, knit 8 foundation plain knitting rows and then follow the pattern chart. When it is a length you like – about 36"/90cm, finish with a balancing line of motifs if need be, so the final placing of motifs matches the starting line, then do 8 plain knitting rows again to complete the *body*. Now, cast on the stitches for an edging, (I think the Doris Edging pairs well with the Trellis Diamond Pattern) and knit it round as explained in "Attaching an Edging", using up the *reserved stitches* from the body first. *Graft* the two ends of the edging together and dress the scarf. You should now be ready to look at the patterns in level * * * *. Look at the teaching patterns first then find one of the easier patterns in this level and try it. Then read Section Four and the "Projects". You should now be able to begin designing for yourself!

*I made a black Elaborated Print O' the Wave Stole this way – I do not advise beginners to knit very dark colours – it's hard on the eyes and should only be done in a good light.

Chart Symbols

| ● | knit stitch. |

| — | purl stitch. |

| ○ | "make 1", (yarn over – y.o.; an *increase*). To make 1 in garter stitch, bring the wool forward *purlwise** and take it over the top of the right hand (R.H.) needle and then knit the next stitch. On the next row, treat the strand you just made doing this, as a stitch. |

| ○○ | "make 2", as above (a *double increase*), but after bringing the wool forward purlwise*, wrap it once around the R.H. needle before taking it back to knit the next stitch. On the next row, treat the two strands created as two stitches. |

◻ or ◻ both mean "knit two together"; when you knit 2 together, you make a slanted *decrease* – the direction of slash shows the direction the slanted decrease lies. Usually this symbol pairs with a "make 1" (○ ∕) the ○"sits" on the slash. This only works well for Shetland 1 and 2 ply yarns. See "Stitch Advice" for how to treat this stitch with thicker yarns.

| ▲ | "slip 1, knit 2 together, pass slipped stitch over" (s.1, k.2 tog., p. s. s. o.). This *double decrease* makes a triangular block of 3 stitches. Usually, it has a "make 1" on either side: ○▲○ so the two new stitches replace the cast off ones. |

| ⊠ | "cast off" (bind off – U.S.). Always cast off loosely, see "Stitch Advice". |

"make 1, knit 2 together", do **both** these stitches at this point, **in the order of working for that row** – see "How to Read a Chart"; only in patterns for experienced knitters.

| > | "slip stitch" (slipped stitch). This occurs at the start of odd numbered rows on edgings and gives a tighter edge. It can be replaced with a knit stitch if preferred. |

| ∴ | "knit into front and back of this stitch" to make a *single increase*. |

| ★ | special instructions – to be explained at the side of the chart or in the text. |

N.B. Blank squares, including those with numbers in pattern outline are to be garter stitched – also referred to as *plain knitted*. Further explanations are given in "How to Read a Chart", the "Glossary", "Stitch Advice" and in individual notes given with the patterns.

* see "Stitch Advice" for a more detailed explanation.

How to Read a Chart

A knitting chart gives knitting instructions in a pictorial form. Reading a knitting chart usually means following two important conventions. The first is that **1 square equals 1 stitch** and the second is that you work or **"read" from the chart in a certain way.**

Here is a chart. It is of a Shetland tree motif and shows a tree (centred) and two half trees. You can knit this now if you want to, in any yarn with suitable needles – see "Knitting Needles and Tension – The Basics"*, for a guide. If using a yarn thicker than a standard 4 ply (Shetland Lace-weight 2 ply) **purl** all the even rows and see "Stitch Advice", for how to work the \ stitches.

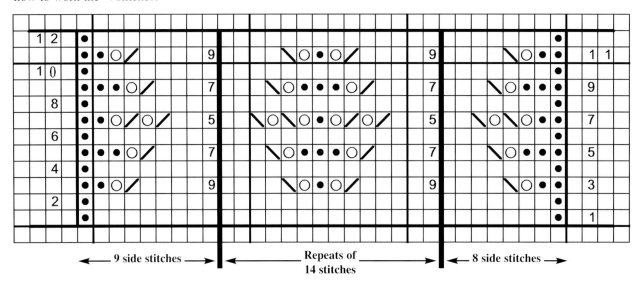

Cast on multiples of 14 stitches + 17 (9 + 8 extra stitches on each side)
e.g. (4 x 14) + 17 = 73 stitches.

Casting On

Look at the information about the stitches directly under the chart (with the arrows). The most important bit concerns the repeat number of stitches, in this case 14. This tells you how many stitches are needed to make one whole motif with spacing. If you want your knitting to be 3 motifs wide, you calculate 3 x 14 stitches. Next, add on the number of stitches given for each side. Doing this, you add on 9 for the left hand (L.H.) and 8 for the right hand (R.H.) sides. So, you should have a sum similar to the one in bold print above, but it will only be for 3 multiples of 14 instead of 4 i.e. **(3 x 14) + 17 = 59 stitches.** Now you know how many stitches to cast on. Use any elastic cast on method you feel happy with and cast on 59 stitches. (Soon you will need to know about special "invisible" cast on methods, these are explained in "How to Cast On".) If you are ready to knit, knit all the cast on stitches once. **Do not count this as row 1.** I call this "confirming" the stitches as you have a chance to check/count them.

Important Tip: You should now be back at the start of the cast on side and there should be a "tail" of the wool trailing down. Get used to leaving a casting-on tail of wool, because it helps you to know if you are working odd or even rows. Note where it hangs in relation to your knitting: usually, if the tail is on the right facing you as you knit, you are working an **odd** row. If it is on the left as you are knitting, you are working an **even** row. This will help as all the rows are usually garter stitched – Shetland lace knitting normally has no "right" or "wrong" side when finished.

* see page 30.

Knitting From a Knitting Chart

Look at the chart again. It is shown on an underlying ten square grid (which helps with counting stitches). Identify the pattern outline. This is usually a rectangle that encloses the symbols and squares. It has a **bold** outline. Outside the pattern outline are the numerals that show the row numbers. Inside the pattern outline there are only symbols, empty squares or numerals.

Pattern Outline Rectangle

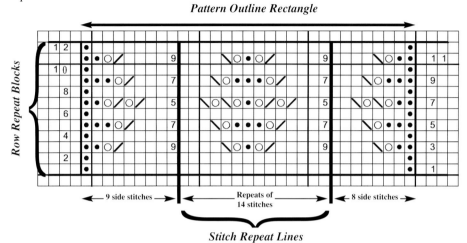

Stitch Repeat Lines

N.B. The numerals in the pattern outline are **not** symbols but are there to help you by counting all the *plain knitted* stitches between the *patterned stitches* (the ones with symbols other than ● marked in) **or** to the sides.

Make sure you have looked at "Chart Symbols" and know which stitch each symbol represents.

Most knitting charts observe the convention of starting at the bottom R.H. corner. Just as when you knit you start at the bottom corner of a piece, so it is with a knitting chart.

Row 1 starts with stitch 1 (in the first, bottom R.H. square in the pattern outline) marked with a knit dot (●). A quick glance along the line shows that the last square on row 1 (on the L.H. side) is marked the same. No other square is filled in on that line with a symbol. **Remember, unless otherwise directed, if a stitch square has not got a symbol in it, it is to be plain knitted. i.e. knit stitched.** This all means that the first row is to be plain knitted. Do this now.

Row 2 when you read a page such as this one, you "break" at the end of each line that you have read from left to right. You take your eyes back to read the next line, again from left to right and so on. **This is not the same with a knitting chart.** When you are knitting, at the end of the row, you swap the needles over and work the stitches just knitted back – starting with the one just made. It is the same with a standard knitting chart. After reading row 1 from right to left, you will now follow row 2 from left to right. With knitting charts, you follow up the pattern in a continuous 'weaving' line – this method of reading lines is sometimes called "with the plough". **All odd rows are read from right to left and all even rows are read from left to right** (this is why you were advised to leave a "tail" of wool earlier, so you can distinguish them). Once you understand this and the symbols, you have mastered knitting charts. It's as simple as that!

After all this, row 2 looks exactly the same as row 1 inside the pattern outline. This means you treat it just the same and knit it. Now you are ready to follow row 3, which is an odd row.

Row 3 shows two knit dots and then a paired increase and decrease ("make 1, k2 tog."). Knit these, and then as shown, knit 9 *plain stitches* and then the *pattern stitches* ("k2 tog., make 1, k1, make 1, k2 tog."). Knit 4 more plain stitches to finish the first pattern stitch block. Look at the stitch repeat lines, which on this chart enclose all the stitches from stitch 9 to stitch 22 on the odd rows. (The "9" means there are 9 plain stitches between the pattern stitches.) These are the 14 stitches to be repeated twice (for 3 whole motifs) before the L.H. side stitches are worked. Knit all these now.

Rows 4 – 11 show how to work each row with pattern stitches. In this book for levels * * and * * * each odd row is a pattern row, each even row is a plain knit row. These even rows may be purled instead e.g. Horseshoe Pattern is worked on a stocking stitch *ground*.

Row 12 shows the first of the three plain *spacing rows* that go between the motifs at the top and bottom. The pattern outline shows extending horizontal lines going out from underneath row 1 and over row 12. This shows how many rows must be knitted for each *row repeat block*. Decide how many repeat blocks of rows you want to work and knit them. Cast off loosely. You should now see you are in charge of how much you knit with Shetland lace. You are making up your own designs; this might seem scary at first but is actually quite liberating!

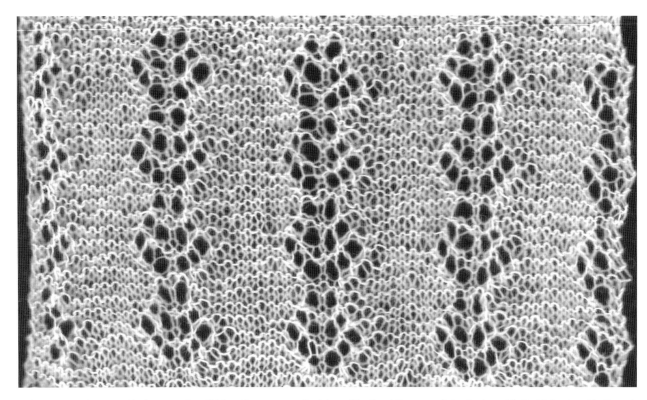

The above photograph shows a Small Tree Pattern worked in a Shetland Lace-weight 2 ply with British size 11 (3mm) needles on 59 stitches for four *row repeat blocks* (4 x 12 = 48) rows. When you have worked the last repeat for the length you want, knit one more plain row to balance the top and bottom ends, then cast off very loosely – the cast off edge should be as stretchy as the rest of the knitting; if necessary, cast off using a much larger sized needle.

As given, this pattern with its pronounced stripe of lace would be a good scarf or stole pattern – when motifs are aligned vertically like this, they are not especially suitable for the squarer items such as shawl centres. **To make a scarf now** with this pattern with the yarn and needles above, I would cast on* enough stitches to make eight whole motif stitch repeats – (8 x 14) + 17 = 129 stitches. As this has a lacy edge to the long sides, I would not necessarily work an additional knitted edging. If worked in a thicker yarn with larger needles, remember to purl the even rows, and work each (\) specially – as "slip 1, knit 1, pass slipped stitch over".

N.B. With larger patterns or for lots of repeats, you might need to check your maths with the Ready Reckoner in Appendix 1 that calculates up to 20 multiples of 11 – 50. Sometimes in level * * * * patterns onwards, two or three symbols will appear in one box. This is because there will have been some *increases* created at that point without matching *decreases* to balance them up. Work the stitches in the order given in the box and don't worry. There will be a row with extra decreases in to compensate, e.g. in the Cat's Eye Pattern, the odd rows contain the increases and the even rows contain the decreases.

* Use the "Knitting Cast On" – see "How to Cast On".

Yarn

Choosing Yarn

I strongly believe that the investment of one's hours and creativity knitting Shetland lace deserves that the piece be done in a *yarn* that is going to stand the test of time. For this reason, I never work in untried or man-made yarns without finding out first by knitting a test swatch, how they look after repeated washing. If the yarn gets furred or *bobbly*, this may spoil the lace effect wanted. So, in general, I advise using only natural yarns, particularly Shetland 1 and 2 ply wool; cotton; mohair; silk and linen mixes. I have found through ten years experience, that the pure Shetland wool – the Cobweb 1 ply and the Lace-weight 2 ply, both knit and launder well and I have used these yarns for the majority of this book. It is also very satisfying to use the traditional wool for these traditional patterns.

Experienced knitters interested in using other yarns should read Section Four, where I give more detail about other yarns commonly used for lace knitting, how to use them and assess their tension effects.

Winding Wool

Many fine yarns are still supplied on a cone or even in *hanks/skeins* and may require winding before knitting. This is a skill in itself. To wind wool off the cone is relatively straight forward following the method below but if you have to wind from a hank, you are going to need one of four things:

1. a friend and up to 15 minutes uninterrupted co-operation as he/she holds the hank;
2. a half-open suitably sized and fronted drawer to place the hank around;
3. an up-turned kitchen chair, the hank looped over the legs;
4. a purpose made wool winder (recommended – see photograph below; I clamp mine to a knitting basket handle as shown).

Purpose made, adjustable wool winders that can be clamped to a table-top (use cardboard pads to prevent marking the table) can be purchased from Jamieson & Smith Ltd. – see "Suppliers' List", or sometimes found second-hand.

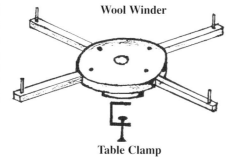

Wool Winder

Table Clamp

Method

Untwist the hank and find the securing knot that ties one end to the other. Undo or break it. Begin winding wool over two or three extended fingers – see photograph. Remember, to wind loosely and evenly, changing the forming ball's position in the hand, every twenty to forty turns; continue to end. Do not wind tightly because the yarn will loose its natural handle, the finished ball should be very "springy" when squeezed.

N.B. If ever you come across a knot, break the thread at that point and start winding a new ball with the remainder – I advise you do this because it is most inconvenient to find a knot as you are knitting; whenever possible, plan ahead and join in new thread only at the start of a row if one cannot *splice join*. All loose threads should be invisibly sewn in after knitting is completed.

Joining Yarn

Next to ugly seams, a bad join or knot can spoil the finished appearance of lace knitting. Making strong yet unnoticeable joins is yet another skill a good knitter must master. A knot alone looks out of place and can easily come undone, causing almost irreparable damage as the stitch loops quickly unravel. Therefore, I strongly advocate joining yarns in the ways suggested below.

Ideally, join in yarn at the start of a row; if you are unsure whether you have enough yarn to get to the end of another row, there are two things that can be tried:

1. Wrap the yarn around the needle (reasonably loosely) the same number of times as there are stitches in a row – if there is enough to do that, then you should be safe. Pull off the winding and continue knitting.

2. If you are knitting an item with too many stitches for that to be practical: when you think you may have enough yarn left to knit two more rows, unwind the ball of yarn to its end, fold the yarn in half and make a *slip knot* at that point. If, when you have knitted the next row you haven't reached the slip knot, you should have enough to do another and final row with that ball. On the other hand, if you have reached or passed the slip knot, you will know that you haven't enough yarn left to knit another full row, so you had better join in a fresh ball now.

Twist Join Method for 2 Ply Yarns

As said before, it's best and easiest to join yarns in at the start of a row. Sometimes though, as is in the case with the middle of a circular shawl, there may be no start of a row to use because you are knitting continuously in rounds, therefore, twist joins are recommended. In the examples below, differently coloured yarns are used for demonstration purposes only. In practice, if joining in differently coloured yarns, you should knot at the appropriate place in the knitting and sew the ends in later.

1. **Overlap new and old thread for 6 to 8 inches (15-20cm). Make a *reef knot* or other non-slipping, small knot to join them (see Picture 1). Pull it tight.**

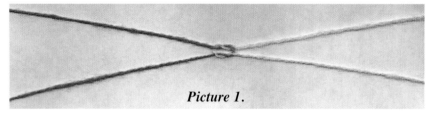

Picture 1.

2. **Carefully untwist the strands of the ply in both loose ends back to the knot; gently break off one strand (or half the number of total strands in the ply – see Picture 2) on each loose end.**

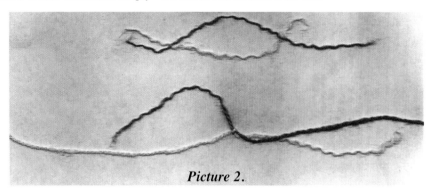

Picture 2.

3. **Discard the broken off strands and twist the remaining strand(s) carefully around the knitting yarn in each direction (see Picture 3); carefully knit with the twisted strands held in place.**

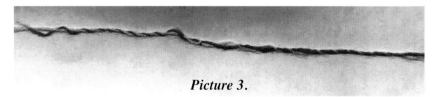

Picture 3.

Splice Join Method for 1 Ply Yarns

One-ply yarns can be very fragile and easily broken; this is why special care must be taken when joining in new yarn. Where possible, join in new yarn at the start of a row with a *reef knot* and invisibly sew in the loose ends when the knitting is completed. If this is impossible, follow the procedure for step 1 of the Twist Join Method (see above).

Now, take a fine, sharp needle with an eye big enough to thread a single end through. Thread in one of the ends and "sew" it through the knitting yarn in one direction for at least 3 inches/8cm. Trim off neatly any excess. Do the same for the other end, but thread it through in the other direction of the knitting yarn. This may look clumsy initially, but it is the safest way to make secure joins in 1 ply yarn. In practice, these joins are usually invisible, particularly when the yarn itself can be slightly irregular in its density.

Alternatively, in very lacy knitting, make a secure knot with long ends and later sew these into place through an available line of decreases in the knitting, where the extra bulk is less noticeable.

Substituting Yarn

The majority of the patterns for this book are worked in the traditional, commercially spun wool, Shetland 1 ply (Cobweb) and Shetland 2 ply (Lace-weight). Section Four has more detail about alternative yarns – including handspun Gossamer – and their suitability. It is important to know that a ply number is only a guide to the thickness of a yarn to the extent that it numbers the total of threads twisted or plied together. As a rule of thumb, the following must be remembered:

Shetland Cobweb 1 ply: a standard 2 ply; this is one of the finest commercially available yarns that I know of.

Shetland Lace-weight 2 ply: a standard 4 ply.

A better indication of the fineness of yarn is its *yardage* per ounce (or metres per 100 grams). Broadly speaking, the higher the yardage per ounce, the finer it is. It will be useful to note the following as a guide:

Shetland Cobweb 1 ply: 215 yards per ½ ounce, 196m per 14g hank/skein approx.
Shetland Lace-weight 2 ply: 230 yards per ounce, 210m per 28g hank/skein approx.

If substituting brands or types of *yarn/thread*, a straight ounce for ounce translation cannot usually be made, because different manufacturing methods produce wools in varying "thicknesses", thereby altering the individual overall *yardage* per ounce/metres per 28g – even though the stated counts of ply are the same. Man-made yarns can be lighter than wool and this too, affects the yardage per ounce/28g. In general, if substituting a yarn* for one of a similar fineness, work out the total yards/metres required for the suggested yarn and buy at least that length of substituting yarn. Always purchase sufficient quantity of a dye lot to knit the item. Before committing yourself, knit a small test sample in the intended *yarn/thread*. Wash, *dress* and handle it several times to assess its suitability e.g. for signs of felting, *bobbling* or *pilling* which will make it unsuitable. Once you are happy with the substitute's durability, try it using different sized pairs of needles to see the lace effect in different densities – see Section Four. Remember though, to *dress* the test piece before assessing; the desired final effect is for lacy openness – not a gauze so open that the pattern is lost, or a piece so dense that the pattern is again lost, due to the tightness of stitches. It's a good idea when trying a new yarn to knit a small item to see how it wears; before using it for a larger project.

N.B. Cotton, silk and other non-elastic *threads* (which may require knitting on larger needles to obtain the lacy openness), cannot be substituted by simply calculating yardage alone; you may require greater lengths of thread for these and so my best advice is to buy in plenty.

Shetland 2 ply (Lace-weight) grey wool and Shetland 1 ply (Cobweb) white wool, as supplied as hanks and then wound into balls – a ball of white 2 ply is placed in the centre to show the difference between the sizes of the 2 ply and 1 ply balls.

Knitting Tips

Always remember to **knit to the end of a row** before finishing. Primarily, this is so you keep the tension of the row even, but it also means that you start the next session with a fresh row and fresh pattern line on the chart.

Obviously, you will always knit with clean hands, but it can really help any knitting you are doing if you also regularly dust your hands with **talcum powder** as you work – I always keep a small container of baby powder in my knitting bag. Doing this helps the stitches to glide smoothly along the needles and so helps with knitting tension, as well as stopping the stitches from bunching or jamming together which they frequently can do, when the weather and you are hot. The talc washes out in the finishing process.

If your **stocking stitch** seen from the back, looks like it has been knitted in groups of two rows, i.e. there are horizontal ridges of pairs of rows in your knitting, it might be because you have slightly tighter tension with your knit or purl rows. Experiment by using a size larger needle for one of these rows, so that you are knitting with two differently sized needles. This doesn't matter at all if the end result is evenly spaced, regular rows.

When **joining in yarn**, leave longer tails of thread than you think you will need so that you have plenty to spare when sewing in the ends later when the knitting is finished. Plan where the best places are for joining in new thread; if not the start of a row, try to include the join in an area of decreasing, where the extra bulk of a knot and the sewn-in ends will be easier to hide. Do not choose areas with increases if at all possible. Spend lots of time on your finishing sewing, the desired result is for a secure, undetectable join that is as elastic as the other knitting – stretch it over your fingers as you sew to ensure you achieve this.

Although casting off isn't usually a problem with Shetland lace knitting because edgings use up the stitches of the main knitting, I was so impressed with this **elastic casting off** that mimics the Knitting Cast On, that I include it here in case you ever need it. It's easiest if the stitches are taken off the R.H. pin and threaded on cotton first:

The Sewing Cast Off

Working from left to right, go down through the front of the **second** stitch from the needle; come up through the back of the **first**; go down through the front of the third; come back up through the back of the second… continue going **down** from the front of every new stitch and coming back **up** through its preceding one in this manner, to the end; fasten off securely.

This **knitted picot cast off** imitates the picot edging made by crocheting "5 chain, 1 double crochet" along a cast off edge. To do this cast off, which has the benefit of being as elastic as the knitting, simply:

Cast off the first stitch in the usual way, then *slip that stitch back from the R.H. needle onto the L.H. needle and knit into it** . Repeat from * to ** four times so that you have a chain of 5 stitches. (It helps to knit the chain stitches quite loosely for this.)

Cast off two more stitches in the usual way, then repeat from * to ** again. Keep casting off 2 stitches then making 5 chain as described, until all the stitches to be cast off are used up. A variation is given right.

If you need hard-to-obtain **smaller size needles**, smaller than the British size 14/ Metric 2.00 mm/American 00, you can always improvise – I found the standard stitch holder that's shaped like an oversized safety pin actually corresponds to an old **British size 16/Metric 1.25/U.S. 0000**. With two of them, straightened with pliers and cut to useable lengths then the cut ends safely capped (rubber bands wound tightly work well) an acceptable set of pins is ready to use. (There is a specialist knitting needle supplier listed in Appendix 6.)

Remember with Shetland lace knitting, it is very important that any **seams and necessary casting on and off should be as elastic** as the rest of the knitting. Use larger sized needles to cast off with if necessary; stretch any sewn seams in both directions to ensure they "give" properly, or try:

The Crochet Seam Method

This can be a quick, secure and handy method to join pieces without sewing. With the appropriate thread or wool and a suitably sized crochet hook for the yarn you are using, make a foundation chain stitch and then crochet pieces together by making a stitch with the hook through the side-loop and then crochet another single chain stitch on the hook. Pick up a side-loop to use from each edge in turn. To finish, pull a length of the wool through the stitch loop on the hook and break off. To check if the seam is elastic enough, pull downwards on each side of the join. If the seam is too tight, undo the crochet seam and redo, using a larger size hook.

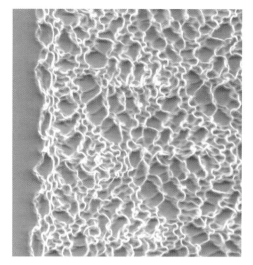

Commence with the light shade of wool; fasten on and work six chain, miss the space of four stitches and loop the wool through the fifth with single crochet; repeat to the end of the stitches. Then join in the darker shade and repeat as shown above.

Knitting Needles & Tension

The Basics

Knitting needles not only give the means of creation, they actually strongly dictate the overall effect of the finished knitting. Using the same wool and a fine gauge (size) of needle, one gets a tight block of knitting; with a thicker gauge of needle and the same wool, one gets a less dense, more open structure to the knitting. With even thicker needles, the structure of the stitches will be so open they can be seen through easily. This can help or hinder the lace effect, depending on what one is aiming for (see "Tension and Lace Design", Section Four).

Tension, ("Stitch Gauge" – U.S.) is the name given to the amount of pressure an individual knitter subjects the yarn to during the process of knitting with needles. Many factors affect tension: tiredness or stress, can cause a knitter to tighten tension unconsciously; a fast knitter usually has a looser than average tension, and so may need to use a smaller sized needle to get the correct tension for a given item. Incidentally, many people often wrongly assume that they need only pay attention to the yarn and the needle size details when knitting to a published knitting pattern. Given needle sizes should be treated as an indicator only; what really should be regarded is the yarn and the stated tension if you want to reproduce an item exactly. The size of the needles should be changed up or down as necessary, until the correct tension is obtained (see "How to Change Tension", below). So strongly did one expert feel about this that he thought that patterns should never give needle size details!

Table Shows Average Tension in Stocking Stitch per Square Inch/2.5cm				
Multiply the boxed figures by 4 to get the count for 4 square inches/10cm square.				
Size of Needle	**Classic 2 Ply***	**Classic 3 Ply**	**Classic 4 Ply****	**Double Knitting**
British 12 Metric 2.75 American 1	9 sts x 11 rows	8½ sts x 10½ rows	-	-
British 11 Metric 3.00 American 2	8½ sts x 10½ rows	8 sts x 10 rows	7½ sts x 9½ rows	-
British 10 Metric 3.25 American 3	8 sts x 10 rows	7½ sts x 9½ rows	7 sts x 9 rows	-
British 9 Metric 3.50/3.75 American 4	7½ sts x 9½ rows	7 sts x 9 rows	6½ sts x 8½ rows	5¾ sts x 8 rows
British 8 Metric 4.00 American 5	7 sts x 9 rows	6½ sts x 8½ rows	6 sts x 8 rows	5½ sts x 7½ rows
British 7 Metric 4.50 American 6	6½ sts x 8½ rows	6 sts x 8 rows	5½ sts x 7½ rows	5¼ sts x 7 rows

* Equates to Shetland Cobweb 1 ply   ** Equates to Shetland Lace-weight 2 ply

Knitting Needles

One of the most useful innovations for modern knitters has been the invention of **circular needles** (around the 1920s, the first circular needles had tiny "ropes" of plaited or twisted wire connecting the arms instead of the drawn plastic flex used today). Although they lack the distinct charm of the earlier bone, bamboo, and even amber or tortoiseshell needles – they do offer several clear advantages to the modern knitter:

- **Safer knitting** knitting left lying around on a circular needle is much less likely to cause injury than traditional long pins.

- **Ability to knit in the round** without sets of pins, so that the construction of Shetland shawls is much easier. This is explained in "Shetland Shawls".

- **The ability to knit many thousands of stitches per row** because a circular needle can be up to a metre long or longer.

- **Safer storage of stitches**; once stitches have been pushed onto the connecting "central flex" they are much less likely to slip off the needle, so avoiding the consequent problems of retrieval.

As you might have guessed, I prefer to use circular needles all the time for these reasons – there's not been anything that I can't knit with them and I prefer their shorter, rigid "knitting arms" in my hands. They come in a choice of lengths per size and generally, I prefer to work with the smaller lengths; but it is up to the individual knitter to experiment and choose. Obviously, **ordinary pins** could be used if preferred, but then slight changes in the knitting procedure I give may be necessary e.g. each of the four borders of a "Cobweb Crepe Shawl, Project 5" would have to be constructed **separately** and then sewn together before the edging is knitted around. Additionally, all even rows would need to be plain knitted and **not** purled (as stated in some of the instructions with methods using the circular needle), to produce the garter stitch pattern.

Sometimes, it is still unavoidable to knit with sets of **double-pointed needles** (as with the centres of circular shawls knitted in the round). I always found this difficult because the stitches would insist on slipping off, especially when they were at their fewest. Then I figured out that wrapping small elastic bands tightly around each of the ends of needles not actually in use, would not only stop this, but save my fraying temper as well!

N.B. Beware of non-standard needle sizes when using old needles and patterns, see page 188.

Care of Knitting Needles

The best needles have smooth rounded shafts and long tapering points. In past days, knitters would grind and file their needles regularly as the points wore down. Although this isn't necessary today with modern needles, you may be lucky enough to find old, finely sized steel needles that are so badly rusted they seem beyond hope. Before passing them by, try rubbing them smooth again with machine oil and fine grade steel wool (wool flannel U.S.) – I had to do this with "Project 6". See tip on page 29 explaining how to make your own small sized needles. Always store your needles properly, in original containers if possible; and use a silicone polish to keep them extra smooth.

Tension Squares and Designing

Boring as it is, a good knitter has to knit the occasional tension square. This is a small rectangle (ideally at least 4 inches/10 cm square) of knitting, which once *dressed* ("blocked" – U.S.) gives a lot of valuable information for the knitter to base work on. You may need to know exactly how many stitches and rows per square inch/2.5cm that a particular yarn or indeed, even colour of yarn (!) makes with you and a particular set of needles. This is not only essential when designing fitted items, it's also useful for non-fitted things such as shawls, as simply changing the yarn or the size of the needles can have a dramatic effect on the size of a dressed item of a given stitch count.

As said, it's particularly necessary to learn the effect of tension both on overall size and lacy appearance when designing garments. Surprisingly, it is possible to make a woman's size jacket from the exact instructions for "Project 1: The Baby Jacket", simply by using larger size needles and much thicker wool. Normally, tension is measured over stocking stitch or the main pattern.

To Knit a Basic (Non-Lacy) Tension Square

Take an intended yarn and a suitably sized circular needle/set of needles (see Table about average tensions above, if you need guidance). Cast on with the Knitting Cast On, about 30 – 40 stitches and knit for 60 – 80 rows, stocking stitch is usual, but if you intend to make a piece with a garter stitch *ground*, knit your tension square in garter stitch. Cast off very loosely.

Now *dress* the square, (do not over stretch). After pinning, leave until thoroughly dry, then unpin and, on a flat surface, use a tape measure (a ruler is better still because it won't stretch) to establish how many stitches and rows per inch/2.5cm you made. It is important to include any fractions of stitches in your calculations; over several hundred stitches they can make a difference; if need be, base your calculations on four square inches/10 square centimetres.

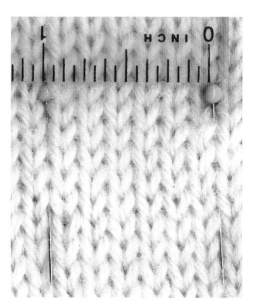

A 6 stitches per inch/2.5cm tension ratio.

How to Change Tension

If it is vital to match a stated tension in a pattern and yours doesn't, try a size larger needle (for less stitches per inch/2.5cm) or size smaller needle (for more stitches per inch/2.5cm) and knit a new square with the same wool and see if this solves the problem.

Another good tip for a tighter tension is to "interlace" the yarn coming from the ball through the fingers of the hand that directs it: – I always thread finer yarn under the R.H. fore-finger, over the next two fingers, under the little finger, then finally, back around the outside, over the little finger to hang down (between the last two fingers) to the yarn ball. This sounds complicated, but I find this really helps control the speed of a fine 1 ply slipping through too fast to the needles and making tension looser than need be. This particularly applies when you are working with the smallest needles, as it may be impossible to find an even smaller size. Remember, a dusting of talcum powder also aids a smooth tension.

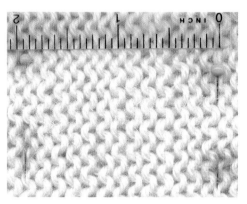

Measure stocking stitch rows from the back, it's easier to count the row "ridges" this way. this has an approximate tension of (13 divided by 2=) 6½ rows per inch/2.5cm.

TIP
A handy rule of thumb with tension is, "the finer the needle, the more stitches and rows per square inch".

How to Cast On

For Shetland Lace Knitting

Two of the prime characteristics of Shetland lace knitting are its elasticity and its lack of obvious beginnings and endings – typically, shawls are knitted on stitches picked up from a long lace edging and grafting replaces seams. This is covered in depth in "Shetland Shawls" and "How to Graft".

"Casting On" is the process of forming the initial row of loops for knitting and is usually done for items of clothing. Traditionally in the Shetland Islands, items of underwear, hosiery, spencers (the forerunners of the cardigan) and baby wear needed casting on. Again, it was and still should be, as unobtrusive as possible – I explain three methods for achieving this.

Knitting Cast On

(Also known as "Knitting On"). As it sounds, this is based on garter stitch knitting and produces an elastic and dainty edging. I use this method for the "Baby's First Jacket – Project 1" and for the "New Shell Scarf – Project 3".

1. Make a *slip knot*. Put it on your L.H. needle. This is your first stitch.

2. Insert the R.H. needle into the **front*** strand of the loop of the stitch from its **left** side – just as if you were going to knit a stitch. Wrap the knitting yarn around the R.H. needle and draw the new loop through with that needle – again, exactly as if you were garter stitch knitting.

3. Now, transfer the new loop onto the L.H. needle by inserting the L.H. needle **into** its **front*** i.e. from the right side of the new loop's front (it should still be on the R.H. needle) and slipping it off the R.H. needle and onto the L.H. needle. Pull on the knitting yarn to tighten the stitch **slightly**. This completes the casting on of one stitch. Repeat steps 2 and 3 as often as necessary.

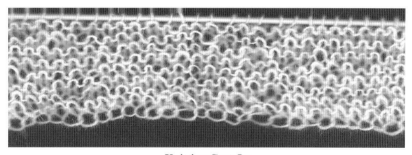

Knitting Cast On

Look at the picture above and notice the initial chain of loops at the bottom edge made by this casting on – if you need to attach an edging, you pick up each little "circle" to knit into.

N.B. It is important that any casting on is done evenly but loosely. The finished casting on should be as stretchy as a normal knitted row when the knitting is pulled horizontally – there should be no additional tightness at that point. You could use a larger sized needle, just for the casting on, to get looser but even stitches – see "Knitting Needles and Tension – The Basics".

* "Front" here means "as you are looking at it" on the pins.

Loop, or "Finger and Thumb" Cast On For Less Than 50 Stitches

Make a *slip knot* a few inches from the end of the yarn to be used. Put it on a needle (A).

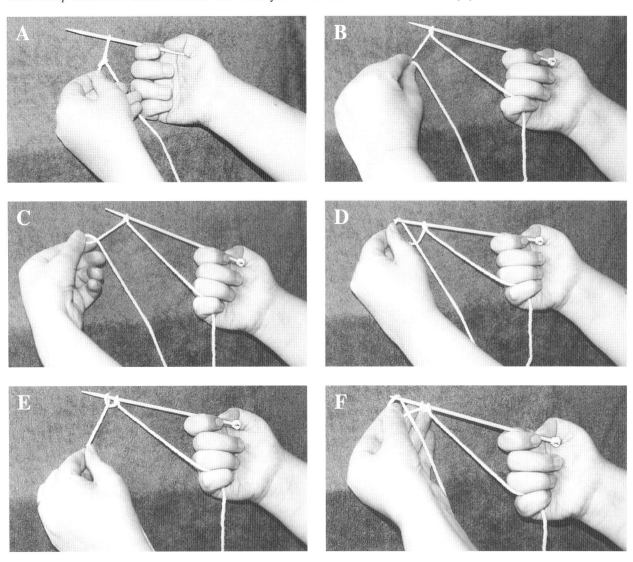

Tighten the knot. With finger and thumb, pinch the strand coming from the ball of yarn (B); turn your wrist back to make a loop in the yarn (C) and insert the needle into this (D). Pull gently on the yarn to tighten the loop (E). Repeat this, adding stitches in the same manner until all the required stitches are made (F). (I am left-handed; you might need to mirror the hand actions pictured above if you are right handed).

Loop Cast On for More than 50 Stitches

Because this method can put an extra "kink" into the yarn if used for a large number of stitches, it may be advisable to do the following modification: **Use a circular needle of the required size.** Unwind the wool for approximately 2 – 3 *yards* for each 100 stitches to be cast on. Make a *slip knot* at this point and then using the yarn with the free end (**not** the end that leads to the ball but the "tail") make the stitches as described above. When the required number of stitches have been made, slide them carefully right around the circular needle and then knit them – this is why a circular needle is used. The knitter can now transfer the stitches to an ordinary needle if preferred.

N.B. The loops made with this cast on must be loose but even. Knitting back this casting on is quite tricky because the base strand opens – ignore this; try practising this method thoroughly first, as it does give a very useful, unobtrusive edge as elastic as possible. Otherwise, use the foolproof Waste Wool Cast On.

Waste Wool Cast On

This rather laborious cast on is worth the effort because it gives the best-finished effect by being totally indistinguishable in the finished knitting.

Generally, with this method you can use any left over **contrasting** yarn of the same weight as that you intend to knit with; i.e. with something to be knitted in a white 2 ply, cast on with a coloured 2 ply. Cast on the required number of stitches in any loose cast on stitch using the waste wool. Knit that row back to confirm the stitches. Now, join in the wool to be knitted with and knit two rows plain before proceeding with the pattern.

This method is recommended when you are going to add a border with a large number of stitches (50+) because it allows the knitter to pick up the desired stitches invisibly – look at the photographs which demonstrate this casting on; a careful look at the lower photograph shows the white strands to be picked up, looping through the contrast cast on.

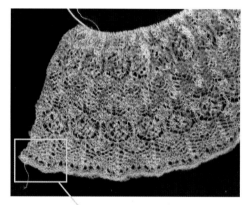

Starting at a side, carefully pick up each white strand that's to be a new stitch on the knitting needle, then snip through its corresponding contrast stitch. By repeating this, all the stitches for a border can be picked up for further knitting.

I used this method for working the Unst Lace Stole's second border which has 185 stitches picked up to be knitted after the initial knitting has been turned upside down. **Check that the right sides of the old pattern match the new as you knit;** adjust, if necessary, by undoing and working an extra plain row before the pattern rows.

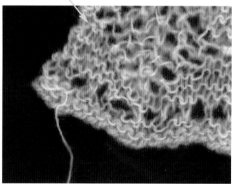

This method can make the tedious and daunting process of grafting large numbers of stitches for Shetland lace knitting unnecessary. See "Shetland Stoles" for additional explanation.

Waste Wool Cast On.

Travelling Leaf Pattern, an 1880s Print O'the Wave pattern, shown up-side-down, so the leaf shapes 'grow' upwards. Suggested for curtains, bread-cloths and anti-macassars.

Stitch Advice

One of the pleasures of Shetland lace knitting is the simplicity of the stitches involved, and with the following words of caution, most knitting in yarns of different "grists" or diameters can be done without any further change to the instructions given with "Chart Symbols". As mentioned, most Shetland lace patterns are knitted in a **garter stitch** ground (knit each row), but if you intend to use a wool thicker than a classic 4 ply, consider changing the pattern slightly by using a **stocking stitch** ground instead (knit odd rows, purl even rows), for the best effects.

Making an Over

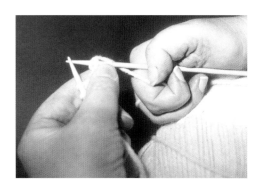

All Yarns: To "make 1" (or an "*over*") is to make a special increase which produces a planned "hole" or *eyelet* in the finished knitting. All the increases indicated by the circle symbols in the charts must be made by **bringing the yarn forward** "**purlwise**"– that is, under the R.H. needle – as if to purl, then taking it back over the top of the needle before knitting the next stitch (see photograph).

On the next row, the strand of yarn over the needle at this point is treated as a stitch and so is knitted or purled into as necessary, without twisting the strand.

The Double Decrease ▲

All Yarns: This is represented in the charts by the solid black triangle symbol. Interestingly, in some early traditional knitting patterns, this was to indicate a simple "knit 3 together" in the knitting. This still works well with the fine yarns, but a better result – with the stitches lying flatter in thicker yarns – is made by doing the following:

"slip 1, knit 2 together, pass slipped stitch over".

Begin by slipping (i.e. transferring the stitch without knitting it) the first of the three stitches *purlwise* from the L.H. needle to the R.H. needle, knit the remaining two stitches together. Then, by inserting the L.H. needle into the front of the stitch previously slipped to the R.H. needle, pull it leftwards right over the "2 knitted together", so the three stitches together resemble a tiny pyramid.

Effectively, you have securely decreased the total number of stitches at this point from three to one – thus getting rid of two stitches – so this is technically known as a **"double decrease"**. Almost invariably, there will be compensating "make 1s" each side of it so that the stitch count for that row will remain constant.

Casting Off/Binding Off ⊠

All Yarns: Always cast off very loosely; if necessary, use a larger size needle for casting off. The number of ✕s equals the number of stitches to be cast off.

Paired Increases and Decreases ⟍◯ ◯⟋

This important advice really only applies to those who are working with yarns thicker than a standard 2 or 3 ply*. With the thicker yarns, it is necessary to adapt the standard single decrease paired with a single increase (the "make 1, knit 2 together" **or** the "knit 2 together, make 1"); purely to make their appearance in the knitting look neater.

In a knitting chart these symbols look like this: ⟍◯ or like this: ◯⟋.

* These equate to Shetland 1 ply (Cobweb) and Shetland 2 ply (Lace-weight) respectively. Remember, with these finer yarns, both these decreases could be simply and traditionally worked as "knit 2 together", without affecting the finished appearance after dressing.

Look at this extract from a tree motif chart.

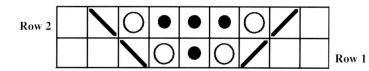

Row 2

Row 1

On the first line – row 1, which **you read from right to left** – the "knit 2 together, make 1" is made before the (knit 1) "make 1, knit 2 together". On the next line, although the symbols are the same on the chart **because you are now reading from left to right** the paired decreases and increases are performed in the same order – **not** reverse order as you might suppose. So, in any row of knitting, the important thing to remember is to watch for which comes first in each pair to be worked, the decrease or the make 1:

When the decrease precedes the "make 1":
actually, no change to the given instructions, simply "knit 2 together", then do the "make 1".

When the "make 1" precedes the decrease:
do the "make 1" as normal and then "slip 1, knit 1, pass slipped stitch over" to perform the decrease; or "knit 2 together through back of loops".

Or do the following tip:

Tip

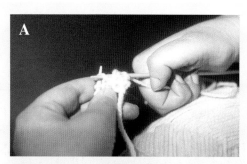

A

With the two stitches to be decreased – go into the stitch to be slipped **purlwise** (picture A); **without transferring the first stitch,** knit the second through it as normal (picture B) then slip both stitches off.

You should have a satisfactory mimic of this type of decrease, which after a little practice, is quick and simple to perform. I thought I had discovered this for myself, then I found it described in Mrs Gaugain's knitting manual of 1846:

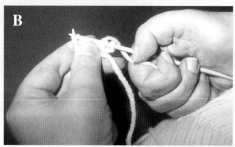

B

"Ti, take in, by inserting the wire as if you were going to pearl the first loop, and catch in the other as if you were knitting a plain one; knit them both off together."

I find this an excellent way to knit the Cat's Eye Pattern that avoids the single strand one can often see crossing the holes created by this pattern.

Attaching an Edging

This method gives the classic elastic edging to Shetland items, and avoids lots of sewing and casting off. For demonstration purposes below, the *body* or main part has been knitted in blue and the edging has been knitted in pink. After the final row or round of the body (blue) has been knitted, keep the stitches on the needle – I call these **reserved stitches** – they are cast off as the edging is worked. Cast on with the "Loop Cast On", the desired number of edging

stitches (pink) – this number is given under each edging chart. Now, knit the edging to the knitting as shown below. To attach an edging (1) to a side: after knitting all the stitches on each return or even row, pick up the last or **outside strand** (side loop) between the *ridges* of the main knitting, (2) and knit a stitch into this (3). Now, **turn the knitting**

and slip the stitch just made onto the right hand needle (4).
Knit the next stitch – the first of that row (5) and then to finish, pass the slipped stitch over (6). Keep knitting the stitches for the edging pattern as shown on the chart, row by row. Continue like this, attaching the edging to the side of the

body, ridge by ridge, until you are nearing one of the corners.

When you are coming to a corner it is necessary to decide if the edging will fit round it without *easing*. **If your edging doesn't have too many cast on stitches (15 stitches or less)** and it has triangular points that will "open" out to allow the edging to spread, then you need do no more than sigh with relief and continue to attach it as shown in pictures 7 and 8 below; simply use up the reserved stitches instead of picking up side strands. Knit the last stitch of the edging "2 together" with the first remaining stitch of the border.

Note how the edging is now at **right angles** to the reserved stitches as you are working along the top of the main knitting. It will do the same at the cast on side of the body, when you will either use up the loops from the Waste Wool

Cast On or pick up a loop for each stitch from the Loop or Knitting Cast On.

If you are knitting quite a narrow edging (20 stitches or less) or one with shallow points, you will only need to knit a few extra rows to get the dressed edging to lie flat around each corner – diagram A below. **If you are knitting a wide edging (20 stitches or more) or an un-pointed edging** such as Twin Holed Diamond With Small Bead Insertion (page 128) then you will need to knit several more rows before and after each side of the corner for it to be successful – diagram B. If you didn't do these extra corner rows, the dressed edging would either not keep flat around the corner, but curl up; or have to be stretched around so forcibly that the effect on the pattern would be disastrous. See also edging

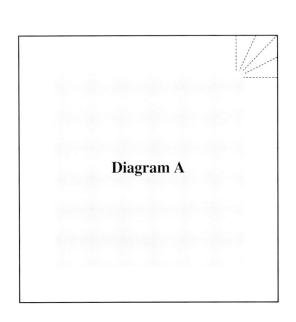

Diagram A

Diagram B

instructions with "Project 5: The Cobweb Crepe Shawl", where this is fully explained.

Different numbers of rows need to be added at corners depending on the depth of the edging.

Note that the pink centre squares are the same size in each case.

When knitting extra rows for corners, instead of attaching the edging to the main part at each return to every stitch (top and bottom edges) or ridge (side edges); do it at every other return, for some rows before **and** after the corner, see picture below.

Unst Lace Stole corner (undressed) 36 stitches deep.

Tip

After working your first corner, stretch it over your knees and pull to shape with your hands to judge the effect. Or dampen, stretch and pin to a flat surface – again to judge the effect. If the corner is successful, you will be able to treat all the other corners in the same way.

This procedure necessarily involves a little trial and error, possibly needing you to *unravel* and re-knit a sizeable section of the edging until you are happy with the effect; this is one of the minor drawbacks of lace knitting and can't really be avoided. My advice here is never settle with second best, if a corner has to be re-knitted, that is much better in the long run than being continually aware that you didn't do your best by it; so grit your teeth and undo the knitting as soon as you are aware it isn't working out.

If you are really clever or particular, you will manage to get the number of edging points to balance each side of the corner. This is something the experts aim for and sometimes manage and I leave this to you. However, I **would** advise you to finish on a full pattern repeat, before uniting the two ends of the edging with *grafting;* you can fit in extra rows or omit rows to achieve this. Doing this, the edging will look properly made rather than an afterthought – though I can report that I have seen expert exhibits where this has been scamped and the edging lace has ended abruptly with a three-quarter point, so spoiling

Unst Lace Stole corner – dressed and finished.

Dealing with Mistakes

the overall beauty of the lace knitting.

1. To avoid mistakes, don't do complicated, fine knitting when tired. Keep an alternative easier project – say in a thicker wool or simpler pattern if you intend to knit at such times. **The most difficult part in lace knitting is the "set-up pattern" row,** when you have to correctly site the pattern motifs for the first time. Use contrast wool thread and markers* to mark the corners, border centre stitch and/or panels of repeating pattern to ensure the motifs are in exactly the right places. Only do this row when you have plenty of time.

2. Get into the habit of stretching the ongoing knitting between your fingers to examine it, section by section, at regular intervals in each knitting session – about every ten rows. A mistake quickly noticed is easier to deal with – this is such an important piece of advice that you will find it elsewhere in this book!

3. It is very important to know that stitches have a correct orientation on a needle; the **front strand on the L.H. needle** of each stitch is usually the **right hand side strand** of the two strands that make a stitch loop. When

Picture 1

picking up stitches, make sure they are all orientated in the same way (see Picture 1).

4. Surprisingly, the odd mistake in very lacy knitting, however complex, is often simpler to repair with needle and thread when the knitting is finished. e.g. A dropped stitch can be secured at the time with a safety pin or contrast thread and later worked into place by using a fine tapestry needle threaded with a long length of the yarn – the ends can be invisibly weaved in. **N.B.** This only applies to one or two stitches at a time – see

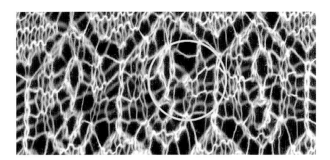 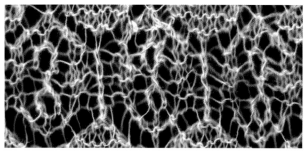

photographs below. Obvious misalignments of pattern **must** be *unravelled**.

The first photograph show a stitch I dropped in the Unst Lace Stole Centre pattern. As soon as I noticed it, I threaded blue yarn through it to stop further dropping or laddering, as the affected stitch's loops undid. After dressing, I sewed the stitch back into place – see second photograph of the identical area – (honestly!) If the stitch had dropped further, I would have used a small crochet hook to work it back into place before sewing.

* See page 43.

5. With lace knitting, there is usually a definite structure of geometric shapes that you can identify (e.g. triangles or hexagons in the design), and you can use these to make sure you are knitting the pattern correctly. Another good thing to do is to keep a running count in your head of the recurring groups of stitches on each row. You will soon notice that a charted row has groups of say, five pattern and then three plain stitches, and that's a help.

6. Stocking stitch and garter stitch areas are the most unforgiving backgrounds for mistakes and they must be rectified by either dropping the affected stitches only and re-picking them up correctly, using the needles themselves or a crochet hook (see Pictures 2 and 3 below) or by undoing to the row affected and re-knitting the entire section.

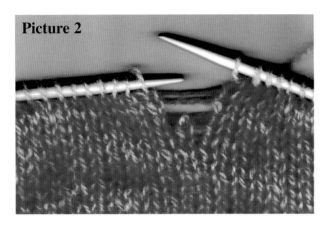 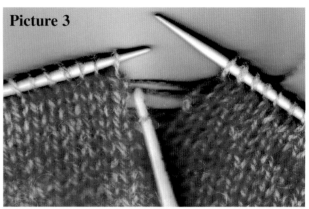

To pick up a dropped stitch in stocking stitch: knit to exactly above the dropped stitch (Picture 2). Catch the dropped stitch by inserting the crochet hook front to back, hook it over the lowest horizontal strand directly above the stitch (Picture 3) and draw the strand back through the stitch on the hook. Repeat till all horizontal strands are replaced in turn, and then slip the recovered stitch back onto L.H. needle. With garter stitch, the process is almost the same but with the alternate rows – that look purlwise in the knitting from the front – you must insert the crochet hook from the back to the front, so that the finished loop appears to be garter stitched.

7. To make it easier to pick up lots of stitches, you can pick them up on a smaller sized needle and then transfer them to the appropriate needle before resuming knitting. This gives you the chance to make sure they are again facing the right way (see Picture 1 on previous page).

8. A very useful technique to learn is "**unknitting**". This is where you reverse the knitting process, stitch-by-stitch, keeping the retrieved stitches on the L.H. needle. This can be done as much as necessary, even row by tedious row (obviously, it is wise to re-wind the yarn onto the ball as you go) and it's sometimes the only way to pick up all the pattern stitches correctly again in complicated lace. I often use unknitting for about 2 rows to pick up stitches after having previously unravelled a lot of knitting. Known in the U.S. as "tinking" because it's "knit" backwards.

9. If you have to do lots of **unravelling** (this means taking the knitting off the needles and pulling it out for several rows – see the photograph on the next page) and you are worried that the stitches will drop or unravel beyond a certain point, mark the row to be unravelled **to,** by threading it loosely with a contrast thread; spray the area beneath it with spray starch and leave to dry before undoing. This helps prevent unwanted unravelling and the starch easily washes out later. Known as "ripping" or "frogging" in the U.S. because you "rip it it, rip it" when you pull the rows out.

10. A row counter or pencil and paper are still very useful with difficult patterns, so that you can keep track of where you are, as initially, all the rows worked can look the same e.g. with the Bird's Eye Pattern. Just mark off the finished rows.

To unravel knitting

Take the work off the pins and gently pull on the knitting yarn to undo the stitches row by row. Wind yarn back onto the ball as you go. If you come to a stitch group that won't undo readily, pinch under that set of stitches with one hand and tease the yarn out with the other by pulling it from side to side. Do not tug, or the yarn may snap. If they still won't budge, gently pick at them with a fingernail to loosen, that should do it.

Don't panic over mistakes. Accept now that you'll make them; the thing is to know what to do next. At the very worst, you can unravel your knitting completely and as you will still have the needles, yarn and pattern, you will have wasted nothing but some time and will have probably learnt something along the way. Attitudes to mistakes vary – I take a strong line about them – and when I do make them, I don't want them left undealt with. More laid back folk say that hand knitting with the odd, noticeable mistake has charm. Historically, the Shetland knitters promoted high standards and properly deplored articles with mistakes being sent out.

Although this might seem a hard counsel of perfection, get into the habit of looking for and rectifying mistakes, so that if they are still present in the knitting, only you and not a beholder know their whereabouts. More personal annoyance and dissatisfaction has been caused me by my deliberately ignoring mistakes at the time of knitting; now they always seem to jump out at me whenever I see the piece that includes them.

A stitch marker marks one of the corners of a shawl border. In the centre of each border I wound a length of contrast thread around the middle stitch. These give bearings about centring pattern motifs and their spacing and are easily moved up the knitting as it grows. (This is the Framed Shawl I describe in Section Four – after knitting the framed centre square, I picked up all the borders' stitches and knitted them outwards, using a long circular needle.)

How to Graft

Grafting or ("Weaving" – U.S.) is the technical name for producing by sewing, a join identical to a row of knitting. It is also known in one form as Kitchener Stitch. Make sure you have the same number of stitches on both sides of knitting to be joined. Keep both sets of stitches on the knitting needles – it's a useful tip to transfer both sets of stitches to a larger sized pair of needles or cotton thread, to stop them slipping off so readily. You could also give a coat of spray starch to the stitches to help stop them *unravelling*. Thread a blunt tapestry needle with sufficient matching yarn – at least three times the length to be grafted.

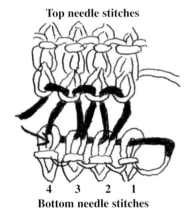

Top needle stitches

4   3   2   1

Bottom needle stitches

Make sure your rows of knitting to be grafted resemble exactly the drawing (left) – knit (or purl) an extra row if necessary.

N.B. The stitches are drawn "off the pins" for clarity. Keep them on the safety pin/knitting needle until you have been through each stitch at least once. (Note, that apart from the first and last stitch, you go into every stitch loop twice before slipping it off the needle).

I give the **garter stitch method for grafting** here; refer to the black thread in diagram left:

Method

*On the bottom needle, sew **down** through the first stitch and **up** through the second stitch. Next, on the top needle, sew **up** through the first stitch and **down** through the second stitch. Withdraw the first stitches from both needles**. Repeat from * to ** to end (the second stitches on both needles have now become "first stitches". Regularly pull the sewing yarn through the stitches to lie in place.

Sometimes, it may be necessary to do **stocking stitch grafting** (with Print O' the Wave, Horse Shoe Patterns etc), so I show it here – I find it easier to do than the garter stitch grafting, and it will always be better to use this than a raw, seamed join.

Top needle stitches

Method

(Again, make sure your knitting to be grafted has the same number of stitches on each side.)

*On the bottom needle, sew **down** through the first stitch and **up** through the second stitch. Now, on the top needle, sew **down** through the first stitch and **up** through the second stitch**.

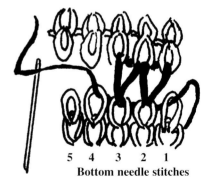

5   4   3   2   1

Bottom needle stitches

Withdraw the first stitches from both needles. Repeat from * to ** (the second stitches on both needles have now become "first stitches"). Regularly pull the sewing yarn through the stitches to lie in place.

I think grafting is one of the hardest processes in knitting, but it more than repays its difficulty by giving a totally indistinguishable join. Consult good knitting reference books to help achieve the best results.

Dressing & Care Instructions

Dressing

Shetland lace knitting in progress looks disappointingly shrivelled, dressing is essential for transforming it to its final beauty. Dressing or Blocking (U.S.) is the final processing of a knitted item. The instructions below explain how to dress a shawl, but equally apply to a stole or scarf. Items which can't be stretched and pinned to shape (e.g. the baby jackets) must be shaped by hand and dried flat instead. It can easily take an hour to wash and dress an item that needs pinning, put aside enough time for this.

After all the ends of yarn have been securely sewn in place with a fine tapestry needle, launder the shawl as per washing instructions (I wash my knitting in the bathroom hand basin, in tepid water with special wool detergent). Then, rinse the shawl in tepid water till the water runs clear. **Sudden changes or extremes in water temperature will cause shrinkage**! Lightly squeeze excess water out and lay the shawl in a large, clean, colourfast towel. With the shawl inside, roll the towel up and blot or press gently using your hands. **Do not wring**. Repeat if necessary, using fresh towels, until the shawl is damp, but not dripping wet.

The shawl is now ready to be shaped and **must** be dried flat (I prefer to dry large knitted items on the double bed, over a colourfast cover; others use a sheet on the carpet; traditionally it was done on special frames). First, spread the shawl so that it is a large square. Then, taking rustless pins, gently pull and pin each point of the edging so the shawl is square and under tension. Although it must not be over stretched, the knitting must be taut. I sometimes give a light coat of spray starch at this point. Adjust the pins till you are happy, then leave to thoroughly dry, which should take about three to six hours. An oscillating cool electric fan may be placed in the room if you are in a hurry.

Warning!

If you have small children or pets and are using pins, shut the door; obviously, pins are a danger to the unwary. **Do not** try to hurry things up by using heat or by putting the shawl in the sun – the colour of the yarn may be affected. Always use an appropriate detergent and **never** machine wash or dry. **Do not** let woollens soak in water or use bleach on them.

When the shawl is thoroughly dry, unpin it and enjoy it. Don't let it become too grubby, wash and dress it again – in all events, the shawl should be inspected and dressed yearly. Do any necessary mending before washing (see "Repair", below).

Aftercare

If the shawl needs to be stored, make sure it is perfectly clean and dry – wash and dress it again if necessary. Fold it lightly and with as few folds as possible, and encase it in white, acid-free tissue paper (available from most stationers and craft shops). Slip the shawl package into a clean pillowcase and store that in a dry cupboard. If you think you may have a moth problem, store bars of lavender scented soap nearby. Do not place anything on top of the shawl package to avoid flattening. I think polythene bags destroy the feel and colour of wool over time and so I don't use them, but this may be just a personal prejudice. When you need to use it again from storage, usually a quick spray of starch, gentle shaping and drying on a flat surface, will restore it.

Repair

Hopefully and with care, the shawl will not come to harm, but if it should get holed, use the same yarn (which, of course being farsighted or cautious, you've saved!) and repair it quickly and securely with a tapestry needle; remember a small crochet hook can be used to return stitches to their correct place – it will be worth keeping any pattern chart with the shawl to help with this.

Contrary to common belief, it is quite possible for totally invisible mends to be made in lace knitting so long as it involves only a few stitches (see "Dealing with Mistakes"). If you are ever in a situation where the repair is too much for you, at least secure all the loose stitches onto an appropriate yarn so that they don't unravel further. When you have gained more experience, it might be that you can repair it yourself.

Remember, properly looked after and stored, a treasured shawl can last several generations and is well worth the making and the care.

Heirloom Knitting

Section Three – Patterns

A Note on the Patterns

As well as presenting the patterns for this book in three approximate levels of skill, each level is additionally sub-divided into type of pattern – centres, borders and edgings.

Centres

These are usually smaller, regularly spaced, repeating patterns normally used for the middles of shawls, stoles, etc. (See note below). The simplest of all of the centres are garter stitched or moss stitched squares or rectangles. Centres can make useful patterns for jumpers, cardigans etc. Another descriptive Shetland term for a centre pattern is an "allover".

Borders

Borders are normally much larger patterns and are often **directional** (this means they have a "right way up"). They can be made up of groups of smaller lace motifs in panels of larger formal geometric shapes. Borders are usually the part where most artistic individuality is shown and it's useful to design these first and then choose complementing centre and edging patterns.

A detail of the Shetland Crepe Shawl – see "Projects". This shows a garter stitch Centre (1), an Old Shell Border (2) and a Clematis Edging (3).

Edgings

Edgings are called "laces" in Shetland. Edgings are what they say, the strip of knitting that traditionally surrounds a piece and are made either first or last. Classic Shetland shawls and stoles do not have any casting on as such: the stitches for knitting the borders or centres are picked up from a long edging strip that's made first of all – the strip itself would either have a very narrow cast-on or an "invisible cast-on". All this care was taken so that the finished item was as elastic as possible and had no detracting seams. (I explain the construction of Shetland shawls and stoles more fully in Section Four). Edgings have an **inside**, or straight edge that joins to the knitting and an **outside**, usually pointed, decorative edge.

---

centre
pattern

← **Plain knitted outside frame**

Please Note

To save space, the centre patterns in this book are presented without any plain knitted "tops and bottoms" being charted – though I do give a suggested number of L.H. and R.H. side stitches.

Normally, if you were making a centre pattern, it would be "framed" with at least, a narrow strip of plain knitting – i.e. garter stitch – all round, see diagram left. A good rule of thumb is to knit twice the number of rows to start and finish as there are side stitches.

e.g. **4** plain knitted stitches each side = **8** plain knitted rows below and the same above.

Field of Flowers Pattern

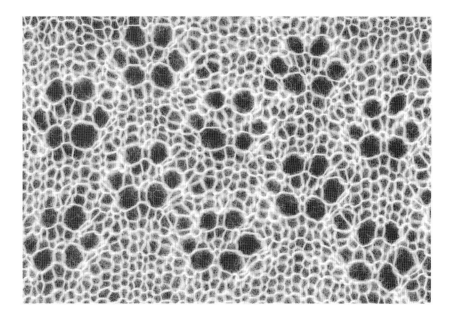

Field of Flowers is my modification of the Cat's Paw Pattern. This is a very simple and pretty *centre* pattern, ideal for those new to following knitting charts. Before pattern row 1, I show 3 of the 6 garter stitch "frame" rows that follow casting on and after the final repeat of rows 1 to 18, I also show 2 of the 5 finishing rows of the garter stitch frame – row 1 is knitted already as row 18.

Experience * * Knitters: Start by working out how many stitches to cast on – multiply a number you want by 12 and then add on the number of stitches for each side. After casting on (see "How to Cast On"), work the 6* foundation garter stitch frame rows, then follow the chart (see "How to Read a Chart"). Remember, each even row is garter stitch or plain knitted, as are all blank squares in the pattern outline. **Remember, the numbers in the pattern outline count *plain stitches* that go between *pattern stitches* or from the sides to the *pattern stitches*.** There are 12 rows in the row repeat block. When you have finished knitting the pattern – after a row 17 so the top and bottom line of motifs balance – make sure you knit 6 plain rows to finish the top of the frame.

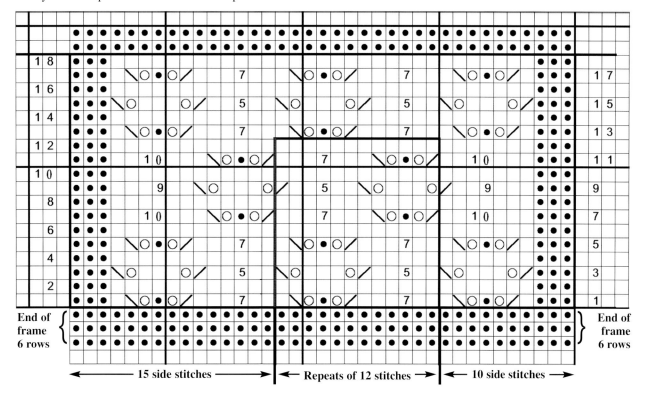

*The last 3 of the 6 frame foundation rows are shown at the bottom of the chart, see page 48.   **Experience ****

49

Chequered Acre Centre Pattern

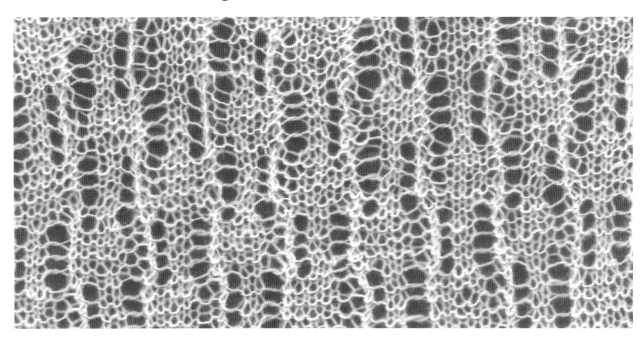

Chequered Acre is a development of a very simple Shetland pattern called Acre – which is just rows 1 and 2 knitted repeatedly; Acre makes an elastic fabric which was often used as the main pattern on socks and other hosiery. Chequered Acre, by staggering the pattern into horizontal bands, produces a less stretchy fabric and is more suited to be a *centre* pattern. Knit all even rows.

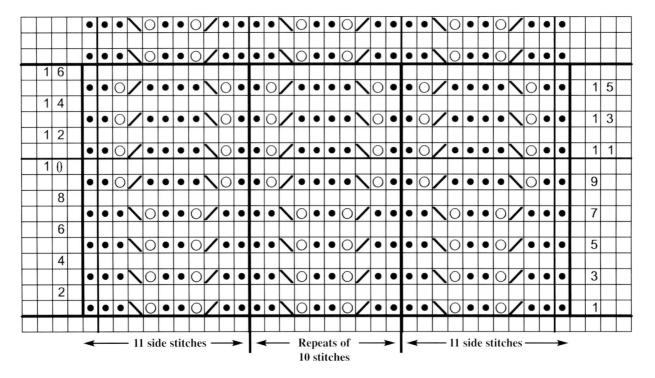

Experience **

Cast on multiples of 10 stitches + 22 (11 + 11 extra stitches on each side)
e.g. (10 x 9) + 22 = 112 stitches.

N.B. You may if needed, cast on 2 extra stitches for each side but be sure to include these in the above sum.

Old Shell Border Pattern

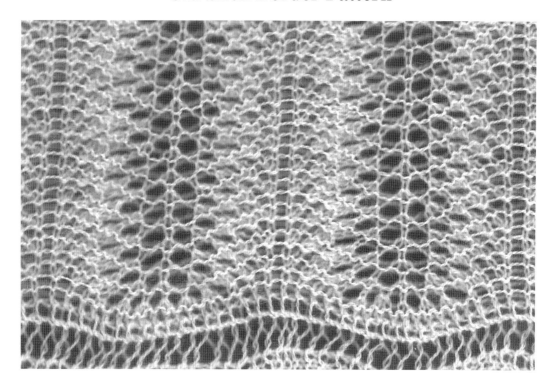

This famous pattern is the one that most people think of as Shetland lace. Another name is Hap Shell, both shell names reflect the fanning shapes created by the *delayed decreases*. There is mild debate over the true name; it actually seems to be Old Shell and not Old Shale (see "Pattern Names"). Anyway, it certainly is a popular pattern, well known in the nineteenth century, then offered bordering *Hap* and *Crepe* shawls. These deceptively simple looking shawls usually had plain knitted centres, sometimes on the diagonal – see "Shawl Centres", Section Four, for how to do this – and were considered a knitting challenge because they would readily show *misknitted* stitches or faulty tension in the garter stitch part. (I have designed my own Cobweb Crepe Shawl with Clematis Edging that can be found in the "Projects Section" of this book).

I give the version below as a four row repeat pattern. It has many variations, it could be six or eight row repeats i.e. one patterned row to five or seven plain knitted rows. Also, instead of six *overs* as below, it could be just four or eight overs; the decreases matching accordingly: e.g. Cast on multiples of 12 stitches – "* knit 2 tog. twice, (m.1, k.1) 4 times, knit 2 tog. twice**. Repeat from * to ** to end of row".

Experience * * Knitters: I have given the pattern below without any plain knitting rows to start or finish. I suggest you knit 4 rows of garter stitch to start. To finish, after a pattern row 1, knit 4 plain rows so that there is a very narrow, plain knitted framing strip all round.

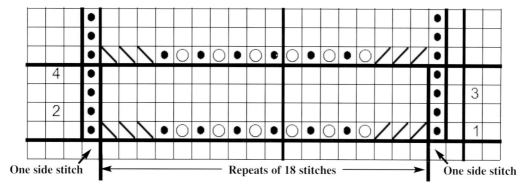

One side stitch ← Repeats of 18 stitches → One side stitch

Experience **

Cast on multiples of 18 stitches + 2 (1 + 1 extra stitch on each side)
e.g. (8 x18) + 2 = 146 stitches.

Crest O'the Wave Border Pattern

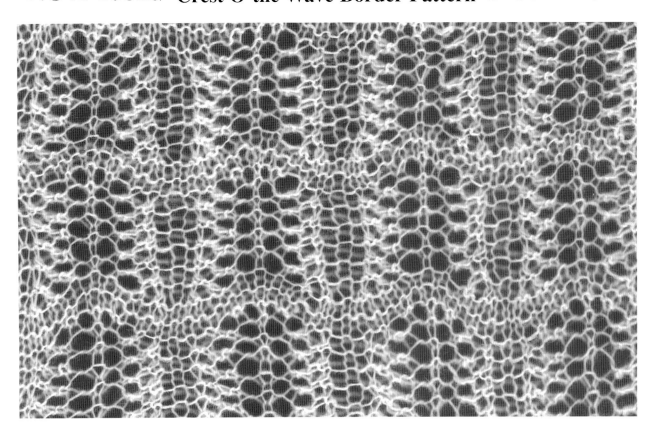

Crest O'the Wave is a variation of Feather and Fan Pattern, inserting bands of garter stitch into that pattern as a feature. This makes a lovely alternative border design to Old Shell. It might be nice to work sections in contrasting colours, by changing the shade of yarn every 16th row.

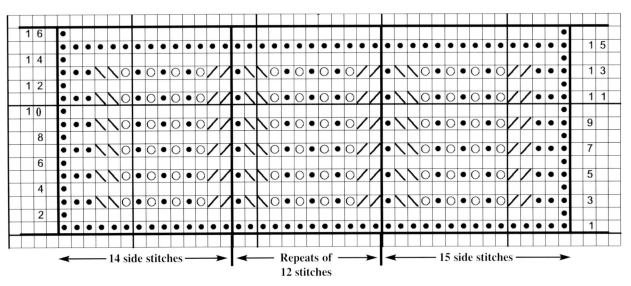

Experience **

Cast on multiples of 12 stitches + 29 (14 + 15 extra stitches on each side)
e.g. (12 x 8) + 29 = 125 stitches.

N.B. If needed, cast on up to 3 extra stitches for each side. Include these in the above sum.

The Brand Iron Edging

This easy edging is one that is over a hundred years old. This is the edging that Mrs A. Hunter of Unst used for the shawl pattern that was one of the few Shetland lace knitting patterns available from wool shops. (I have two copies of this, one in black and white from the 1950s and another I bought to knit for my family in the 1980s. That's the one that started my interest in this form of knitting.)

I chart the edging exactly as it is given to be worked finally around the completed shawl, this means the first stitch on odd rows is shown as *slipped*, it could just be plain knitted should you prefer.

Experience * * Knitters:

Row 11: The number 13 tells you to knit 13 plain stitches after the "knit 2 together", to the end of the row.

Row 12 is "cast off 5 stitches, knit to end. (13 sts.)" As always, cast off very loosely.

Remember: Knit stitch all the blank squares in the pattern outline on the even rows – the first and last stitch on these rows are marked with dots – get used to remembering that empty squares (and stitches with numerals) in these patterns are always plain knitted this way. By omitting unnecessary symbols like this, the patterns are easier to read and follow.

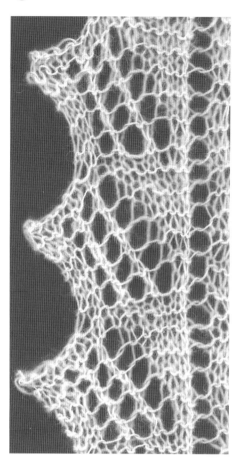

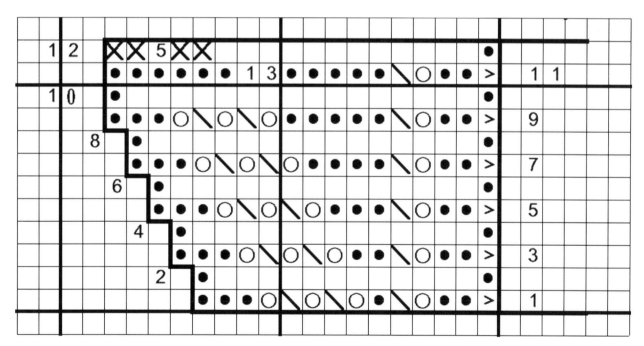

Cast on 13 stitches

Experience **

Traditional Scalloped Edging

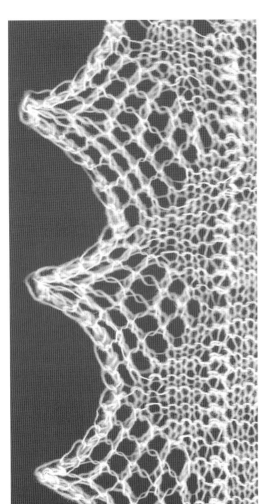

Traditional Scalloped Edging is a favourite Shetland pattern used frequently for Old Shell bordered shawls. It is also called Fan Edging.

I chart the edging as a strip to be worked initially for a shawl, this means the last stitch on even rows is shown as knitted, it could be knitted "2 together" with a stitch from a shawl border should you prefer to knit it around a shawl to finish it.

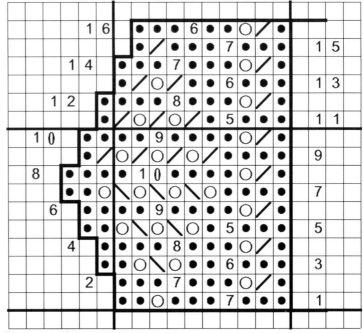

Cast on 9 stitches   Experience **

Experienced Knitters:

This edging is very easy to change, here is a much larger version coupled with the *Lacy Edge Stitch*. Other variations in this book are Scallop Shell Edging and Double Scallop Shell Edging.

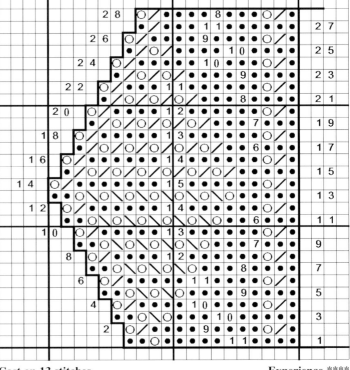

Cast on 13 stitches   Experience ****

54

Cat's Paw Pattern

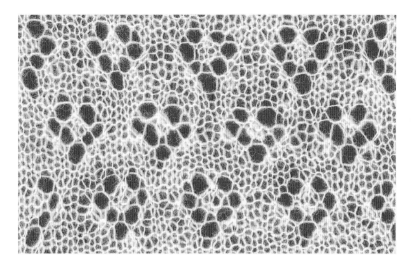

This is from a late nineteenth century knitting pattern for a shawl centre, but I have traced it back to at least the early 1800s in Central Europe. Cat's Paw is a regular arrangement of bead motifs in plain knitting; experienced knitters could change the spacing of the motifs. Remember to knit all blank and numbered squares in the pattern outline.

The outside pattern stitches on each side on row 7, show \ and / ("knit 2 together") replacing ▲ ("slip 1, knit 2 together, pass slipped stitch over") this keeps the number of stitches consistent.

Experienced Knitters: You might like to know the original centre was worked in a fine classic 3 ply with British size 10/3.25mm needles. It had 17 whole motif stitch repeats per row – 143 stitches were cast on, and it began with two rows of plain knitting and then as from row 13 on my pattern. Rows 13 to 12 (20 rows) were then repeated 11 times so the top and bottom balanced; then an extra row of plain knitting was done to finish.

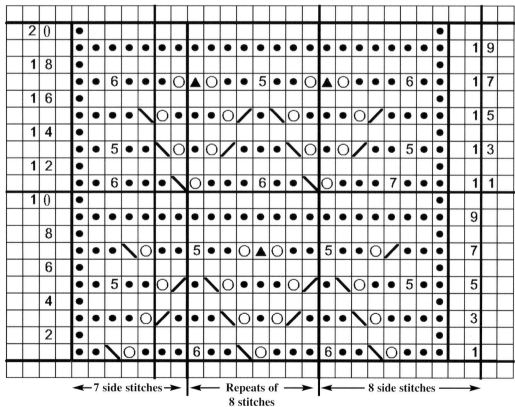

Experience ***

Cast on multiples of 8 stitches + 15 (7 + 8 extra stitches on each side)
e.g. (8 x 8) + 15 = 79 stitches.

Shetland Fir Cone Pattern

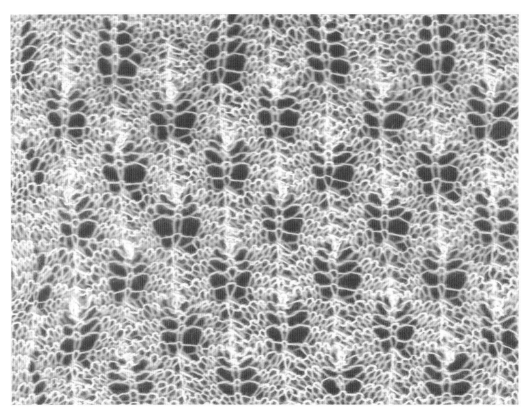

This effective *allover* lace is made by *delayed decreases* giving the curving shapes; otherwise it would be very like the Chequered Acre Pattern. Excellent for scarves and *un-bordered* shawls.

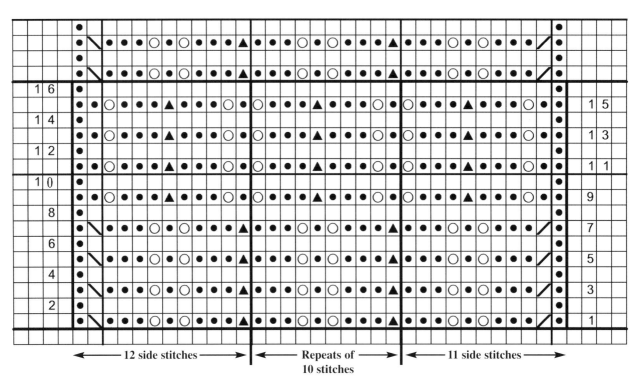

Experience ***

Cast on multiples of 10 stitches + 23 (12 + 11 extra stitches on each side)
e.g. (10 x 15) + 23 = 173 stitches.

N.B. You may if needed, cast on extra stitches for each side. Include these in the above sum.

Small Leaf Pattern

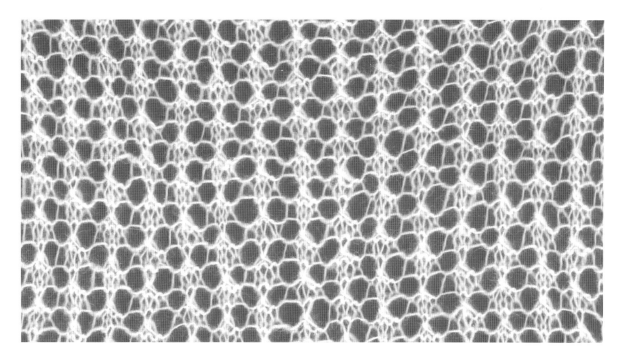

Small Leaf Pattern makes a basic *fill-in* pattern for larger elements and can be a useful mesh to bed other motifs on, see "Unst Lace Stole – Project 7". It is one of the simplest of the Shetland centres and is basically like a tiny bead stitch. It could be used as a centre pattern for a scarf or a stole with a similar dainty edging such as the Cyprus Edging or the Traditional Peaked Shawl Edging.

Experience * * * Knitters: This is a simple 4 stitch and 4 row repeat pattern. Only the third stitch in from each side on row 1 is altered from the rest. A careful look at the chart shows that all the increases are vertically aligned, the "knit 1s" and "*double decreases*" alternate. Once you've learnt this, remembering the pattern is simple. **There are 4 rows in the row repeat block.**

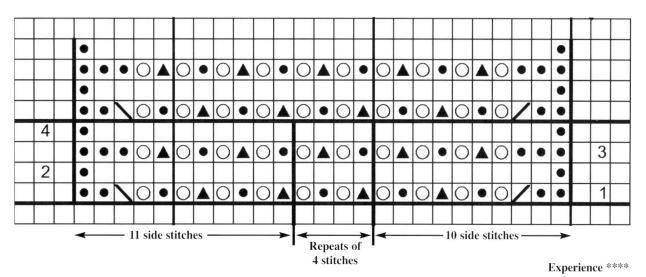

Cast on multiples of 4 stitches + 21 (11 + 10 extra stitches on each side)
e.g. (4 x 20) + 21 = 101 stitches.

N.B. If needed, cast on extra stitches for each side. Include these in the above sum.

Bead Faggot Pattern

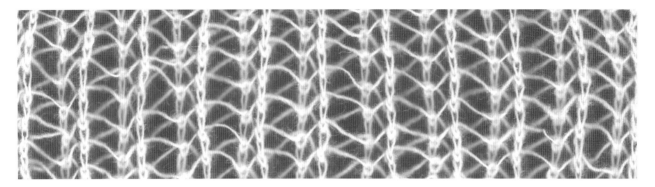

This very simple two row pattern is made by *close-working* Small Leaf Pattern, page 57, I include it because it is still useful for making dainty baby socks as it was used originally; and I use this as a demonstration pattern for the baby bootees (see "Project 1").

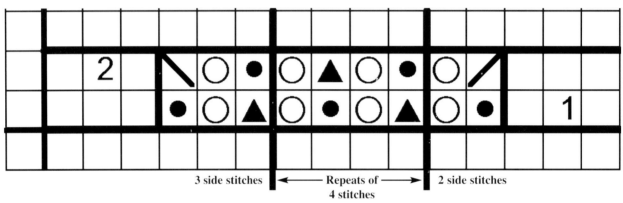

3 side stitches   ← Repeats of →   2 side stitches
4 stitches

Cast on multiples of 4 stitches + 5 (3 + 2 extra stitches on each side)
e.g. (9 x 4) + 5 = 41 stitches.

N.B. You may if needed, cast on extra stitches for each side. Include these in the above sum.

I used this pretty and very simple faggot stitch to work the main pattern on these bootees, see "Project 1" for instructions on how to make them.

Two Razor Shell Patterns

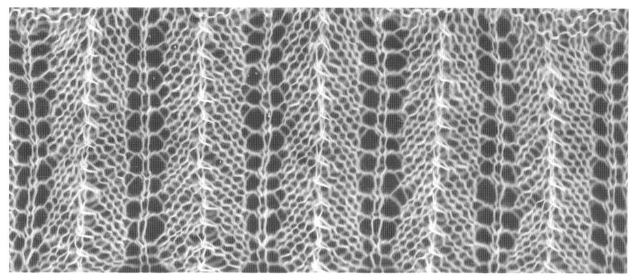

Interestingly, I have found this pattern described in an old knitting brochure as Feather And Fan, but more consistently I have found it recorded as Spout or Razor Shell. It is a pattern that is easily experimented with and I give one alternative below. This two-row pattern is one that is very pretty when knitted in bands of complementing colours because, as with any pattern with markedly *delayed decreases* (e.g. Old Shell, Horseshoe Pattern), the lines of colour undulate accordingly. See "New Shell Scarf, Project 2". **N.B.** Purl all even rows for the pattern chart below, to get the above pattern.

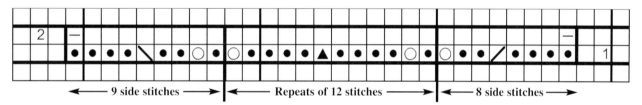

← 9 side stitches → | ← Repeats of 12 stitches → | ← 8 side stitches →

Experience ***

Cast on multiples of 12 stitches + 17 (9 + 8 extra stitches on each side)
e.g. (12 x 8) + 17 = 113 stitches.

N.B. You may if needed, cast on extra stitches for each side. Include these in the above sum.

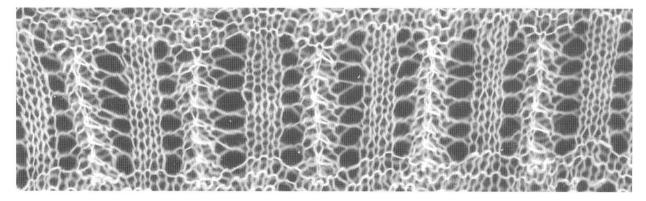

This is one of many variations of the Razor Shell, and the pattern row is as follows:

Cast on multiples of 8 and 3 extra L.H. side stitches.

"*knit 3, make 1, knit 1, slip 1, knit 2 together, pass slipped stitch over; knit 1, make 1**. Repeat from * to** to end, finishing with a knit 3." Each even row is purled, each odd row patterned.

This would be a suitable pattern for the leg of a sock, or a scarf pattern.

Mrs Montague's Pattern

This pattern is a very early lace, it was the pattern on fine silk stockings belonging to Queen Elizabeth I, and a Mrs Montague was her silk woman and would have knitted stockings for the Queen. This is a simple *allover* design and would make an excellent shawl centre (either with or without borders), especially when combined with an equally modest edging such as the Doris Edging. **This is a 16 row repeat block pattern.** Up to seven more side stitches can be added left and right – remember to include these in the casting on sum.

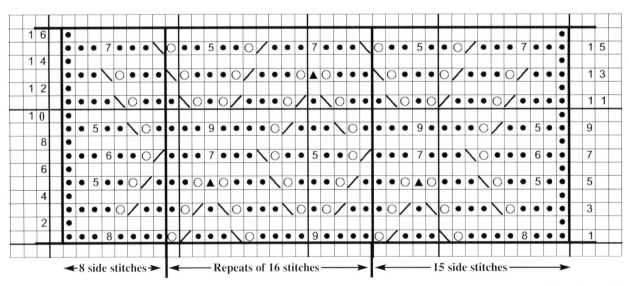

Experience ***

Cast on multiples of 16 stitches + 23 (8 + 15 extra stitches on each side)
e.g. (16 x 10) + 23 = 183 stitches.

Mrs Montague's Pattern II

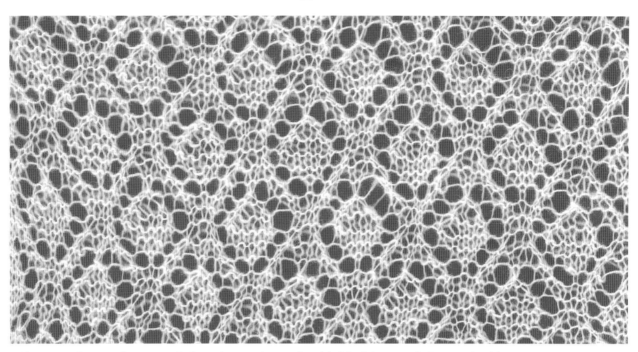

This pattern is one of many variations that can be made with Mrs Montague's Pattern; in this example I have set the diamonds closer together. You might try this as a centre pattern with the Doris Edging for harmony of design. **There are 20 rows in the row repeat block.**

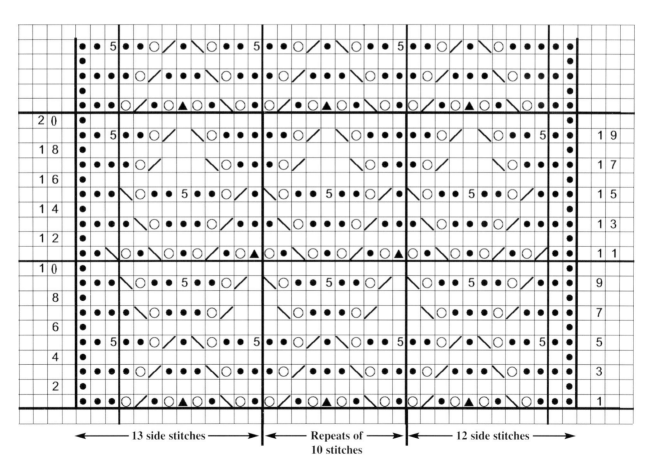

13 side stitches — Repeats of 10 stitches — 12 side stitches

Cast on multiples of 10 stitches + 25 (13 + 12 extra stitches on each side)
e.g. (10 x 8) + 25 = 105 stitches.

Trellis Diamond Pattern

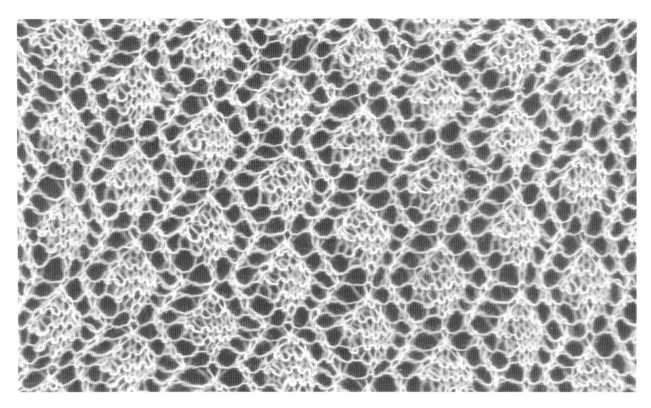

Trellis Diamond, which I have seen as the *centre* of a Victorian Shetland lace shawl, is a pretty and simple *allover* design which seems a direct descendent of the well known Mrs Montague's Pattern. It gives an airier lace that experienced knitters could easily modify by enlarging; the diamonds could be 7 or 9 stitches wide instead of the 5 shown here. In one enlarged version and combined with an eyelet pattern (Rosebud) it makes a traditional Shetland design, Rose Lace. Knit all even rows.

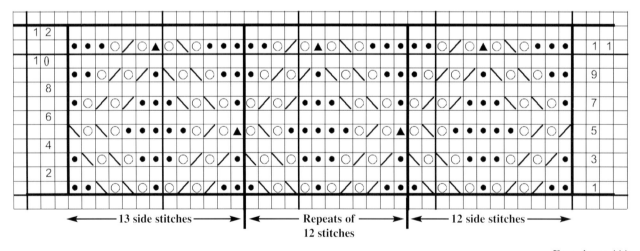

Experience ***

Cast on multiples of 12 stitches + 25 (13 + 12 extra stitches on each side)
e.g. (12 x 10) + 25 = 145 stitches.

N.B. You may if needed, cast on extra stitches for each side. Include these in the above sum.

Trellis Diamond Pattern II

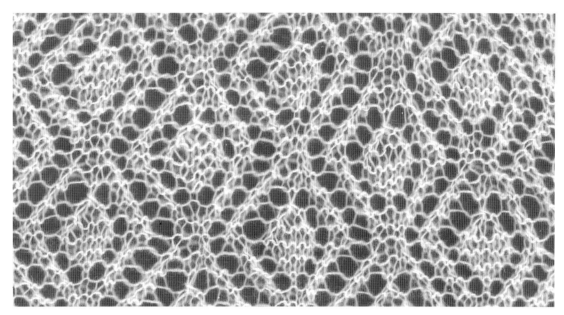

Trellis Diamond II is a wider version I made of Trellis Diamond Pattern, and would make a good *allover* for a shawl, etc. Experienced knitters could try working this by omitting the plain knitting rows and working the pattern rows only i.e. making existing row 3 into a row 2, row 5 into a row 3, row 7 into a row 4 and so on. I call this "**close-working**" a pattern; technically speaking, it makes a **lace knitting** pattern into **knitted lace**. This is very similar in appearance to Mrs Montague's II Pattern. This is a 20 row repeat pattern; close-worked, it would only be a 10 row repeat.

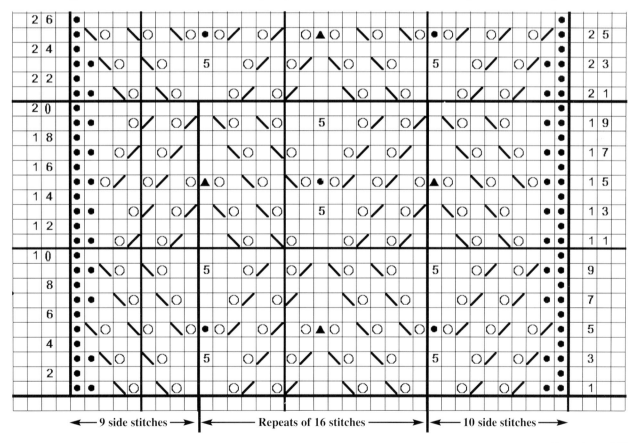

← 9 side stitches → ← Repeats of 16 stitches → ← 10 side stitches →

Experience ***

Cast on multiples of 16 stitches + 19 (9 + 10 extra stitches on each side)
e.g. (16 x 11) + 19 = 195 stitches.

N.B. If needed, cast on extra stitches for each side. Include these in the above sum.

Rosebud Pattern

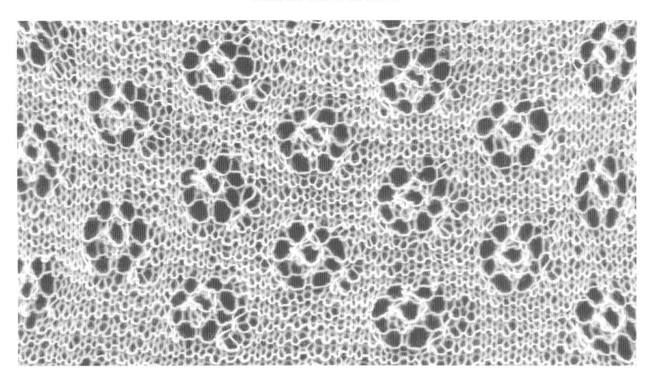

Rosebud is one of a group of *Eyelet* designs. On its own like this, it might also be called a Shetland Eyelid Pattern. Again, this could be modified by experimenting with the spacing or be combined with other patterns as it has been with Rose Lace. This would be a lovely *allover* for the centre of a shawl, especially if the border or edge has other eyelet groups included.

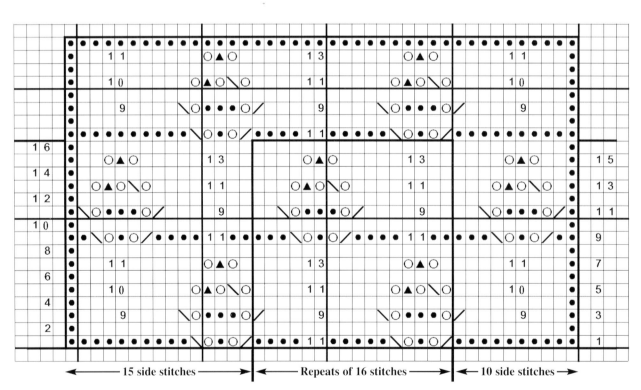

15 side stitches ← Repeats of 16 stitches → 10 side stitches

Experience ***

Cast on multiples of 16 stitches + 25 (15 + 10 extra stitches on each side)
e.g. (16 x 5) + 25 = 105 stitches.

Leaf Lace Pattern

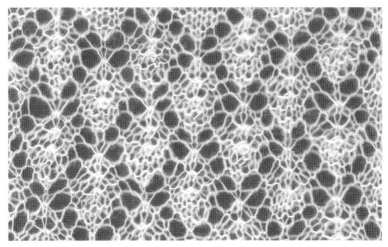

Leaf Lace is a basic but lovely pattern and seems related to the Horseshoe Pattern. It is easily experimented with – instead of the leaves being only five stitches at their widest, they could be seven or nine stitches. Also, experienced knitters might like to make it a *close-worked* pattern by omitting the plain knitted rows. Three or more knit stitches may be added to each side.

N.B. Here the pattern is photographed from the "**back**" – but remember there is no wrong side with garter stitched Shetland lace. The "**front**" is shown on page 19 for comparison. Knit **or** purl all even rows, I have not put in symbols on these rows as either a stocking stitch or garter stitch *ground* would look lovely; see Large Leaf Pattern which is stocking stitched.

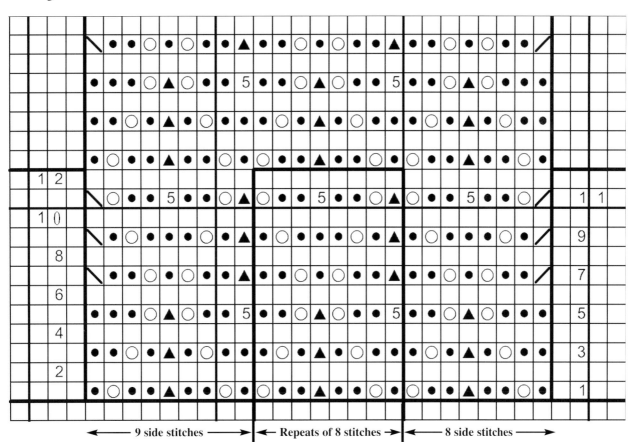

←——— 9 side stitches ———→ ←— Repeats of 8 stitches —→ ←——— 8 side stitches ———→

Experience ***

Cast on multiples of 8 stitches + 17 (9 + 8 extra stitches on each side)
e.g. (8 x 14) + 17 = 129 stitches.

N.B. You may if needed, cast on extra stitches for each side. Include these in the above sum.

Candlelight Pattern

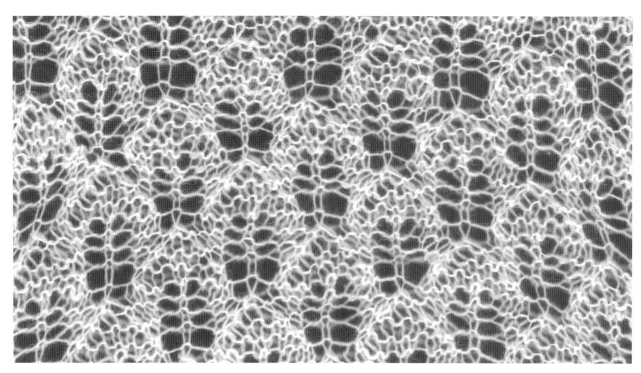

Candlelight is another famous old pattern – I have traced it back to at least the first half of the nineteenth century. In Shetland, it is also known as Fern Stitch Pattern. This is usually worked with purled even rows (stocking stitch) which gives a pronounced diamond shape to the "flame" but I give it here as garter stitched throughout because it is in 1 ply (see "Stitch Advice").

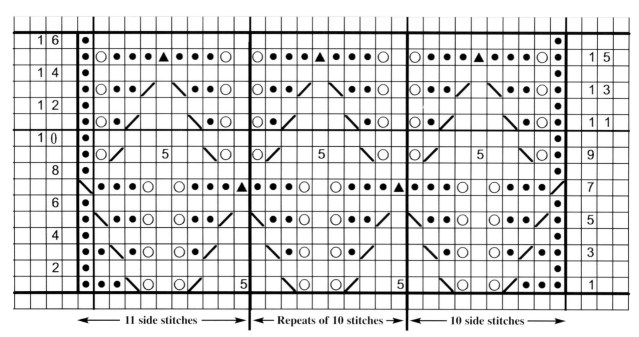

Experience ***

Cast on multiples of 10 stitches + 21 (11 + 10 extra stitches on each side)
e.g. (10 x 12) + 21 = 141 stitches.

N.B. Cast on up to 4 extra stitches for each side. Include these in the above sum.

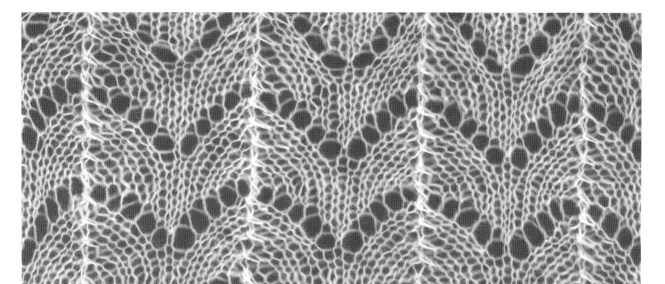

This is a classic Shetland lace pattern (I have also found it called Fishtail Pattern), easy to make and remember. I show the pattern above in a stocking stitch ground but it can be worked in a garter stitch one (as charted below), in the finest yarns. Like many of the patterns involving *delayed decreases,* it lends itself to being knitted in bands of colour to give an "arches of colour" result. Just change the yarn colour at the end of every row repeat block. It's interesting to see that simply by *half-staggering* the pattern after row 10, one gets the Large Leaf Pattern. This pattern is very easy to alter; a variation can be obtained if one just knits from rows 5 to 10 inclusive.

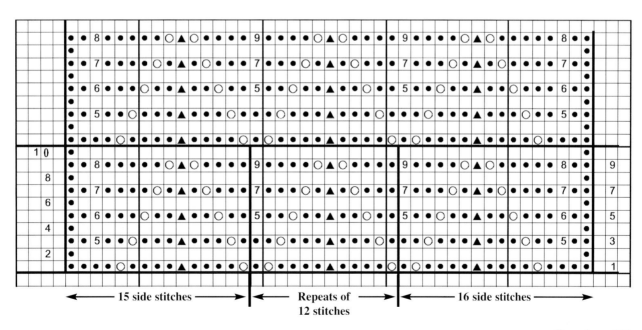

← 15 side stitches → ← Repeats of 12 stitches → ← 16 side stitches →

Experience ✳✳✳

Cast on multiples of 12 stitches + 31 (15 + 16 extra stitches on each side)
e.g. (12 x 8) + 31 = 127 stitches.

N.B. You may if needed, cast on extra stitches for each side. Include these in the above sum.

Large Leaf Pattern

One can see how this pattern was developed by comparing it with the Horseshoe and Leaf Patterns. In the above example, I have knitted odd and purled even rows (stocking stitch) but this is just as effective in a garter stitch ground, as it's charted – remember, most of the Shetland traditional fine 1 ply Shetland lace was made in garter stitch. Experienced knitters might like to try *close-working* this pattern by omitting the plain knitted or even rows and working just the ten pattern rows to obtain a finer knitted lace.

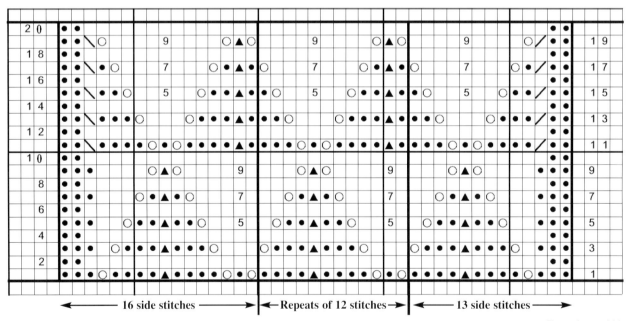

← 16 side stitches → | **←Repeats of 12 stitches→** | **← 13 side stitches →**

Experience ✳✳✳

Cast on multiples of 12 stitches + 29 (16 + 13 extra stitches on each side)
e.g. (12 x 8) + 29 = 125 stitches.

N.B. If needed, cast on extra stitches for each side. Include these in the above sum.

Madeira Pattern

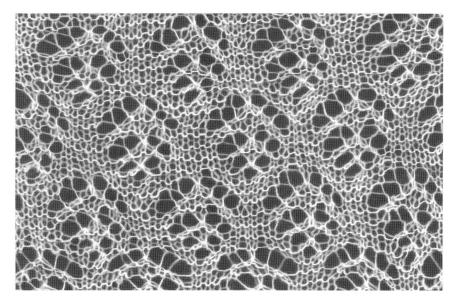

This pattern motif is traditional in Shetland lace, and seems to be a variation of the fern motif; used like this it makes an attractive *allover*. Experienced knitters could alter the spacing easily. This is a 28 row repeat block pattern.

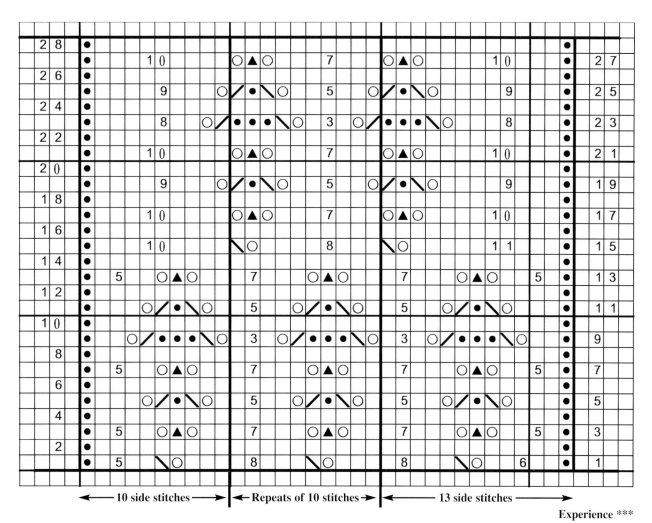

◀—— 10 side stitches ——▶ ◀— Repeats of 10 stitches —▶ ◀—— 13 side stitches ——▶

Experience ***

Cast on multiples of 10 stitches + 23 (10 + 13 extra stitches on each side)
e.g. (10 x 12) + 23 = 143 stitches.

N.B. You may if needed, cast on extra stitches for each side. Include these in the above sum.

Mrs Hunter's Pattern

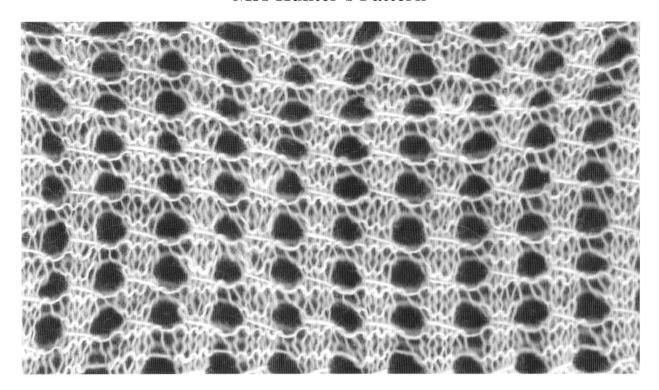

To me, this seems to be a most unusual pattern to be a Shetland one because it involves a large looped decrease that encases three stitches. It was traditionally used as the centre of plain *hap* shawls or scarves with very simple borders and basic triangular edgings – like the plain triangle in the Triangle with Vandyke Edging (but without the faggoting start and edging). The borders were usually made of the plainer lace knitting designs such as Old Shell and Crest O'the Wave. This is a 4 row repeat pattern and makes a very elastic lace.

Row 1 The ★ symbol means that you must do the following special *decrease*: "slip 1 stitch *knit wise*, knit 3, then pass the slipped stitch over the 3 stitches just knitted" – this makes the large loop bundling the 3 stitches together, as a careful look at the photograph shows. Effectively, this is a decrease row, losing a quarter of the total stitches. New stitches to compensate are on row 3.

Row 3 This is the increase row which places a "make 1" above each of the star symbols on row 1 to rebalance the number of stitches.

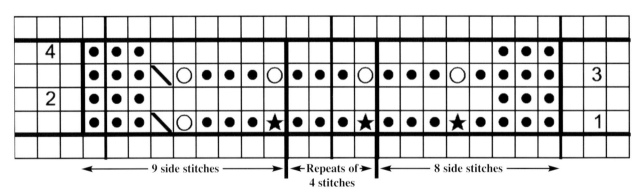

Experience ***

Cast on multiples of 4 stitches + 17 (9 + 8 extra stitches on each side)
e.g. (4 x 20) + 17 = 97 stitches.

N.B. If needed, cast on extra stitches for each side. Include these in the above sum.

Print O' the Wave Pattern

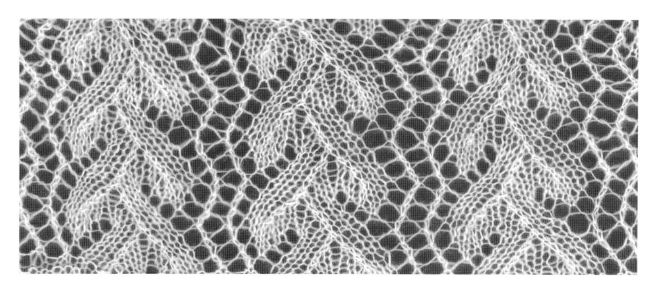

Print O' the Wave is another of the classic Shetland lace patterns and one of the most graceful. It has zigzagging lines of *faggots* combined with a travelling leaf motif; indeed, Trailing Leaf Pattern is one of this pattern's alternative names. By continuing the lines of the zigzags and repeating the leaf shapes, we get more "fronds" on each side. Doing just this, I re-created an old Shetland design which I have called Elaborated Print O' the Wave. The pattern here, could be easily adapted by adding pairs of stitches to make more lines of zigzag separating the main vertical motifs. Experienced knitters will see an *insertion* could be made by working up odd row stitches 1 – 27, just change stitch 27 on row 1 to a "knit 1", instead of the "make 1" and stitch 27, rows 9 and 11; to a "knit 2 tog.". Purl all even rows.

N.B. This pattern is best worked in stocking stitch as charted; all ＼ symbols should be worked as "slip 1, knit1, pass slipped stitch over", so the pronounced line of the "spines" of the decreases become a design feature.

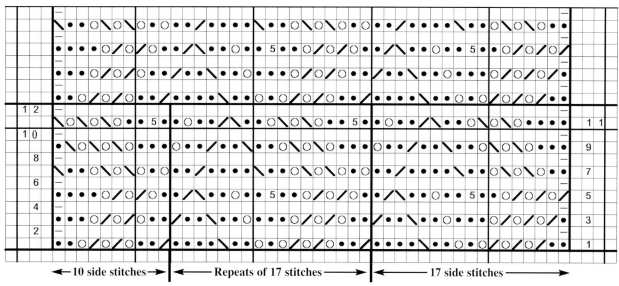

Experience ***

Cast on multiples of 17 stitches + 27 (10 + 17 extra stitches on each side)
e.g. (17 x 7) + 27 = 146 stitches.

N.B. If needed, cast on extra stitches for each side. Include these in the above sum.

Feather and Fan Border Pattern

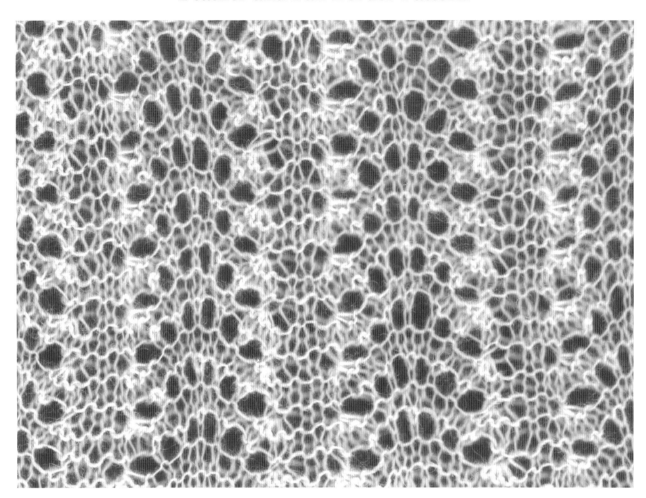

It's easy to see that this pattern is a variation of the famous Shetland lace Old Shell. By comparing the two, it can be seen that the decreases only, have been compressed into one stitch action each side of the increases. This is a simple pattern, the **black stars** mean "knit 4 together"; the **white stars** mean "knit 4 together through back of loops" or could be worked as "slip 2, knit 2 together, pass slipped stitches over" if the knitter finds that version easier. **The pattern below is only a 4 row repeat pattern.**

Experienced Knitters might like to try putting in more pairs of knit rows between the pattern rows or try purling each second row. This was how these traditional patterns were knitted in Shetland; many knitters had their personal versions of this pattern and of Old Shell. Feather and Fan is another good pattern to try changing the colours with, i.e. by making each pattern repeat in a different shade or contrasting colour.

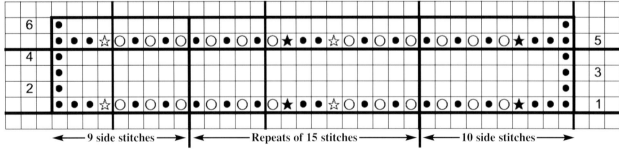

Experience ***

Cast on multiples of 15 stitches + 19 (9 + 10 extra stitches on each side)
e.g. (15 x 8) + 19 = 139 stitches.

N.B. You may if needed, cast on extra stitches for each side. Include these in the above sum.

Old Spanish Lace Border

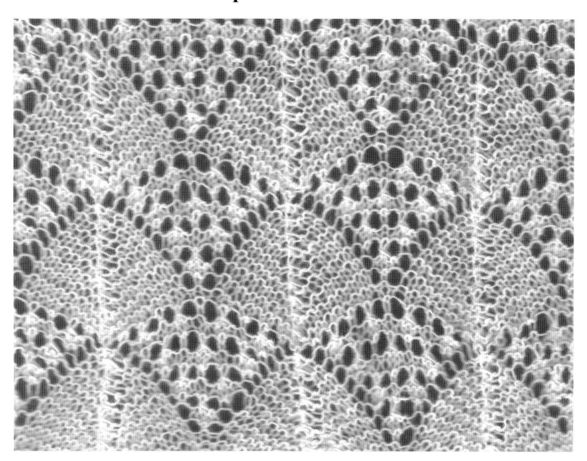

This is a dainty lace design whose large plain knitted triangles have been constructed using *delayed decreases*. It is like a Horseshoe Pattern combined with a small bead stitch, and is another that would look effective if knitted in bands of toning colours. It is also known as Madeira Cascade Pattern and makes a very striking lace for a border, or could be used as a suitable centre for large simple scarves or shawls without border panels; just a simple knitted edging. Knit all even rows for the pattern photographed here.

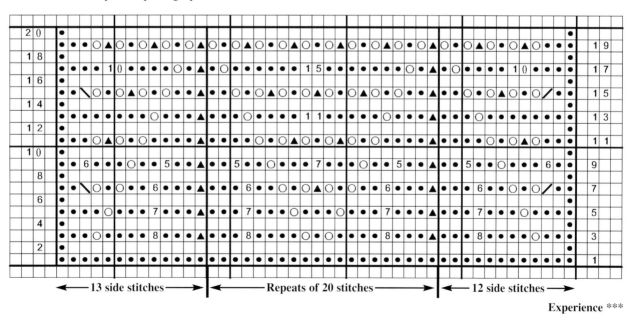

Experience ***

Cast on multiples of 20 stitches + 25 (13 + 12 extra stitches on each side)
e.g. (20 x 7) + 25 = 165 stitches.

N.B. You may if needed, cast on extra stitches for each side. Include these in the above sum.

Doris Edging

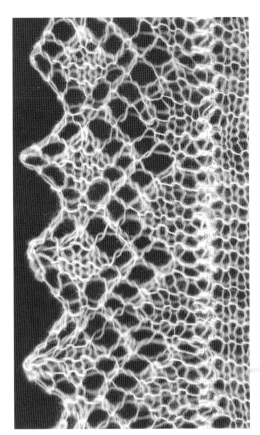

This old but lovely pattern comes from a 1910s needlework magazine, which dates from the last days of that high-fashion period of "white knitting" as lace knitting was then also known. Unfortunately, the demand for patterns meant there were usually lots of mistakes in the text, which were often rushed translations of European patterns. Doris though, has all the features of a Shetland lace pattern, with its diamond and zigzag combination.

Experienced knitters: You might like to try combining the Doris Edging with one of the charted *insertions* e.g. the Ring Insertion on the Ring Shawl Lace. This is easily done with either a panel of *faggots* or just knitted straight on. See "Adapting an Edging Pattern". You will then get a wider lace edging to use.

You might like to try the *Lacy Edge Stitch* with this.

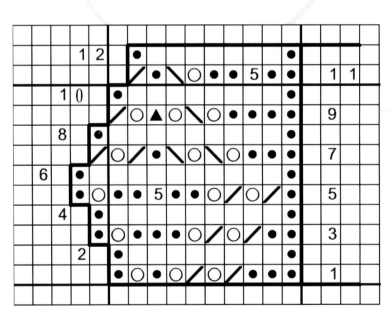

Cast on 9 stitches   **Experience ✳✳✳**

Rippled Diamond Edging

I created this edging by experimenting with a large Trellis Diamond Pattern and a bead motif. It makes a simple and basic edging for shawls or stoles with diamonds in the main part. It could be made even simpler, without the centred bead in the large diamond; simply replace that element's pattern stitches with knit stitches.

Experienced knitters would be able to adapt this pattern further by adding more zigzag lines or by putting a spider or other small motif in the place of the bead.

Experience * * * Knitters it is advisable to knit the last stitches at the outside (pointed) edge very loosely, so that the maximum stretch can be achieved when finally *dressing* the knitting to *ease* this wide edging around corners.

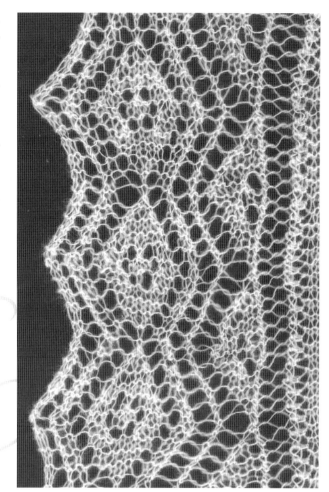

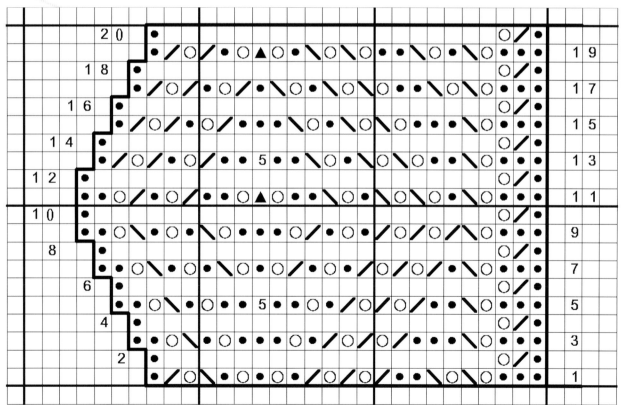

Cast on 23 stitches

Experience ***

75

Traditional Peaked Shawl Edging

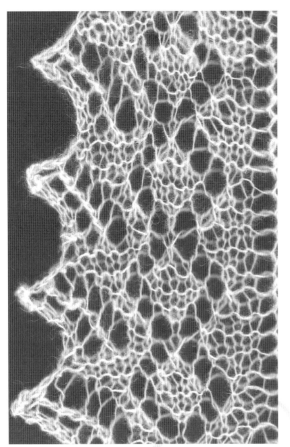

This beautiful edging is very similar to the Doris Edging but with a tiny faggot stitch edge at the outside. This comes from an end of the nineteenth century knitting pattern where it edged a Shetland *Crepe* shawl very like "Project 5".

Traditional Peaked Shawl Edging would be especially suitable paired with centres and borders using diamonds in the main pattern or with an Old Shell bordered shawl.

Experience * * * Knitters: This 10 row pattern has a slip stitched straight edge. Usually, this was done to give a slightly tighter inside edge; these slipped stitches could be plain knitted instead. Row 10 reads "cast off 5 stitches, knit to last 3 stitches, make 1, knit 2 together, knit 1. (17sts.)"

Experienced knitters could try altering this pattern by enlarging the centre diamonds (to seven or nine stitches wide instead) or perhaps even by omitting the plain knitted rows and altering any stitches accordingly. If you do this, I recommend adding in a plain knitted row 6 to keep an even number of rows – this means all the patterns first rows remain odd, outward rows.

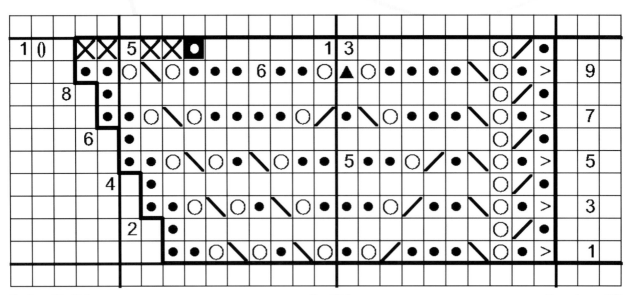

Cast on 17 stitches   > = slip stitch   **Experience ***

◙ = Casting off *Lock-stitch*

When you cast off you have to knit the next stitch along to pass the first cast off stitch over. This anchor stitch I call the "lock stitch" because it stops the casting off undoing itself. When you cast off 5 stitches, the lock stitch is the stitch the fifth cast off stitch is passed over – so here it's the sixth from the beginning of the cast off row.

Scallop Shell Edging

This large edging is a late nineteenth century variation of the well known edging I have called Traditional Scalloped Edging. I find it is a very useful and pretty edging for fine knitted lace items that include tree motifs. I developed Double Scallop Shell Edging from this pattern, by changing the direction of the *faggoting* in the top of the inside triangle.

Experienced knitters could adapt the pattern by changing the number of plain knitted stitches that divide off the outside shell component of the design. Instead of the three as first shown, there could be one or many more; obviously for each stitch omitted or created, the number of cast on stitches must be adjusted accordingly. By omitting the first 5 stitches and changing the inside *faggot* triangle into plain knitting, one gets a much larger version of the Traditional Scalloped Edging.

The first stitch of each odd row could be slipped for a tighter edge. See advice with the Wave Edging about the Lacy Edge Stitch.

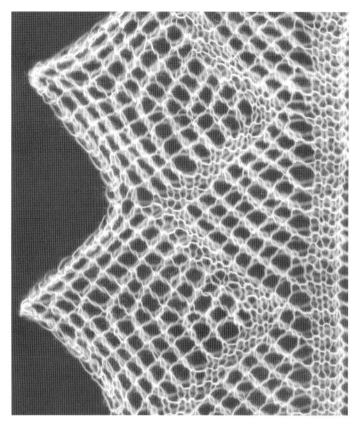

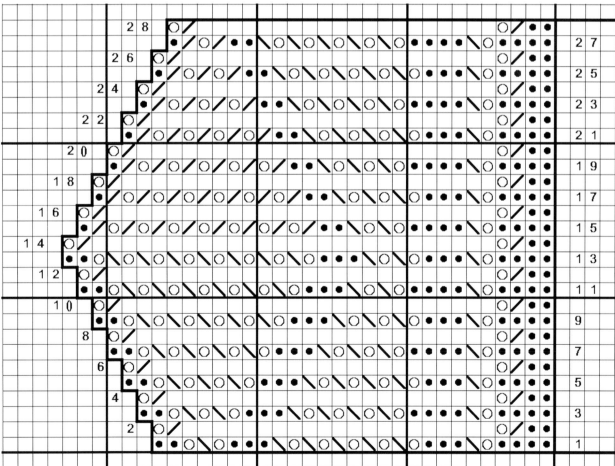

Cast on 26 stitches   Experience ***

77

Ocean Wave Edging

This simple edging is designed to go with Print O' the Wave Pattern – page 71, and like that pattern, has to be knitted on a stocking stitch *ground* (see note below, for how to knit the even rows). As this is a narrow edging by itself, I added a tiny leaf *insertion** worked on the first 5 stitches down each straight side; I have placed a dividing bar over each chart to mark the join. This insertion may easily be omitted if preferred – in which case, simply cover over these five stitches (so you don't work them); the pattern directions would then start: "Cast on 13 stitches".

Because this is such a *directional* edging, I have included charts for **both** sides of the centre pattern. If necessary, the centre and both sides for the edgings could be cast on at the same time and knitted up together, (top and bottom edging strips would have to be added on separately, and their ends *grafted* together to the side edging's two strips to finish).

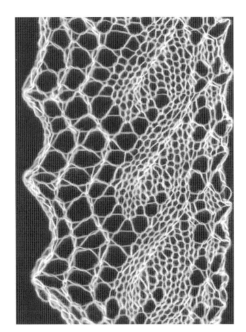

Left Side Edging

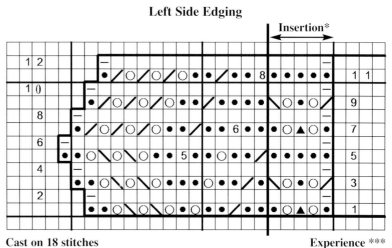

Cast on 18 stitches   Experience ***

N.B. Purl all even numbered rows, as indicated by the first and last purl stitch symbols (—) on those rows.

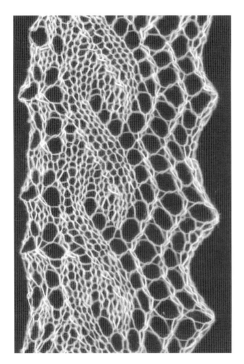

Right Side Edging

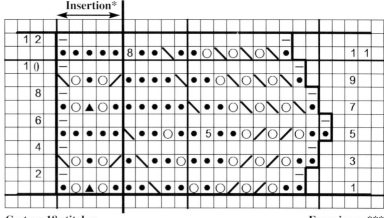

Cast on 18 stitches   Experience ***

This right hand side edging starts at the outside edge for the patterned, odd rows.

78

Shetland Bead Lace Pattern

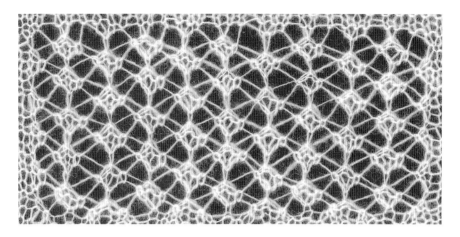

The Shetland bead is one of the classic Shetland lace motifs. It occurs in several sizes where it can be like a diamond; it can be used as a closely worked *allover* (as above) or it can be regularly spaced in plain knitting – Mrs Montague's Pattern. The beads can be in groups by themselves (see Bead Diamond) or in larger geometric shapes – here, it is used as a rectangle in plain knitting. On its own, it can be the centre pattern of a shawl or a bordered scarf/stole and would work best when combined with a border or edging which also includes bead motifs, to give a unity of design e.g. with Queen's Lace Edging.

Experience * * * Knitters: Try this **only** when you are confident at experience * * *. This is one of the first pattern-every-row designs given; if it seems daunting, try alternating the four pattern rows below with four plain knitting rows. If tackling it straight as given below, work this in a Shetland Lace-weight 2 ply yarn or equivalent for best results, as you can then treat each decrease as a knit "2 together". For thicker yarns, read "Stitch Advice" for help on working decreases.

N.B. When finishing the pattern section, stop after row 4. Doing this balances the top and bottom bead positions.

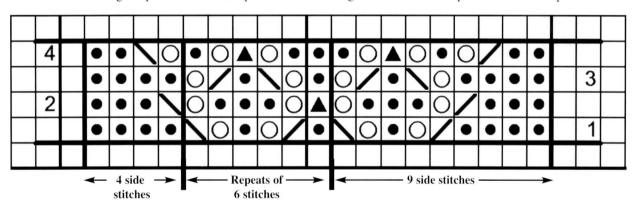

Experience ***/****

Cast on multiples of 6 stitches + 13 (4 + 9 extra stitches on each side)
e.g. (20 x 6) + 13 = 133 stitches.

Bead Diamond Pattern

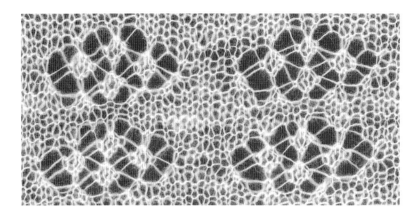

The Bead Diamond is an example of a small *fill-in* pattern that could be put in an area of plain knitting between larger motifs on borders. I show it here as two beads high and wide. It can be much larger – one famous recorded form is the Steek Diamond, see page 113. Here, it is a 14 row repeat pattern.

Experience * * * Knitters: Remember, knit stitch all blank squares in the pattern outline. The patterns now may have pattern stitches on every row, so you need to be confident at this level. If you intend this to be an *allover* pattern, add on extra stitches for each side – I suggest 5, do twice that number of plain knitting rows for the start and finish of the frame; see "A Note on the Patterns".

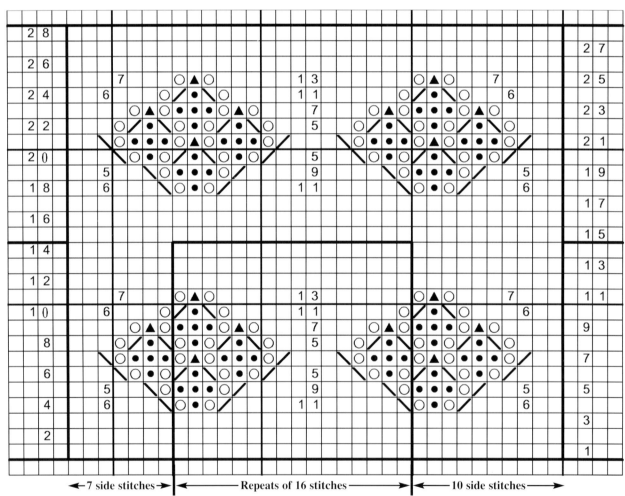

←7 side stitches→   ←——— Repeats of 16 stitches ———→   ←—— 10 side stitches ——→

Experience ***/****

Cast on multiples of 16 stitches + 17 (7 + 10) extra stitches on each side)
e.g. (8 x 16) + 17 = 145 stitches.

N.B. If needed, cast on extra stitches for each side. Include these in the above sum.

Bead and Madeira Pattern

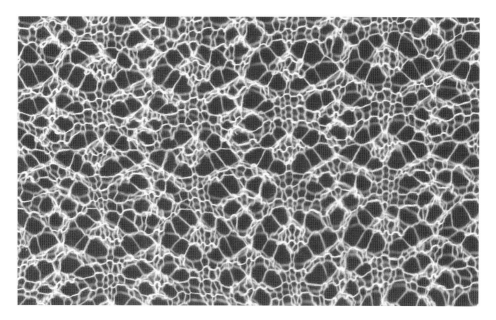

This is a traditional and very pretty centre design, suitable for a fine shawl. It's made with a small bead and a tiny Madeira or fern motif. It isn't a hard pattern to knit and experienced knitters could modify the pattern by moving the fern motif two more stitches (squares) apart, see "How to Adapt a Pattern". I have also found this also called a Puzzle Pattern, but I think that name belongs to the spider's web motif.

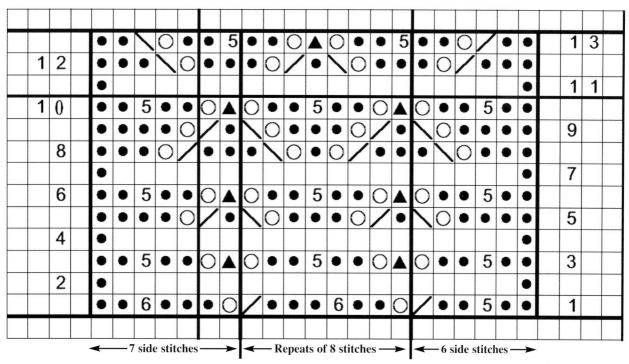

← 7 side stitches → | ← Repeats of 8 stitches → | ← 6 side stitches →

Experience ****

Cast on multiples of 8 stitches + 13 (7 + 6) extra stitches on each side)
e.g. (8 x 15) + 13 = 133 stitches.

N.B. If needed, cast on extra stitches for each side. Include these in the above sum.

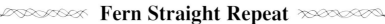

Fern Straight Repeat

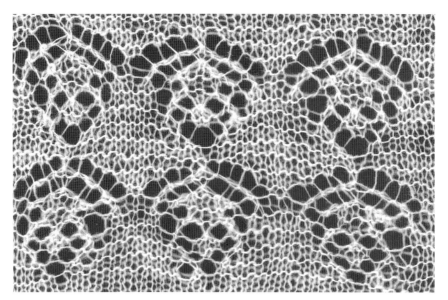

This is one example of the Shetland fern motif in use in a simple *allover* pattern. It is given as three squares at its closest – on row 13; and between rows 18 and 20. Obviously, it can be spaced closer or moved (in odd numbers of stitches/squares) further apart e.g. one stitch, 5, etc. depending on how lacy the finished lace should be. This is one of the backbone motifs of Shetland lace, a variant is the Madeira and it's interesting to compare them to see how motifs evolve.

N.B. Remember, each blank square including those with numbers in the pattern outline should be knitted in plain garter stitch.

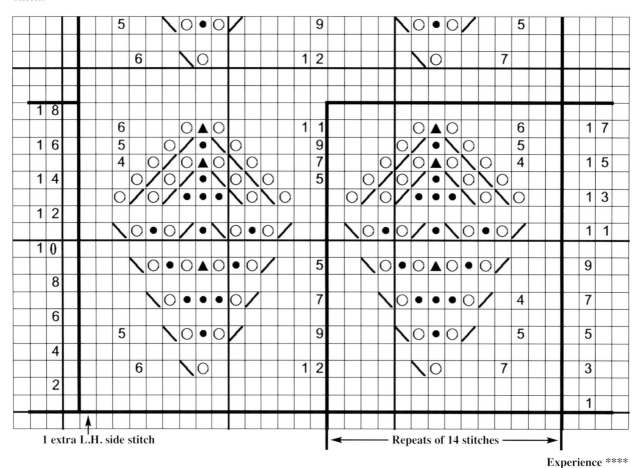

1 extra L.H. side stitch

◄——— Repeats of 14 stitches ———►

Experience ****

Cast on multiples of 14 + 1 (L.H. side stitch)
e.g. (14 x 8) + 1 = 113 stitches

Fern Staggered Repeat

This is exactly the same pattern as Fern Straight Repeat but with this, I have put alternate lines of ferns *half-staggered* and closer together. This makes a lovely *allover* lace; again, this could be re-spaced as suggested in the Fern Straight Repeat. In the chart, I give half motif designs that can be used if required – they are not shown in the photograph. **Cast on multiples of 14 + 1**. Add side stitches to this pattern if wanted, include them in the sum.

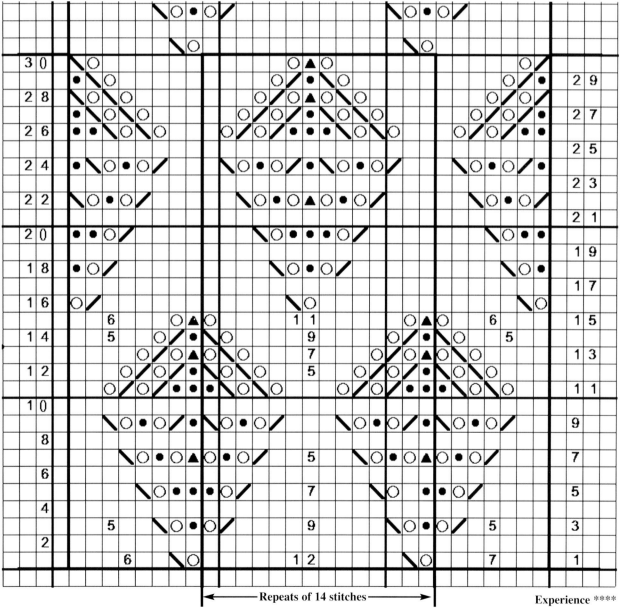

←——— Repeats of 14 stitches ———→

Experience ****

83

Madeira Lace Pattern

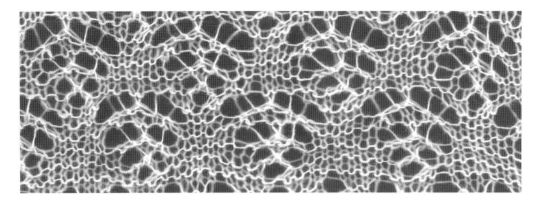

Madeira Lace is a pattern I made with the Madeira motif. This is suitable for a shawl centre pattern or as a *fill-in* in larger motifs and has a 20 *row repeat block*. This little motif can be used in combination with others to make additional centre patterns – it is given with a small bead to make Bead and Madeira Pattern.   Looking at the chart below and ignoring the two outside lowest Madeiras, a useful triangle of six small Madeiras can be found, I have faintly outlined a triangle over the chart to show this; this element may be of help to experienced knitters arranging motifs for composition in a shawl border, see page 207.

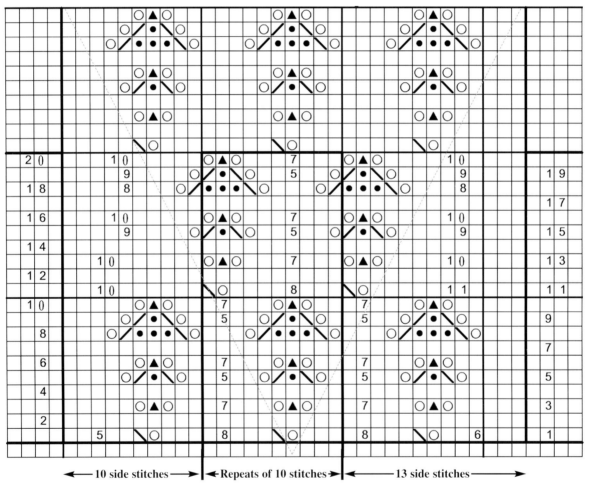

see page 207.

Experience **

Cast on multiples of 10 stitches + 23 (10 + 13 extra stitches on each side)
e.g. (10 x 12) + 23 = 143 stitches.

N.B. You may if needed, cast on extra stitches for each side. Include these in the above sum.

This graceful, traditional lozenge pattern I found on a very old knitting pattern for a lady's jumper. This is easily experimented with, e.g. by changing the number of beads in the lozenge, see the following three designs which show two *allover* or centre patterns and a smaller lozenge pattern.

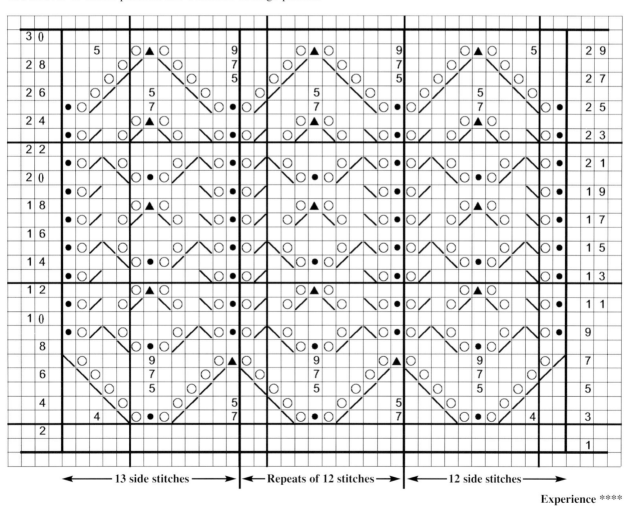

←——— 13 side stitches ———→ ←— Repeats of 12 stitches —→ ←— 12 side stitches ———→

Experience ****

Cast on multiples of 12 stitches + 25 (13 +12 extra stitches on each side)
e.g. (12 x 10) + 25 = 145 stitches.

N.B. You may if needed, cast on extra stitches for each side. Include these in the above sum.

Twin Bead Lozenge Pattern

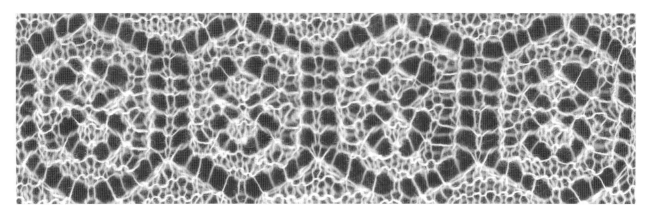

It's easy to see that this adaptation of the Bead Lozenge Pattern produces a useful "shield" shape to be used as an individual motif or as an *allover* pattern, as above. This would make an attractive element in bordering a scarf or stole, especially if the main pattern is comprised of bead groupings or motifs. This lozenge pattern is given elsewhere in the book with one, two and three beads contained in the hexagonal outline; you could put four or more. It would work just as well with columns of spider or cat's paw motifs replacing the beads (see "Design Library").

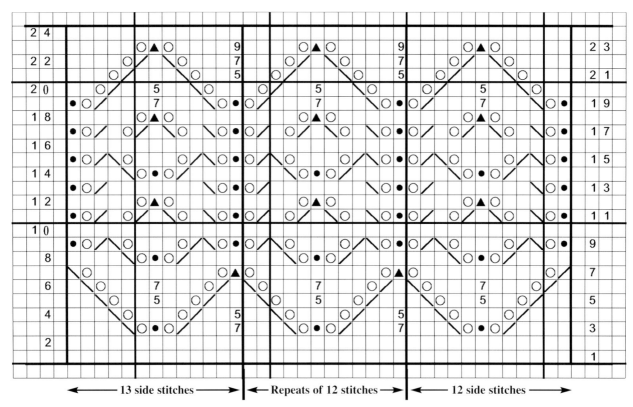

Experience ✳✳✳✳

Cast on multiples of 12 stitches + 25 (13 + 12 extra stitches on each side)
e.g. (12 x 10) + 25 = 145 stitches.

N.B. You may if needed, cast on extra stitches for each side. Include these in the above sum.

Bead Lozenge and Plain Hexagon Centre Pattern

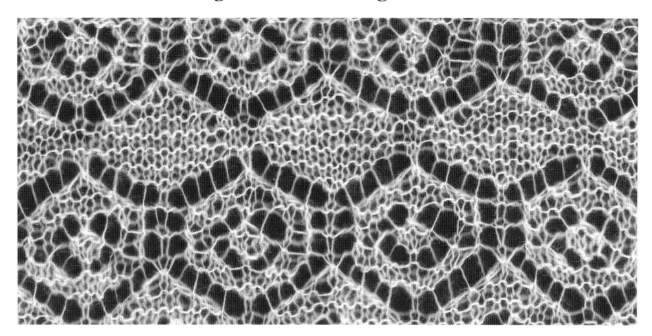

This very pretty combination of classic Shetland lace motifs makes a good centre pattern for a shawl. It can be easily adapted, perhaps by increasing the three plain rows distance to five between the lozenges, or perhaps by centring another bead or spider motif in the plain hexagon.

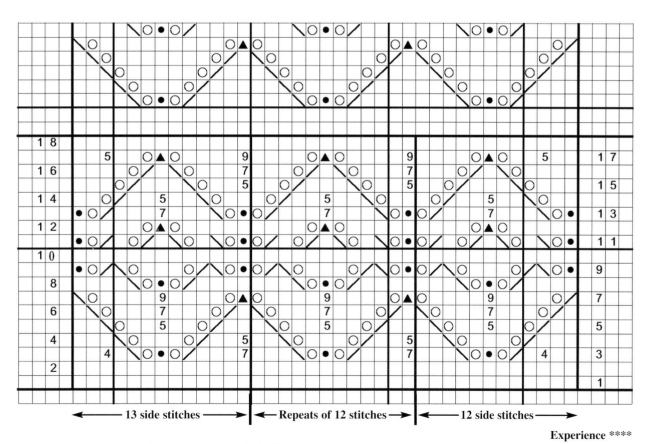

Cast on multiples of 12 stitches + 25 (13 +12 extra stitches on each side)
e.g. (12 x 10) + 25 = 145 stitches.

N.B. You may if needed, cast on extra stitches for each side. Include these in the above sum.

Bead Lozenge Centre Pattern

This scale-like lace I made by working small bead lozenges/hexagons only, as an *allover*. This is a 20 row repeat pattern and would look very well combined with other bead lozenges in the borders and edging. I used this as a pattern for a white cotton child's jacket, see page 205.

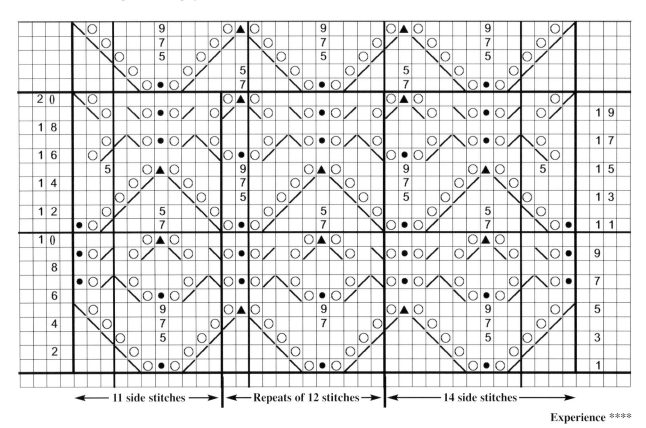

←———— 11 side stitches ————→ ←— Repeats of 12 stitches —→ ←———— 14 side stitches ————→

Experience ****

Cast on multiples of 12 stitches + 25 (11 + 14 extra stitches on each side)
e.g. (12 x 10) + 25 = 145 stitches.

N.B. You may if needed, cast on extra stitches for each side. Include these in the above sum.

Diamond Lace Pattern

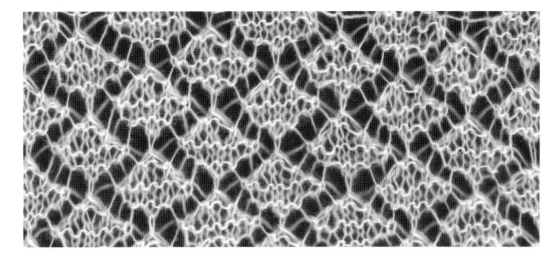

This pretty lace pattern is made in Shetland Cobweb 1 ply with British size 13/2.25mm needles. It produces a fine centre pattern by itself and would work particularly well with a bead stitch edging such as Queen's Lace Edging. Looking at the photograph above, it is easy to see regular, large diamond groups of four and nine individual diamonds; taking these, one can set them into otherwise plain knitting to make *fill-in* elements in a border panel – see "Design Library", where this is shown, page 226. Alternatively, one can obtain a larger centre pattern (or again, an element for a border) by taking the chart pattern below and alternating each pattern row with a plain knitting row.

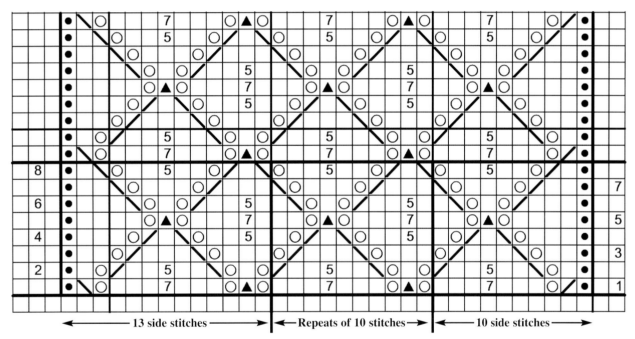

← 13 side stitches → ← Repeats of 10 stitches → ← 10 side stitches →

Experience ****

Cast on multiples of 10 stitches + 23 (13 + 10 extra stitches on each side)
e.g. (10 x 9) + 23 = 113 stitches.

N.B. If needed, cast on extra stitches for each side. Include these in the above sum.

Mirrored Fern Pattern

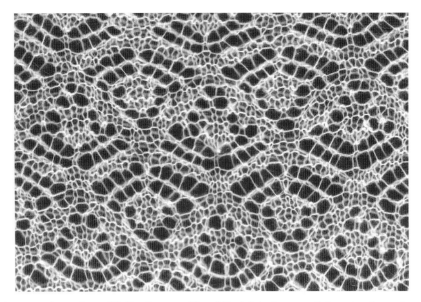

I made this pattern by experimenting with the fern motif and find it to be a useful centre for a shawl or scarf. It could be further adapted by moving the motifs nearer or further apart.

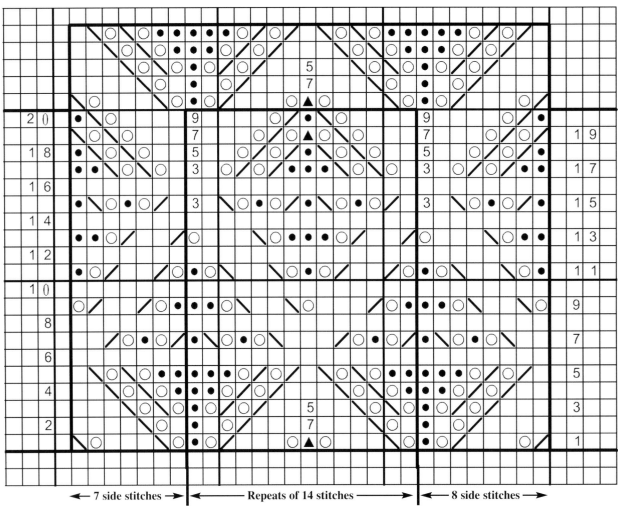

← 7 side stitches →   ← Repeats of 14 stitches →   ← 8 side stitches →

Experience ****

Cast on multiples of 14 stitches + 15 (7 + 8 extra stitches on each side)
e.g. (14 x 10) + 15 = 155 stitches.

N.B. Cast on up to 5 extra stitches for each side. Include these in the above sum.

Fern Lace Stitch Pattern

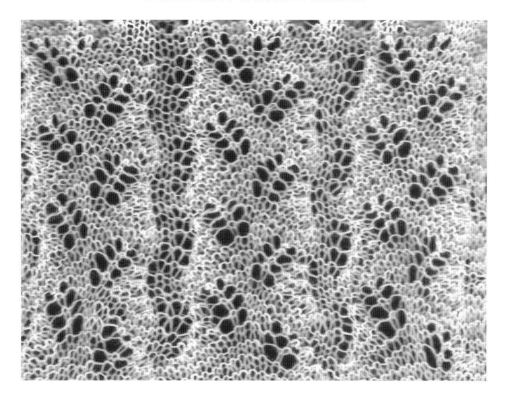

This pretty design is an early lace; the main part (the wide lace "columns") also appears on a mid-European lace-knitting sampler dating from the first half of the nineteenth century (now in the Boston Museum). With that, the panels were separated by lace *faggot* stitches instead of the two knitted stitches as shown above. This would be a lovely scarf pattern.

N.B. The **stars** in the chart **represent "knit three together"** so that the *double decrease*s on either side of the two purl stitches reflect each other.

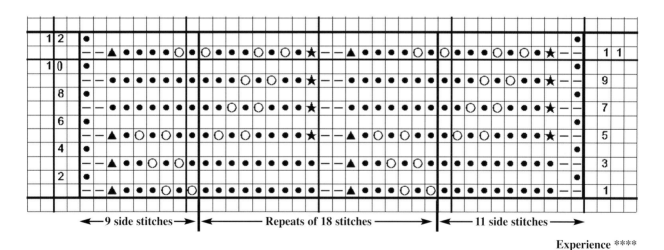

←—— 9 side stitches ——→ ←————— Repeats of 18 stitches —————→ ←—— 11 side stitches ——→

Experience ****

Cast on multiples of 18 stitches + 20 (9 + 11 extra stitches on each side)
e.g. (18 x 5) + 20 = 110 stitches.

N.B. You may if needed, cast on extra stitches for each side. Include these in the above sum.

91

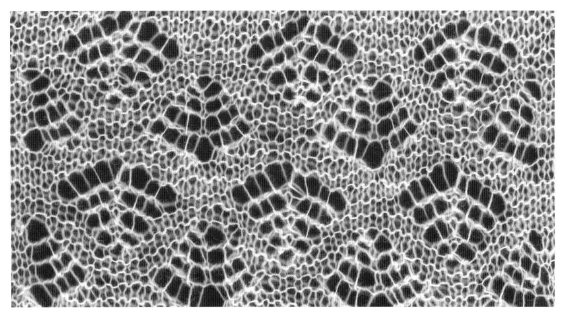

This pretty two-way lace I made by experimenting with the small tree motif. Experienced knitters might like to continue along this line by adjusting the spaces between the motifs. This would be most suitable for a shawl centre with tree motifs in the borders, or as a stole pattern with a Traditional Scalloped Edging. This pattern is shown on the chart with the minimum number of side stitches, you may add up to four more to each side – allow this in the sum when casting on.

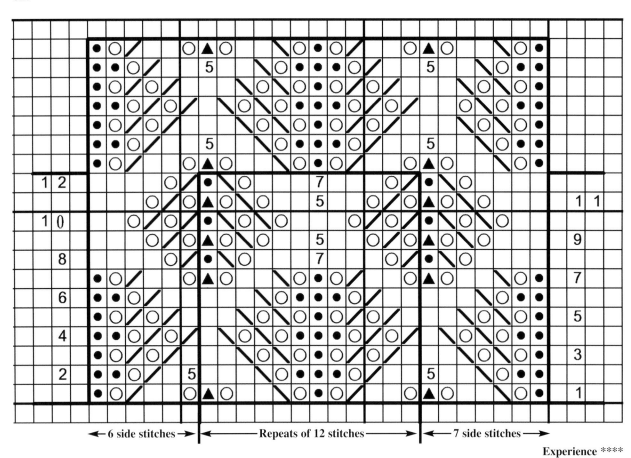

Experience ✳✳✳✳

Cast on multiples of 12 stitches + 13 (6 + 7 extra stitches on each side)
e.g. (12 x 10) + 13 = 133 stitches.

N.B. You may if needed, cast on extra stitches for each side. Include these in the above sum.

Small Trees Lace Pattern

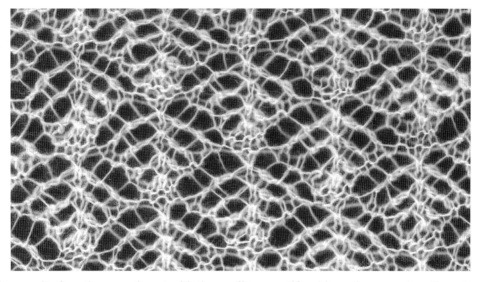

This pattern is a result of another experiment with the small tree motif and it produces an airy *allover* lace. This is the closest you can space the motifs, but they can be further apart – I explain this in "How to Adapt a Pattern".

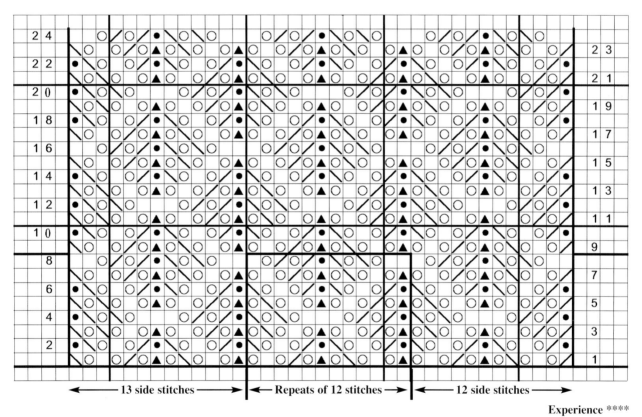

← 13 side stitches → ← Repeats of 12 stitches → ← 12 side stitches →

Cast on multiples of 12 stitches + 25 (13 +12 extra stitches on each side)
e.g. (12 x 10) + 25 = 145 stitches.

N.B. You may if needed, cast on extra stitches for each side. Include these in the above sum.

Alternating Small Trees Lace Pattern

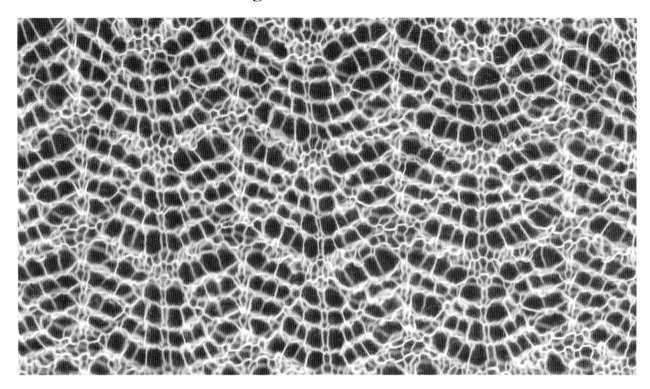

This pretty and airy lace is one more result of my experimenting with the Small Trees Alternating and Staggered Pattern by changing the spacing between the motifs. This would be a suitable *allover* for a stole or a shawl featuring tree motifs in various sizes and forms, perhaps with a scalloped edging.

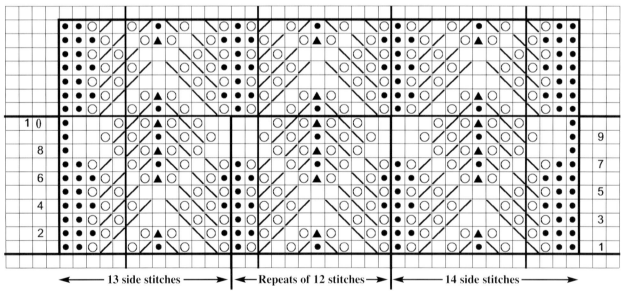

Experience ✳✳✳✳

Cast on multiples of 12 stitches + 27 (13 + 14 extra stitches on each side)
e.g. (12 x 10) + 27 = 147 stitches.

N.B. You may if needed, cast on extra stitches for each side. Include these in the above sum.

Mrs Montague's Pattern – as a Fine Lace

I made this pattern by omitting the plain knitting (even) rows on the Mrs Montague's Pattern II, so that it was *close-worked*. It makes a pretty centre pattern when worked in the finest needles and yarn; this was made in Shetland Cobweb 1 ply with British size 14 (2mm) needles. It is reminiscent of a nineteenth century veil pattern I have seen, that had a Lace Holes Edging and seemed about a *yard* square. This has a 10 row repeat block.

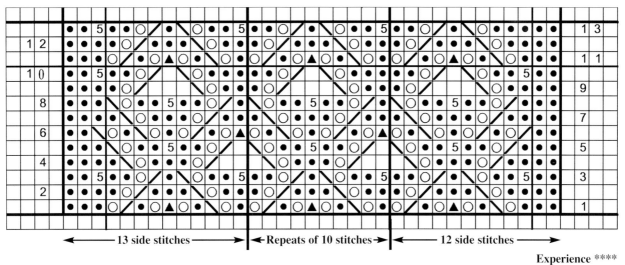

Experience ****

Cast on multiples of 10 stitches + 25 (13 + 12 extra stitches on each side)
e.g. (10 x 8) + 25 = 105 stitches.

N.B. You may if needed, cast on extra stitches for each side. Include these in the above sum.

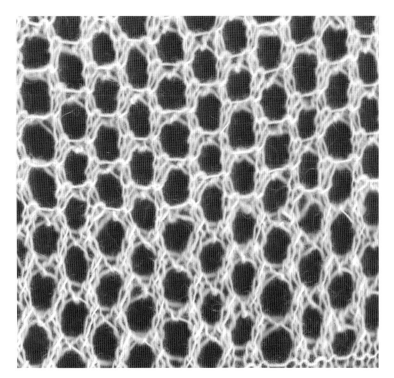

Cat's Eye is one of the most famous Shetland lace mesh patterns. It is a simple four row repeat using *double increases* on the odd rows, which aren't correspondingly decreased until the even rows. Because it looks complex on the chart below, I give the following written directions as well.

N.B. By looking closely at the photograph it is possible to see that the top and bottom sections are slightly different. This is because the even rows have been purled first (as the chart suggests) but finally, the even rows are knitted (top of photograph). The knitter must decide which even row stitch to use throughout.

Cat's Eye Pattern

Row 1 Knit 4, (make 2, knit 4), repeat stitches in brackets to end.

Row 2 Purl 2, (purl 2 together, knit 1, purl 1, purl 2 together) repeat stitches in brackets to last 2 stitches – purl 2.

Row 3 Knit 2, make 1, (knit 4, make 2) repeat stitches in brackets to last 6 stitches – knit 4, make 1, knit 2.

Row 4 Purl 3, purl 2 together, (purl 2 together, knit 1, purl 1, purl 2 together) repeat stitches in brackets to last 5 stitches – purl 2 together, purl 3.

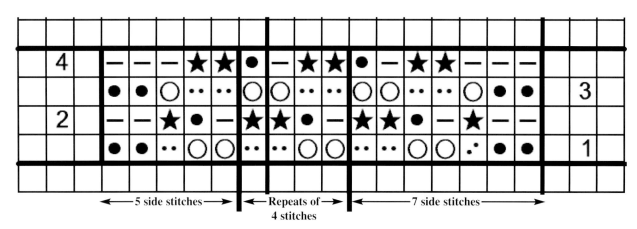

Stars = "purl 2 together"

Experience ****

Cast on multiples of 4 stitches + 12 (5 + 7 extra stitches on each side)
e.g. (4 x 16) + 12 = 76 stitches.

N.B. If needed, cast on extra stitches for each side. Include these in the above sum.

Madeira and Diamond Pattern

This is a lovely centre pattern alternatively known in Shetland as Diamonds and Small Trees. It combines two basic Shetland motifs and could best be used for stoles or scarves. I have seen it used as a centre square for a 1 ply lace shawl (retailing at just under £400) with a Tree of Life and Steek Diamond and Roache (Strawberry) Diamond border.

This pattern could be modified easily; I show it one way as Madeira and Diamond Lace, a variation created by omitting the plain knitted rows. I believe this pattern is well over a hundred years old.

There are 52 rows in the *row repeat block*.

Madeira and Diamond Chart

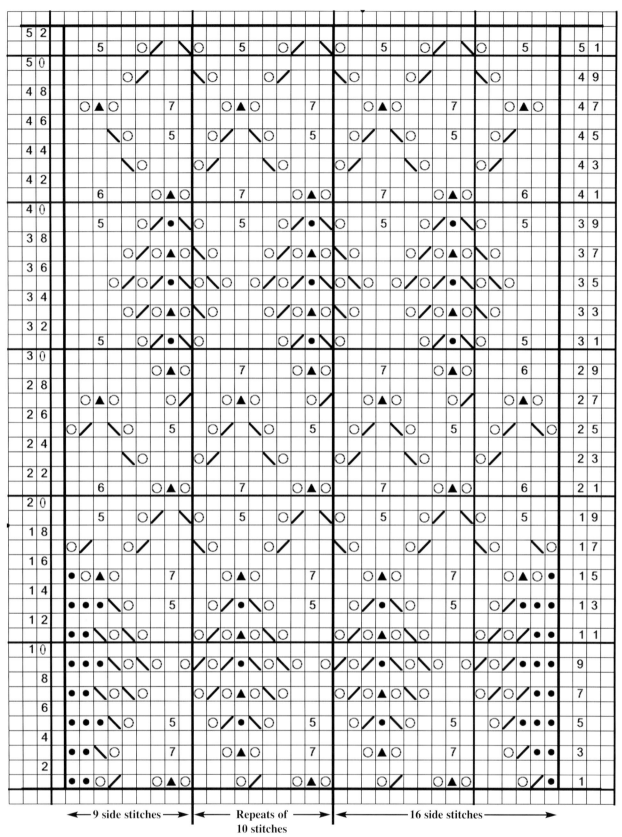

9 side stitches ← → ← Repeats of → ← 16 side stitches →
10 stitches

Experience ****

Cast on multiples of 10 stitches + 25 (9 + 16 extra stitches on each side)
e.g. (10 x 11) + 25 = 135 stitches.

N.B. If needed, cast on extra stitches for each side. Include these in the above sum.

Madeira and Diamond Lace Pattern

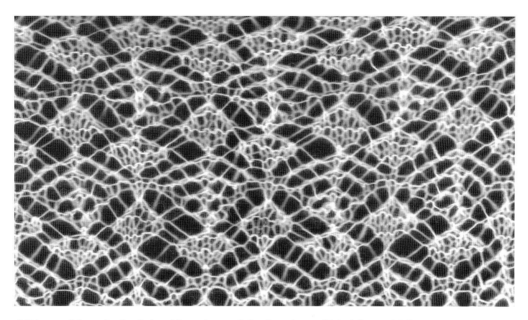

Madeira and Diamond Lace is the *knitted lace* form of the *lace knitted* Madeira and Diamond Pattern – one just omits the even or knit rows of that pattern to get this; any standard pattern-every-other-row pattern can be **close-worked**. This makes a fine lace, suitable for an *allover*.

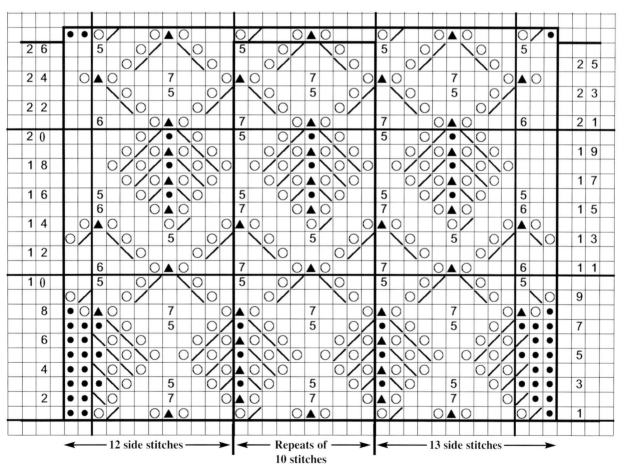

← 12 side stitches → ← Repeats of → ← 13 side stitches →
10 stitches

Experience****

Cast on multiples of 10 stitches + 25 (12 + 13 extra stitches on each side)
e.g. (10 x 11) + 25 = 135 stitches.

N.B. If needed, cast on extra stitches for each side. Include these in the above sum.

Dewdrops and Hexagons Pattern

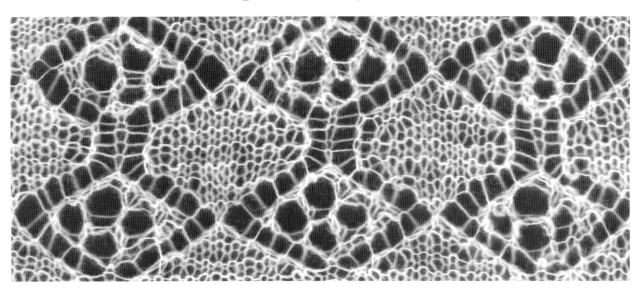

This paired grouping of lace hole diamonds with plain hexagons would be suitable as a centre pattern or for an element in a stole border. Ideally, there should be other lace hole motifs in the edging. To make it with diamonds instead, leave out the repeat rows 11 and 12.

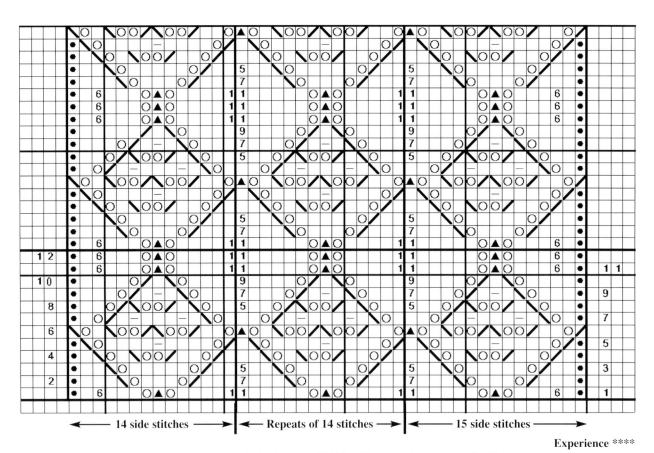

← 14 side stitches → ← Repeats of 14 stitches → ← 15 side stitches →

Experience ****

Cast on multiples of 14 stitches + 29 (14 + 15 extra stitches on each side)
e.g. (14 x 8) + 29 = 141 stitches.

N.B. You may if needed, cast on extra stitches for each side. Include these in the above sum.

Allover Tree and Bead Diamond Pattern

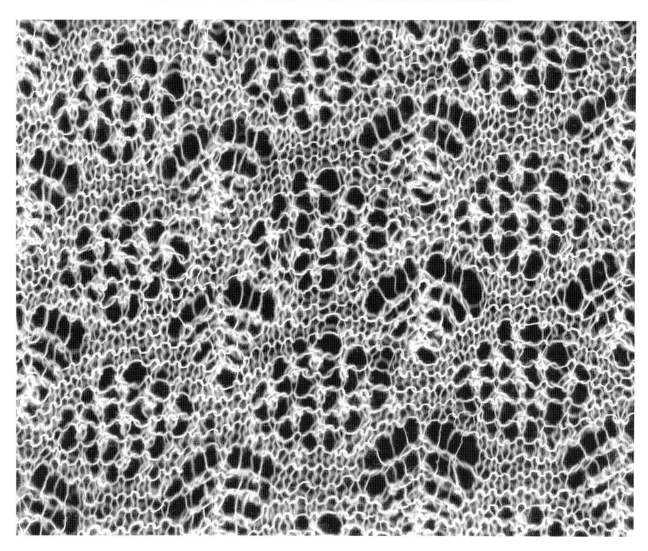

This beautiful *allover* or centre pattern is a most satisfying Shetland lace. It's pleasingly balanced and simple, with just two alternating design motifs. Like quite a few Shetland lace patterns, it's *directional*, but it still makes a lovely shawl or stole centre pattern, especially when made in one ply yarn. It could be adapted by replacing the small tree motif with a Madeira or fern, or by experimenting with the spacing of the motifs e.g. try spacing the diamonds five stitches apart instead of three at their nearest (see little chart). This modification can be tried with other allover patterns.

N.B. Remember when you enlarge a pattern like this, it ought to get taller as well as wider, so will need more pattern rows. This example has increased from 18 to 22 pattern rows.

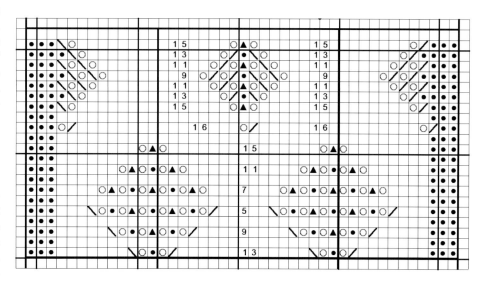

Cast on multiples of 18 stitches + 13 RH and 12 LH side stitches.

101

Allover Tree and Bead Diamond Chart

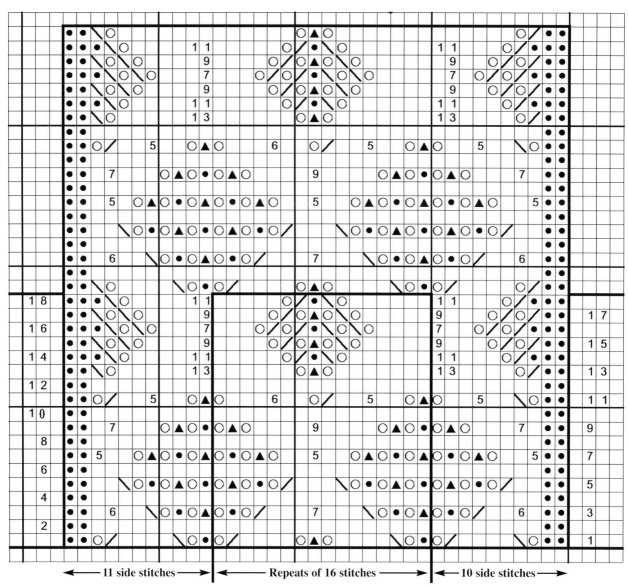

←—— 11 side stitches ——→ ←—— Repeats of 16 stitches ——→ ←—— 10 side stitches ——→

Experience ****

Cast on multiples of 16 stitches + 21 (10 + 11 extra stitches on each side)
e.g. (16 x 10) + 21 = 181 stitches.

N.B. If needed, cast on extra stitches for each side. Include these in the above sum.

Elaborated Print O' the Wave Pattern

I recreated this pattern from one of the nineteenth century stoles in the collection of the Lerwick Museum and Library, Shetland. By comparing this with the Print O' the Wave Pattern and chart, it can be seen how this pattern was originally developed, and how it could be additionally altered. Although this is quite an easy design to knit, chart reading skills need to be quite good and for this reason I have graded this a level * * * * pattern. It is advisable to work this in stocking stitch throughout; also, work each ＼especially as "slip 1, knit 1, pass slipped stitch over" to get the unbroken slants on the spines of decrease.

N.B. Because this is such a large pattern to chart, **I have had to omit all the even rows,** please be aware of this and **remember to purl the even rows**. Charting pattern rows only, is quite a conventional practice with very large patterns in knitting charts; but I won't do this without bringing it to the reader's attention each time. Experienced knitters might like to try the chart as given i.e. pattern every row – this would involve "purling 2 together" etc. This should produce a lacy version of the design.

Elaborated Print O' the Wave Chart

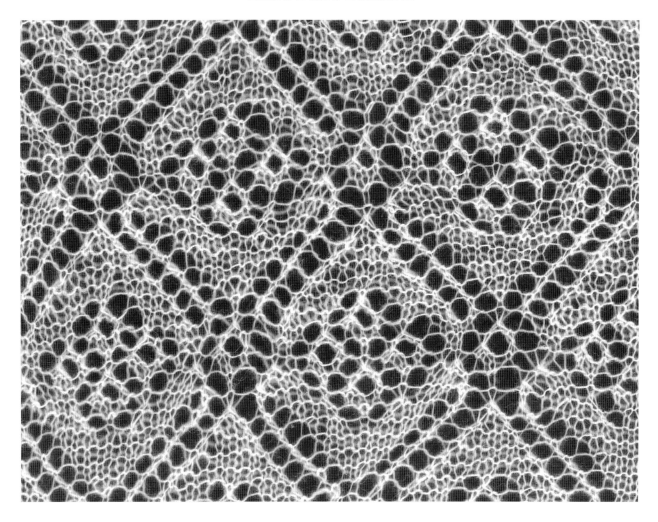

Also known as Rose Trellis Lace, Rose Lace is a descendant of the famous sixteenth century pattern, Mrs Montague's Lace. Firstly, that became a Trellis Diamond Pattern and then, when that was enlarged and combined with Rosebud Lace (an eyelet pattern) Rose Lace evolved, as shown.

The above pattern could be both a centre pattern in its own right, or a border pattern to items with other eyelet patterns as their centres e.g. Rosebud Pattern.

This pattern looks simple but the *delayed increases* around the interlocking diamonds need special attention and concentration when knitting – look at row 15 for example. Luckily, every even row is plain knitted. I developed Rose Diamond Lace from this pattern by leaving out the plain knitting rows. One way of extending knitting skills is by knitting Rose Lace first and then variations e.g. replacing the centre group of four rosebuds with groups of beads or laces holes. The enlarged interlocking diamond background to this pattern is often a useful element in border patterns with alternating centre patterns of trees, beads, etc. See "Lace Christening Robe" border. The basic grid is in the "Design Library".

Rose Lace Chart

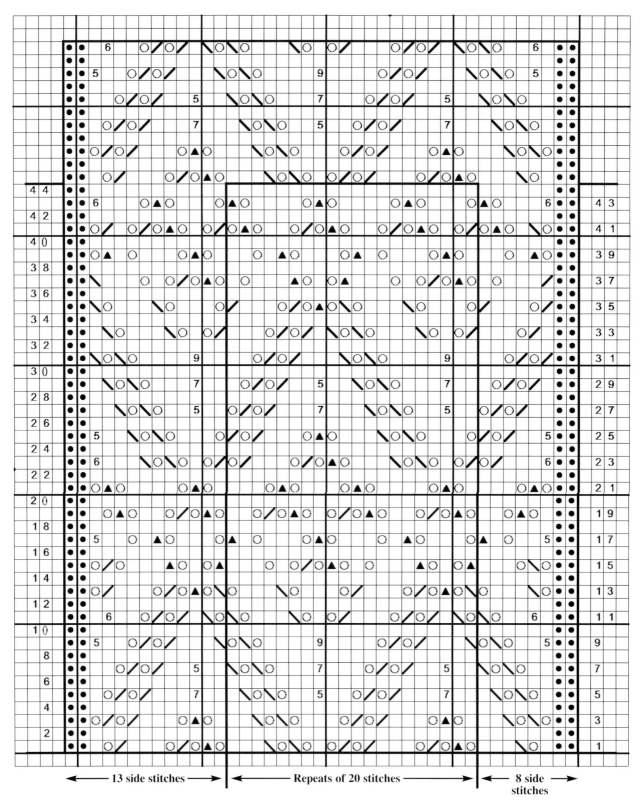

◄——— 13 side stitches ———► ◄——— Repeats of 20 stitches ———► ◄—— 8 side stitches ——►

Experience ****

Cast on multiples of 20 stitches + 21 (13 + 8 extra stitches on each side)
e.g. (20 x 5) + 21 = 121 stitches.

N.B. If needed, cast on extra stitches for each side. Include these in the above sum.

106

Large Trees and Diamonds Border Design

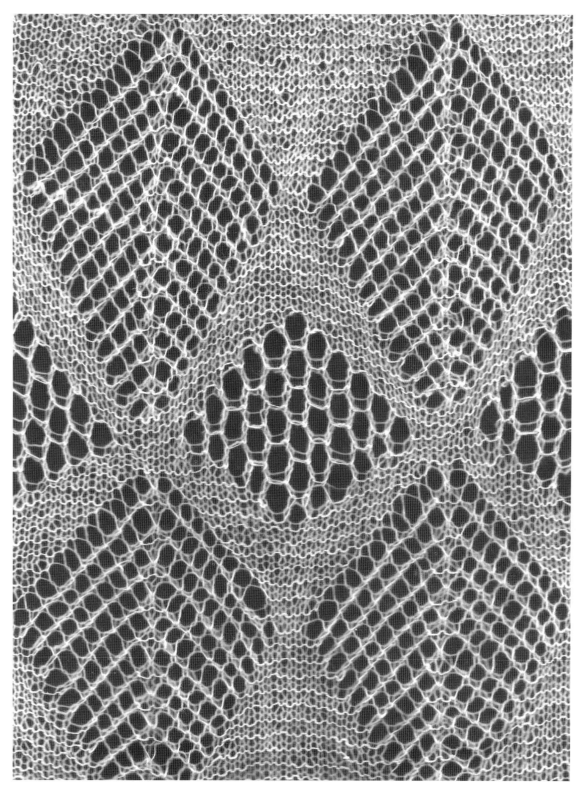

This is a recreation of a nineteenth century Shetland stole border – see the museum photograph on the following page. It has a centre that is an intricate version of Print O' the Wave and I have charted this separately as Elaborated Print O' the Wave. The borders consist of three rows of ten trees alternating with two rows of the nine lace hole diamonds plus two half-side diamonds, as shown on the chart. The "heads and tails" of the borders were plain (as shown on the charts) and therefore I have separately plotted the end of the border's knitting. So, the order of the knitting for this piece is as follows: from chart A, knit rows 1 – 10 (the plain foot); then knit rows 11 – 66. Repeat rows 11 – 66 once and then rows 11 to 28; **now** knit chart B (the end piece), which replaces the starred row 29 to row 50 on chart A. The knitting itself is relatively simple, but as chart reading skills must be reasonable, I have graded this pattern as a level * * * *.

Large Trees and Diamonds Border Chart A

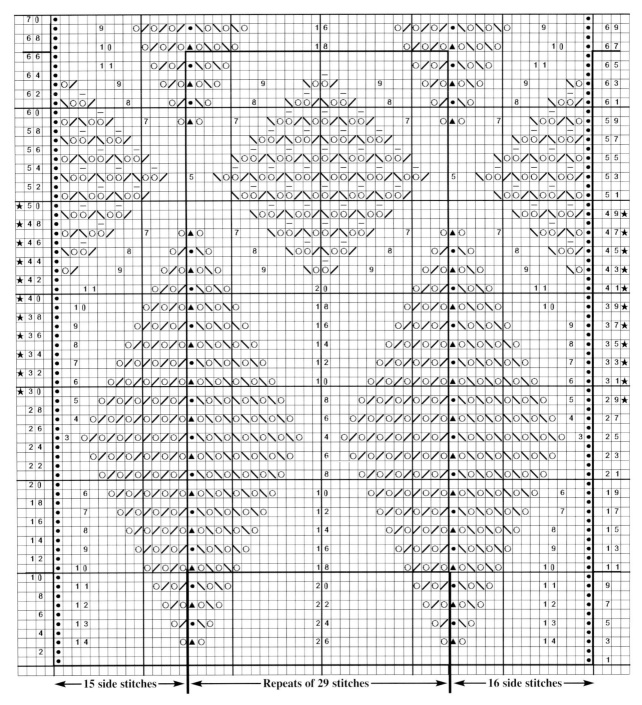

← 15 side stitches →   ← Repeats of 29 stitches →   ← 16 side stitches →

Experience ****

This is the start and main section of the border design.

The shawl border had
(9 x 29) + 15 L.H. and 16 R.H. side stitches = 292 stitches.

N.B. On even rows 44 – 62: knit and purl into each of the previous row's *double increases* – i.e. into the ◯ ◯s of the odd numbered rows 43 – 61.

Large Trees and Diamonds Border Chart B

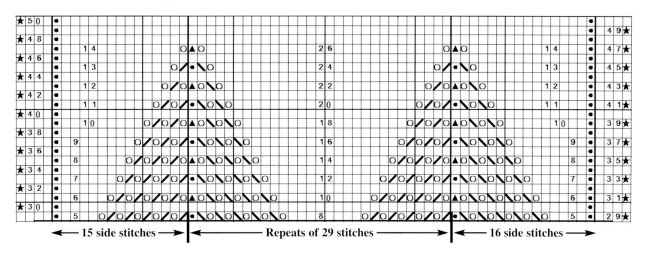

← 15 side stitches → ← Repeats of 29 stitches → ← 16 side stitches →

This chart gives the plain end section or top, of the border design

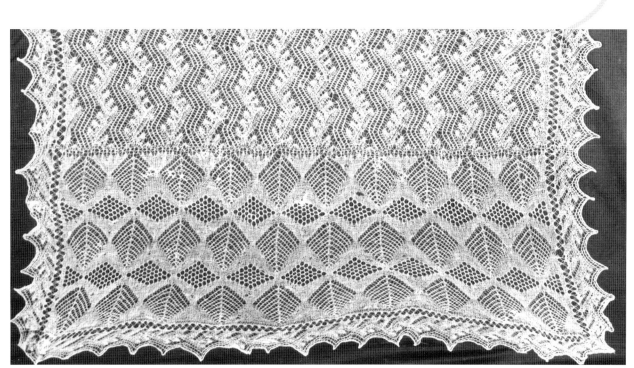

This is a photograph from the Lerwick Museum and Library, Shetland, and is of a Print O' the Wave Stole. The effective border composition is of Lace Hole Diamonds and Large Trees. (Note – the centre pattern is shown "upside-down" here).

Pattern and Lace Hole Stripe Design

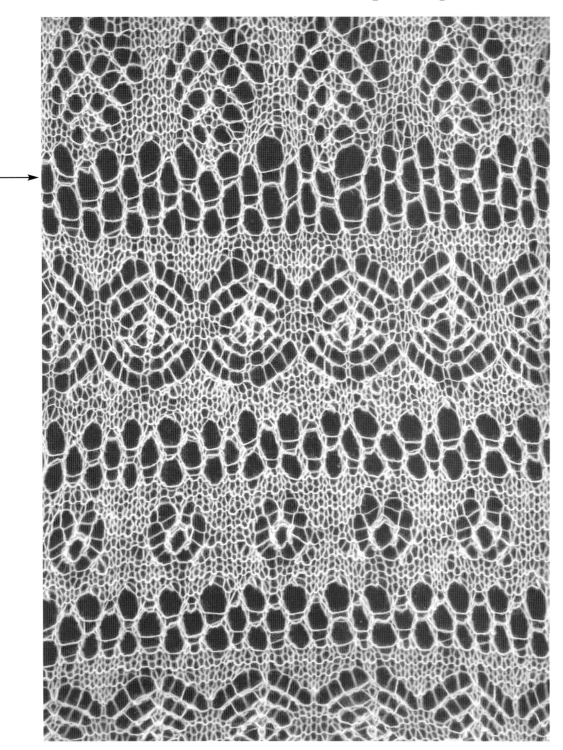

This interesting composition of bands of contrasting pattern alternating with bands of lace holes makes a good stole centre or border pattern. Any motif from the "Design Library" could be similarly grouped with a contrasting horizontal stripe of lace stitches set in panels of plain knitting – e.g. Bead Lace, Cat's Eye or Bird's Eye Pattern. I have charted an upright tree motif (that's not on the photograph) as another example. Extra lace holes might be worked, see the top band (arrowed) which has four lines of lace holes instead of three.

 I created this pattern by developing on a traditional stole pattern that alternates spiders (1) and webs (2) only with lace holes (0), in the manner above. Using this as a model, I suggest that only two of the motifs could be chosen and alternated with the Lace Hole Stripe in the following manner: 1-0-2-0-1-0-2-0-1 etc., making sure you finish with the starting motif repeat to balance. Or it could be worked as given for a scarf pattern that's constructed in the "make two matching halves and graft them together" method described in "Shetland Stoles and Scarves".

Pattern and Lace Hole Stripe Design Chart A

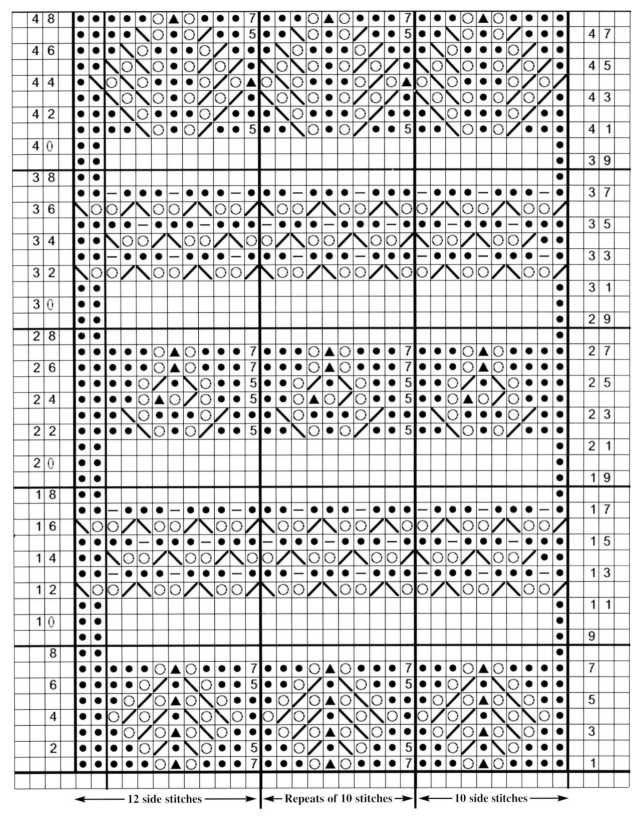

←———— 12 side stitches ————→ ←— Repeats of 10 stitches —→ ←———— 10 side stitches ————→

Experience ****

Cast on multiples of 10 stitches + 22 (12 + 10 extra stitches on each side)
e.g. (10 x 10) + 22 = 122 stitches.

N.B. If needed, cast on extra stitches for each side. Include these in the above sum.

Pattern and Lace Hole Stripe Design Chart B

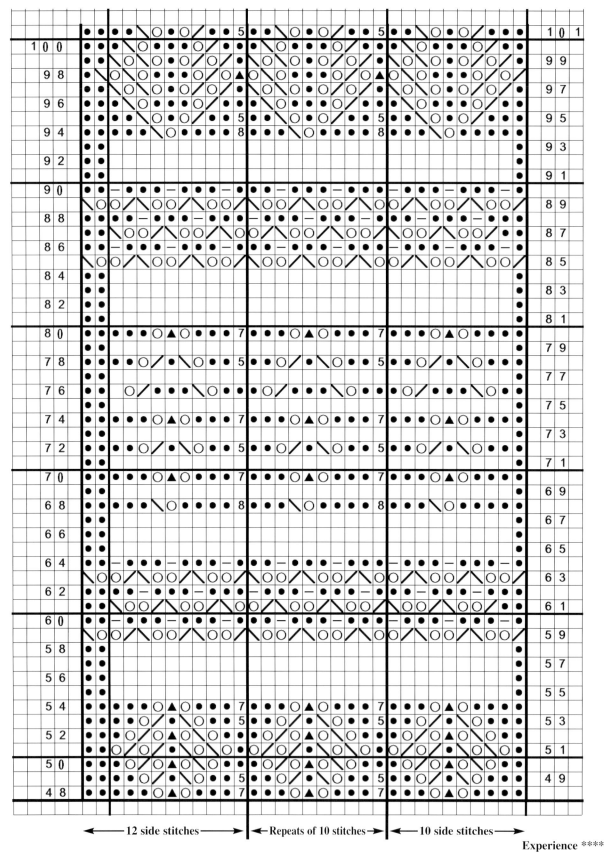

←——— 12 side stitches ———→ | ←— Repeats of 10 stitches —→ | ←—— 10 side stitches ——→

Experience ****

Cast on multiples of 10 stitches + 22 (12 + 10 extra stitches on each side)

e.g. (10 x 10) + 22 = 122 stitches.

N.B. If needed, cast on extra stitches for each side. Include these in the above sum.

The Tree of Life is an ancient motif widely used throughout Indo-European art. It is also easily identified in the Fair Isle knitting that was made in Shetland. This border design is a typical, easy border with horizontal lines of repeating motifs that could readily be exchanged for others from the "Design Library". Starting from the bottom, the motifs in this composition are Peerie Flea Pattern, the Roache (Strawberry) Diamond, the Steek (Bead) Diamond, the Tree of Life and a Madeira Pattern. An interesting, large centre pattern could be made, by just alternating the Roache and Steek Diamonds only, as set out on the chart. This border chart is for those who want a rectangular border for a stole, and a Tree Of Life Border Chart II, (given on page 163) is for those who wish to make a mitred border for a shawl.

I have seen this border used for a shawl with the Cat's Paw centre and a Brand Iron Edging.

Tree of Life Border Chart

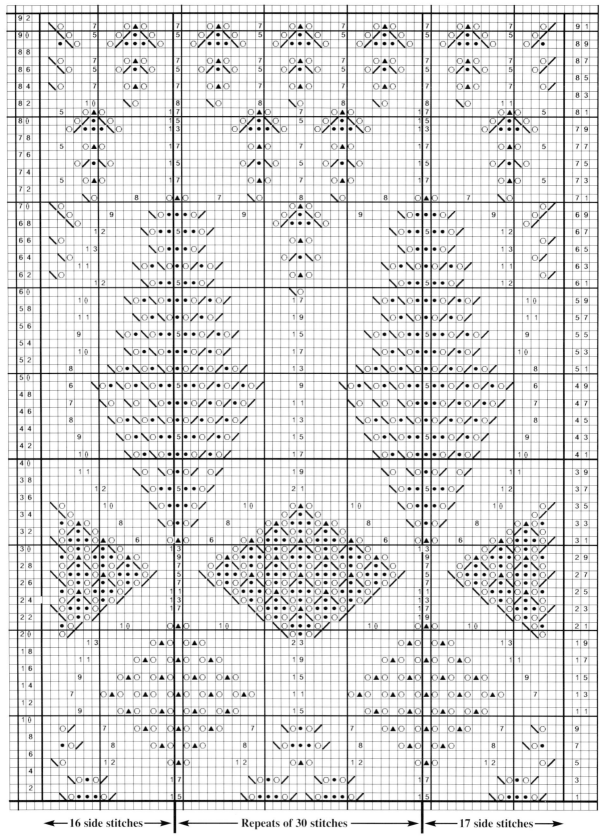

← 16 side stitches →   ← Repeats of 30 stitches →   ← 17 side stitches →

Experience **

Cast on multiples of 30 stitches + 33 (16 + 17 extra stitches on each side)
e.g. (30 x 3) + 33 = 123 stitches.

N.B. If needed, cast on extra stitches for each side. Include these in the above sum.

Cyprus Edging

This is a dainty, useful narrow edge. Again, experienced knitters might like to combine this with an *insertion* after replacing the slipstitches on the odd rows with knit stitches.

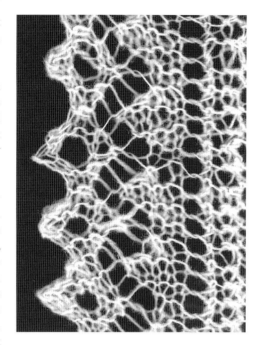

Experience * * * * Knitters: This pattern needs a little extra concentration and a word of explanation. On both of **rows 6 and 8** there is an increase without a matching decrease next to it. This has pushed part of each of those rows one square to the left on the chart. Don't worry about this, just knit them as shown, the diagonal line of four increases (shaded) should be apparent.

Row 5 and 6: **Row 5** shows a *double increase* (O O). Do this by bringing the wool forward *purlwise* and then wrapping it once around the needle. Keep the wool at the front, then take it over the top of the needle to the back and do the next of the two knit stitches. On **row 6,** knit the first two of the three stitches as shown, then knit and purl into that same large strand of yarn twisted around the needle. Then, carry on with the chart. What you have just done has made two stitches in a large loop that makes a large, planned hole in the centre diamond of this pattern. You do this double increase quite frequently in Shetland knitting e.g. in all lace hole patterns. Sometimes, charts will show that the knit stitch precedes the purl stitch, the order doesn't matter, so long as you have knitted and purled once into the large loop.

Row 8: This row shows two cast off stitches at the beginning. Remember when casting off, you have to knit two stitches before passing the loop of the first stitch over the second stitch just made. When you have cast off the second stitch in the same way, there should be three stitches on the R.H. pin before you do the yarn forward or "make one" (O) i.e. one stitch left over from the casting off the lock stitch and two stitches from the stitches knitted as charted.

Each even row ends up with a paired increase and decrease (O ╱) before the final knit stitch. This makes a simple *faggot* edging.

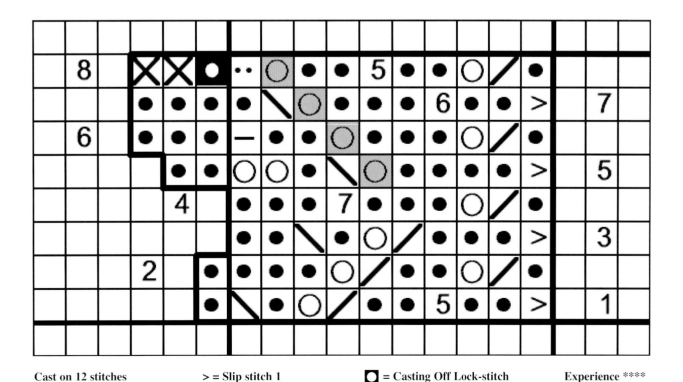

Cast on 12 stitches   > = Slip stitch 1   ◨ = Casting Off Lock-stitch   Experience ****

Sarah McComb Rawson's Edging

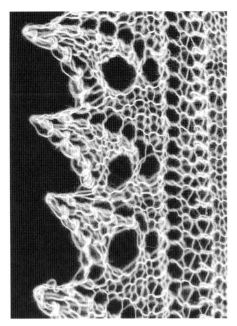

I don't know if this edging is a traditional Shetland lace but I include it because it is linked to a story that concerns the spread of lace knitting to America. Sarah McComb Rawson's family emigrated to America from Scotland in the early nineteenth century. Taking part in the rush to the newly discovered Californian gold mines in 1849, they eventually settled in a ranch, west of Sacramento. Around this time, the middle-aged Sarah became severely injured when trying to restrain a horse and wagon team. She lived the rest of her life in a chair, where she passed some of the spare time knitting the beautiful lace that she probably learned in her Scottish childhood. Three of her finely edged handkerchiefs are in The American Museum in Bath, Britain. The above edging is a near recreation of one of the edgings. It is a famous old pattern; a collection of old patterns calls it Eye Spot Edging or Wagon Wheel Edging. Enlarged, it appears combined with a bead diamond as Candle Flame Scallop – which I believe to be an American adaptation. Another recreation of one of the patterns Sarah knitted that is typical of Shetland lace, is Bead Insertion with Plain Vandyke Edge and I use this for a handkerchief edging in the "Projects". On the handkerchief edges I have seen, the knitted lace work is in finest cotton or silk, and the fullness is *eased* carefully around the corners.

Tip

Experiment with the "multiple yarn overs" on row 1. If you do the four as the pattern shows, you get a really large hole. I worked only three yarn overs, but made sure I did the four stitches in them on the next row as charted below; so that the right number of stitches was maintained. This gives a slightly smaller hole, which can be preferable. This can apply to "any multiple yarn over" pattern. See advice with Wave Edging regarding the Lacy Edge Stitch. The pattern as given here, advises purling above the single increases to "open" the loops. In practice, with fine yarn I find it makes little difference.

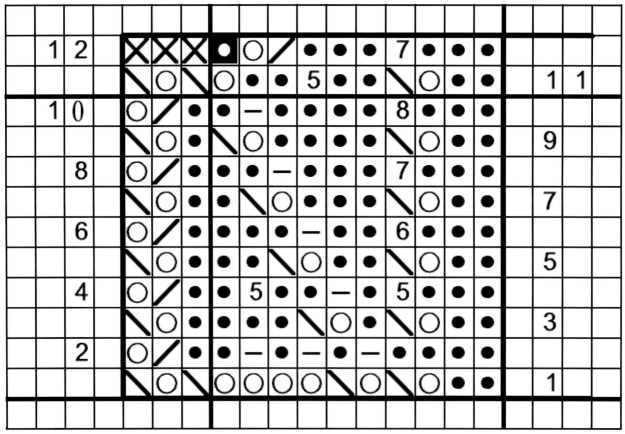

Cast on 10 stitches   ◘ = Casting Off Lock-stitch   Experience ****

116

Elaborated Print O' the Wave Edging

This edging is based on the centre pattern Elaborated Print O' the Wave found on an intricate and finely knitted antique stole in the Lerwick Museum and Library's collection. The centre and border patterns for this are given on pages 103 and 107.

This beautiful edging needs careful dressing to display the frond-like pattern.

Experienced knitters could adapt this further by trying just one, two or four fronds on each side, instead of the three given here. A narrower edging can be obtained by ignoring the first ten odd row stitches (amending the decreases and increases as necessary) – see "Adapting an Edging Pattern", where this is demonstrated.

Compare this to Ocean Wave Edging. You might need to "mirror" this in a similar manner for a R.H. side version. Because this pattern is so large, I have only charted the odd/pattern rows, it has 36 rows.

N.B. Work all \ as "slip 1, knit1, pass slipped stitch over". **Purl all even rows (not charted)**.

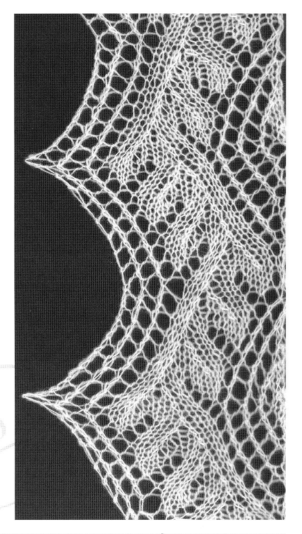

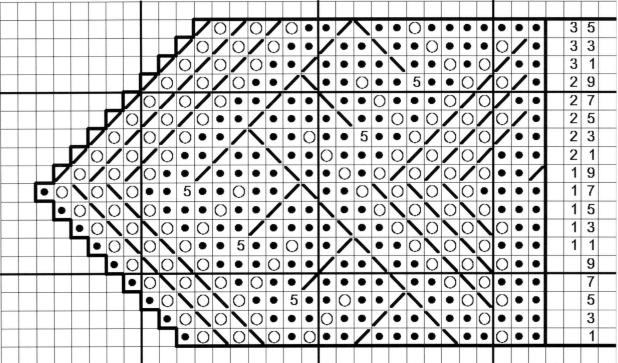

Cast on 20 stitches

Experience ****

Wave and Wave Lace Edgings

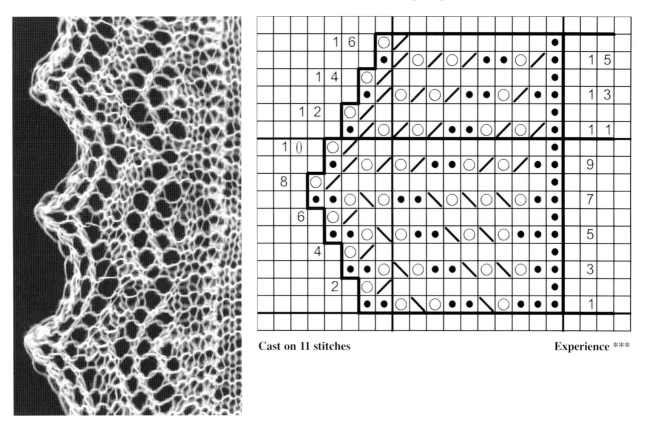

Cast on 11 stitches **Experience** *****

This example of Wave is one of many forms of this pattern. This version is another of the patterns collected in the late 1800s.

Lacy Edge Stitch: All the even rows begin with a "yarn over and knit 2 together". To do this, put the wool round the right hand needle first and then do the knit two together. On the odd rows, treat this last stitch especially by knitting into the back of it. Doing this 'opens' the lace loop on the edging and makes it more elastic, which can be very useful when stretching around border corners.

Experienced knitters will see that I made Wave Lace below, by *close-working* the Wave Edging above. Knitters wishing to extend their skill might like to try first Wave and then Wave Lace. This makes an airy, delicate edging. **N.B.** The first stitch on even rows is shown one square **out** on rows 2 to 4, and one square **in** on rows 6 to 8. This keeps the lines of increases and decreases in their proper positions.

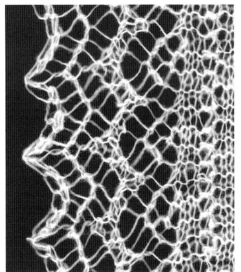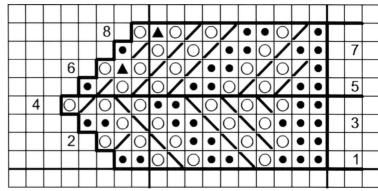

Cast on 11 stitches **Experience** ********

118

Coburg Edging With Faggot Insertion

This edging was one collected in the late 19th century but I have combined it with a *faggot insertion* on the first ten stitches at the straight edge. It is a simple pattern, in fact very similar to the Brand Iron Edging, apart from the *double increase* at the pointed outside.

Remember, this could also be worked with the *Lacy Edge stitch* to make it a little more fancy. Otherwise, it could be made as a narrower edging by omitting the first ten faggot stitches (see advice below). It could be made correspondingly wider by continuing on with increase rows, so row 13 would be like row 11, but have 7 knit stitches before the pattern stitches, and a row 16 would begin with "cast off 7 stitches".

Experience * * * Knitters: might care to try this pattern from the large knitted triangles on – i.e. from stitch 11 outwards on the odd rows. Cover over the stitches on the right of the dividing bar and ignore the numerals, by simply knitting them.

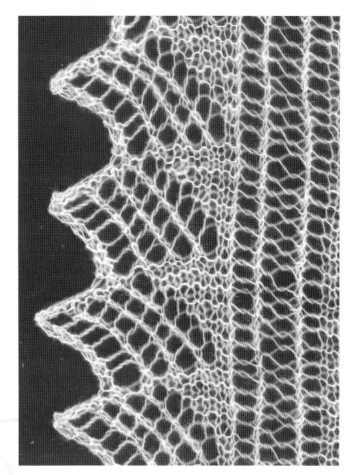

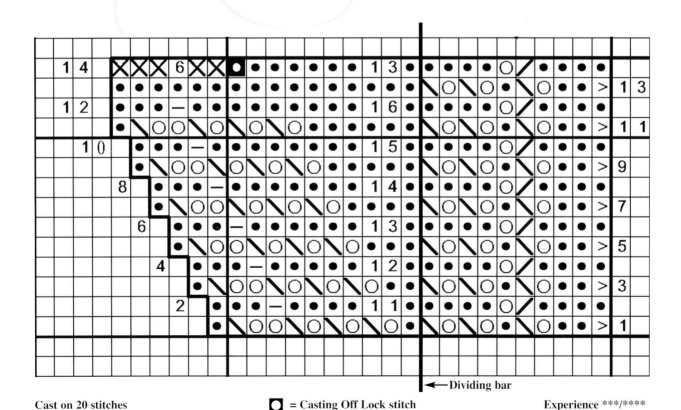

←— Dividing bar

Cast on 20 stitches   **⬛ = Casting Off Lock stitch**   Experience ***/****

Dewdrops Edging

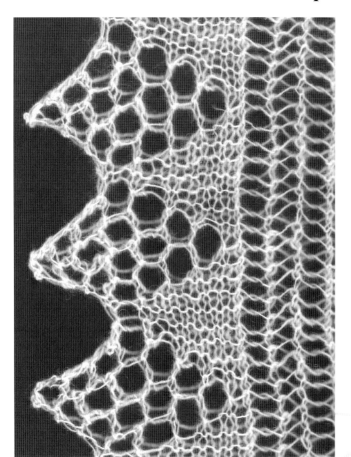

This also could be known as Lace Hole Diamond Edging, but as one of the Shetland names for this stitch is "Drops" reflecting its naturalistic name, I have called it Dewdrops Edging. It is a simple edging and would work well paired with a centre or border pattern, which includes lace hole diamonds in the main knitting.

Experienced knitters will see that the vertical lines of faggots at the beginning could be omitted. Doing this, a narrower edging could be made by working from stitch 8 outwards, replacing the 8 "knit 2 together" stitches (shaded) in that column with knit stitches. I have placed a dividing bar at this point (after stitch 7) to help. See "Adapting an Edging Pattern".

This pattern's lace hole diamond is often found combined with other elements to make more elaborate edgings – see Mrs Sutherland's Fine Lace Edging.

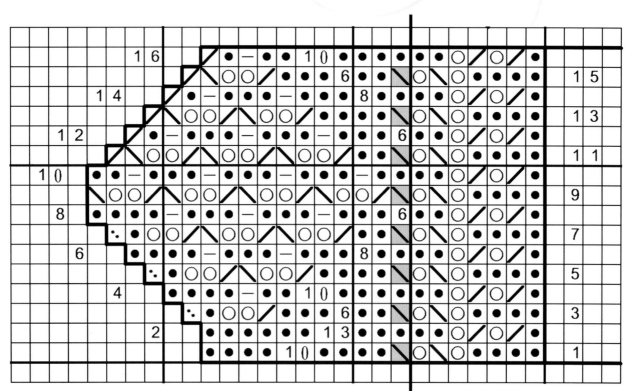

Cast on 18 stitches

Experience **

This is a classically simple, traditional edging that usually finishes large shawls with Old Shell Pattern borders and plain knitted centres.

Experienced knitters might like to experiment by changing the size of the triangle; by removing some of the "Vandyke edging repeats" (i.e. the zigzag lines); or by omitting the first six stitches upwards from the inside edge and knitting it plain.* Alternatively, place a small bead motif or similar in centre of the plain triangle – this would then make a similar edging to one commonly used in the nineteenth century.

Using the Faggot Insertion:
I show this pattern with quite a nice *faggot* insertion on the inside, which could be used in combination with any of the simpler edgings e.g. Doris, Traditional Scalloped or Wave. What you would need to do is simply knit the first six faggot stitches as given in each odd row below, before working the chosen pattern's odd row stitches. Then, end each even pattern row with the extra last six faggot stitches as they are given below on the even rows. Remember to include the extra six stitches in the casting on. e.g. with the Doris Edging, cast on 9 + 6 = 15 stitches.

*Add an extra R.H. side stitch and plain knit it, till row 24 when it will be a "knit 2 together," as shown here – shaded.

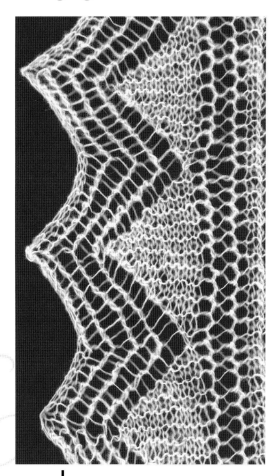

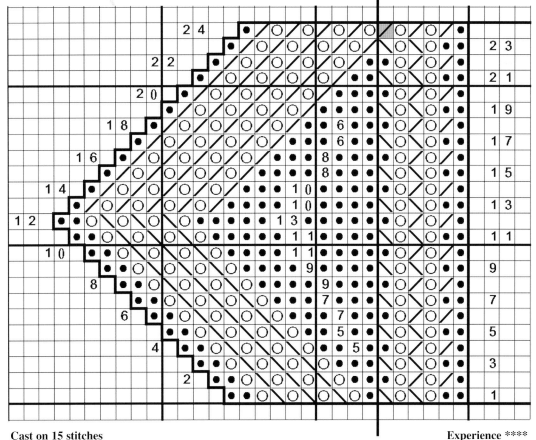

Cast on 15 stitches   **Experience ****

Irish Lace Edging

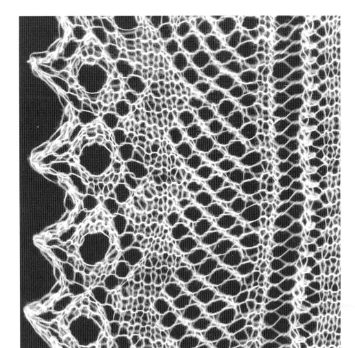

At the end of the nineteenth century this Shetland lace edging was also known in early ladies magazines as the Elaine Edging, (see "Pattern Names"). The large, open diamond part of the edge (from stitch 12 outwards on odd rows) could be recombined with any *insertion* with a simple row of *faggoting* (see "Adapting an Edging Pattern").

Additionally, the first 11 odd row stitches (the *insertion*) could be recombined with a smaller edging e.g. Doris, to make a different wide edging. **Very experienced knitters** would be able to make a faggoted edging from this alone.

The *Lacy Edge Stitch* worked on the first two stitches of every even row could be replaced by two knit stitches instead.

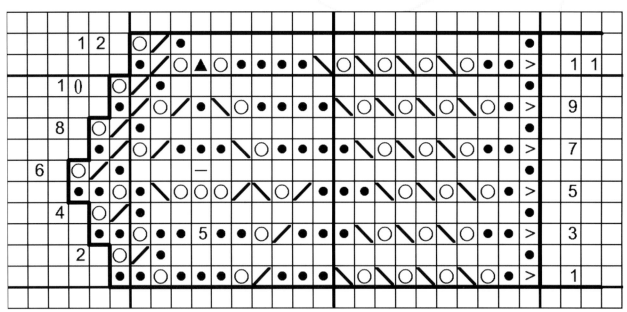

Cast on 20 stitches   > = Slip stitch 1   **Experience ****

122

 Double Scallop Shell Edging

Double Scallop Shell Edging is a comparatively simple edging to knit but as the *row repeat block* is so large, I have graded this at a higher level. I made this design by changing the direction of some of the stitches in the Scallop Shell Edging. This makes a suitable edging to borders, which include large trees because, to a certain extent, it echoes their forms. Experienced knitters might like to add the Lacy Edge Stitch to this. A lacy variation could be made by *close working* this pattern.

N.B. Knit the outside edge stitches very loosely, so the edging dresses well around corners. You could try slipping the first stitch on the odd rows for a tighter inside, or straight, edge.

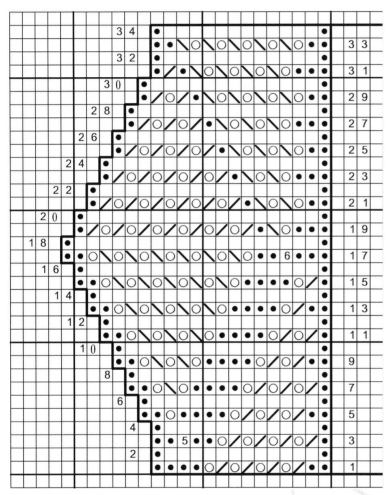

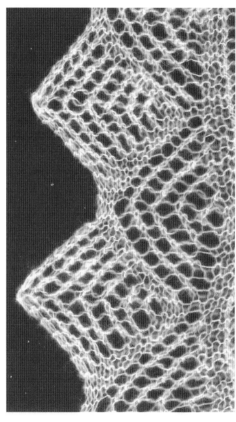

Cast on 14 stitches   **Experience ****

The Brand Iron and Grand Eyelet Edging

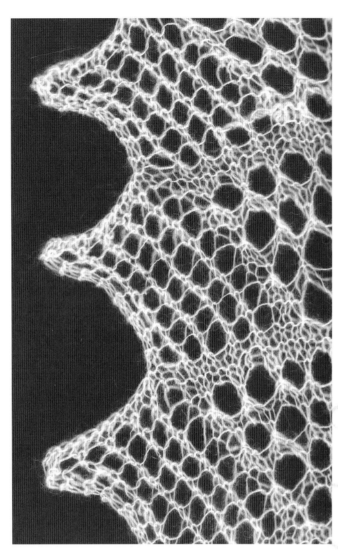

I found this edging on a very old knitting pattern for a baby's shawl. This edging combines two popular elements in Shetland lace knitting, as the name I have had to give it suggests. It makes a dramatic, large edging and would suit the plainer centres such as Mrs Hunter's. Experienced knitters will be able to make this pattern five lace holes wide instead of four, by continuing the sequence of the rows.

N.B. The photograph shows the edging without the faggoted straight side that is charted below on the first 8 stitches. Some of the rows have unusual necessary decreases e.g. row 3 at stitch 12; and this has thrown the charting relationships slightly out. Have a look at the Brand Iron Edging itself to see how this section is worked, if you need to.

Row 18: As with all casting off in Shetland lace, cast off the ten stitches very loosely. See advice with the Wave Edging for help with the Lacy Edge Stitch that is worked at the outside edge on the even rows.

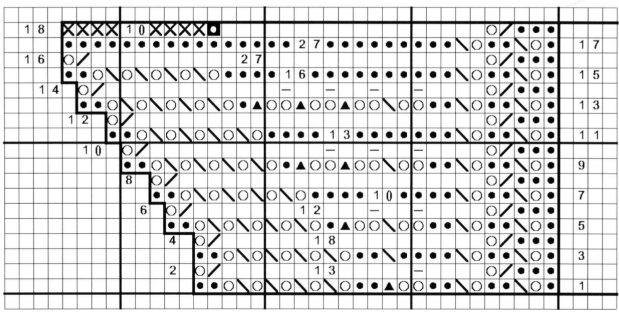

Cast on 24 stitches   ◘ = Casting Off Lock-stitch   Experience ****

Victorian Zigzag Insertion and Edging

This simple but elegant edging dates from the middle of the nineteenth century and is useful for its zigzag insertion element. This is charted from odd stitches 7 – 18 and can be reused with another edging. To help, I have put two bars through the chart to mark the insertion.

Experience * * * * Knitters: Odd row stitches 19 to end (i.e. from the bar 2 outwards) give the necessary stitches to make a very small triangular edging. Again, these could be reused by adding them on to any other insertion; perhaps with a faggot pattern like that worked up on the first three straight edge stitches. Use a piece of squared paper and copy the relevant sets of stitch symbols onto that, so you have made your own pattern chart to work from. Do this whenever necessary with your own edgings.

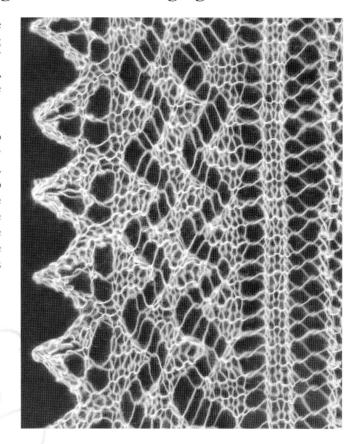

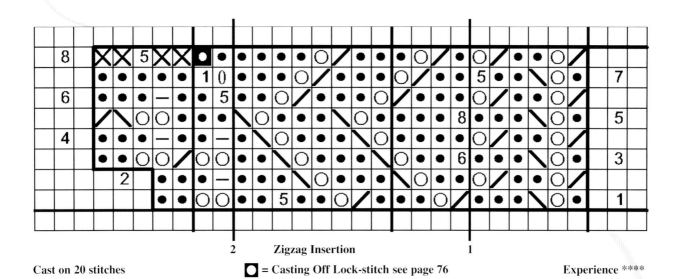

2   **Zigzag Insertion**   1

Cast on 20 stitches   ◻ = **Casting Off Lock-stitch see page 76**   **Experience ****

Two Insertions with Small Triangle Edging

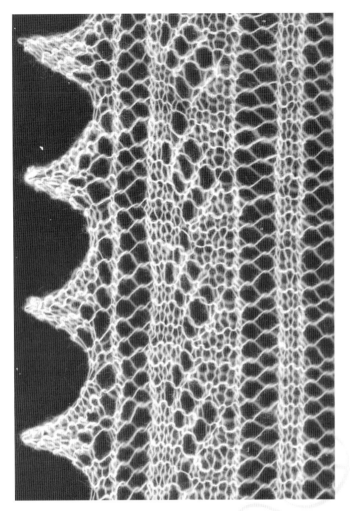

This edging is comprised of three main vertical elements – an inside faggoted strip (1), a diamond insertion (2) and a faggoted triangular edging at the outside.

This composition dates from the end of the nineteenth century, when it was suggested that it was useful for items of underclothing and infant wear.

Experienced knitters will be able to identify and use the elements as they wish. I have put dividing bars on the chart to mark the diamond insertion; the faggoted insertion is worked on the first seven stitches. Also, it is possible to obtain a narrower pointed edging by just working from the diamond insertion outwards.

N.B. This edging doesn't have the deep triangles that are so useful for easing round corners. If the edging is to be used for this, I suggest easing the edging carefully around – see advice in "Attaching an Edging".

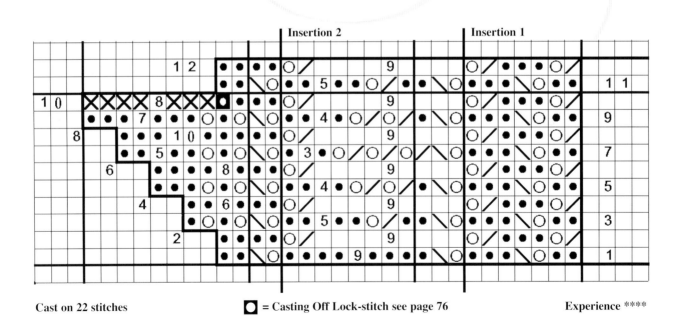

Cast on 22 stitches

▣ = **Casting Off Lock-stitch see page 76**

Experience **

Fern Leaf Edging

Fern Leaf Edging is a useful, uncomplicated edging that I have adapted to use as an edge on a Shetland Fir Cone patterned shawl – see detail photograph below. To do this, I omitted the faggoted inside edge and just worked the triangular outside pattern.

Experienced knitters will see that the first 11 stitches on the inside edge could be knitted up as a separate insertion strip, or coupled to another edging.

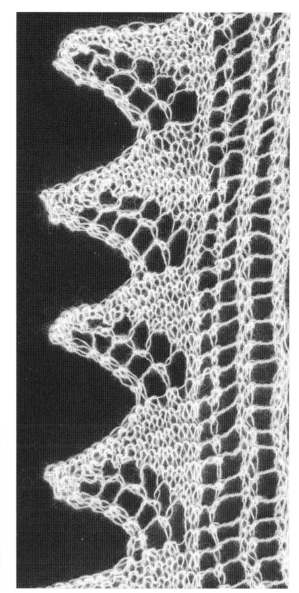

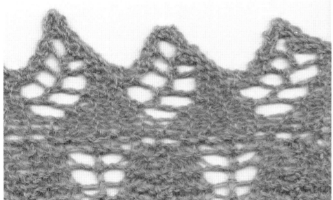

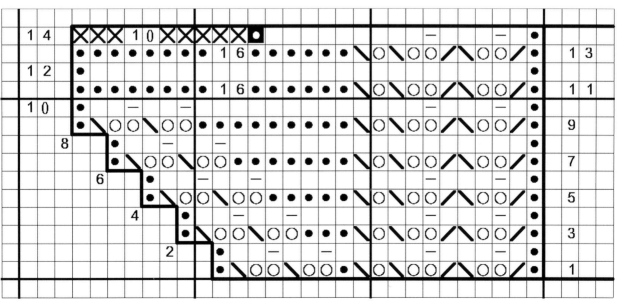

Cast on 17 stitches   ▢ = **Casting Off Lock-stitch page 76**   **Experience ****

Twin Holed Diamond with Small Bead Insertion

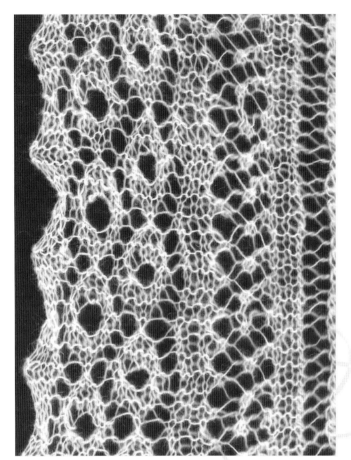

This pretty and elaborate edging is a combination of an insertion and an old edging. The insertion (worked on the first ten stitches at the straight edge side) makes a neat element that can be re-combined with other edgings. This a particularly nice edging to make in the finer yarns, and is, I think, more suited to adult designs.

N.B. The edging itself has no pronounced point, and so must be carefully pinned when being dressed to get the tiny peaked outside edge. Experienced knitters could work this from stitch 11 up as an insertion in its own right – changing the double decrease on row 9 to a single decrease – and by stopping after odd rows' stitch 24 and turning to knit the even rows back (a second dividing bar has been put in to mark the place).

Again, this edging must be carefully gathered at the corners because there are no deep triangles in the design to open and spread the edging around.

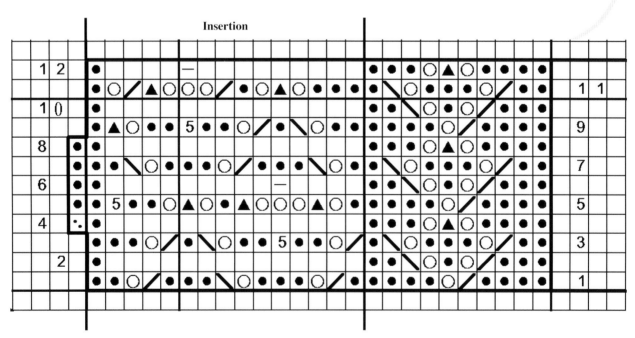

Cast on 25 stitches

Experience **

128

Queen's Lace Edging

This reasonably simple yet beautiful lace is well over a hundred years old. It has a very attractive four-row insertion on the straight inside worked up on the first six stitches; this could be coupled with any plain edging.

Conversely, the remaining stitches knitted up, would make a pretty, narrow edging in itself i.e. starting with stitch 7 on the odd rows and working up (to help, a dividing bar is ruled between stitches 6 and 7 to mark off the insertion, to work or not as wanted).

Use this edging with patterns that include groups of small bead stitches to give unity of design.

Experienced knitters might like to exchange the insertion element for another – perhaps the Bead Insertion that is given with the Snail Shell Edging.

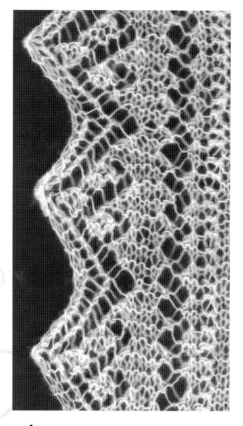

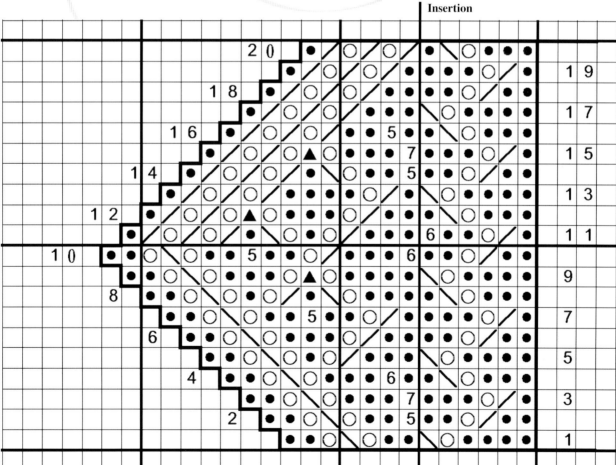

Cast on 12 stitches

Experience ****

Traditional Scalloped Edging with Lacy Edge

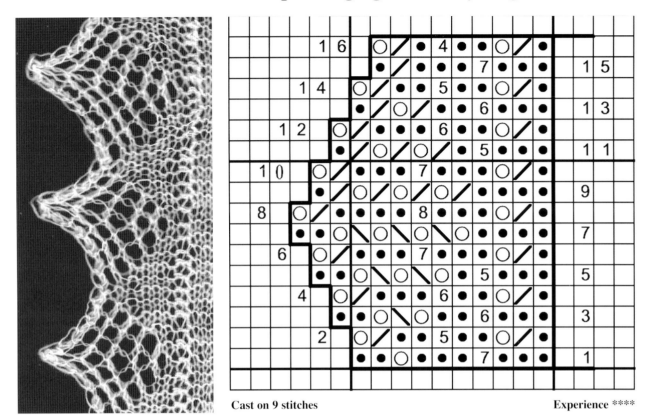

Cast on 9 stitches   **Experience ****

This classic Shell Edge is a very popular edging for Shetland lace shawls. It can be made wider by casting on extra multiples of two stitches (see Large Scalloped Edging page 54). It could also be combined with an insertion. See advice with Wave Edging for help about Lacy Edge Stitch.

Lace Holes Edging

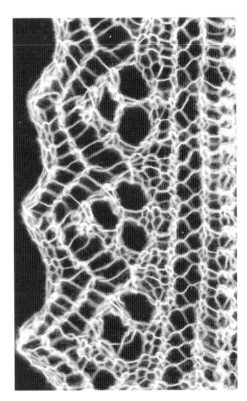

Another classic edging that can be adapted as suggested above (see Ring Shawl Edging where this is combined with an insertion). Most suited to edge items that include lace hole groupings to give unity of design.

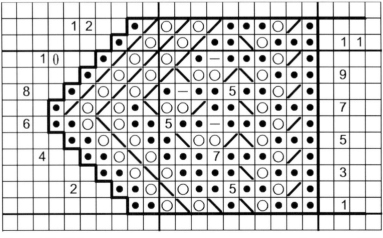

Cast on 12 stitches   **Experience ****

Finely Scalloped Lace Edging

This graceful and beautiful fanned lace is an early lace, I have seen it used as an edging for a very fine lace knitted sampler from the early 1800s. It is quite easy to knit and displays very well when dressed. Experienced knitters will see that the pattern itself is easy to adapt, and I give it here first as a simple narrower fanned edging, without the double zigzag. The chart for the photographed edging is given afterwards.

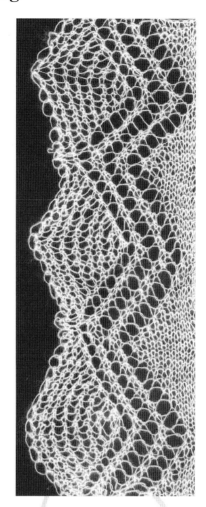

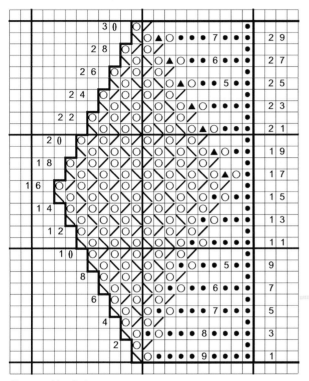

Cast on 11 stitches

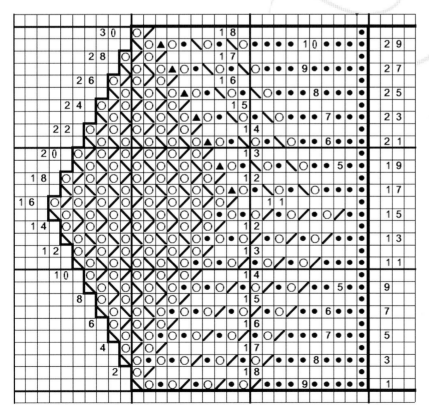

Cast on 20 stitches   **Experience ******

131

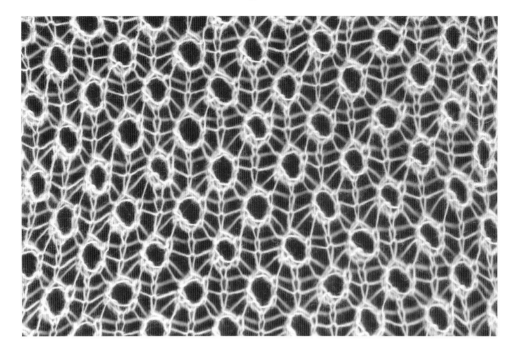

This amazing pattern, which doesn't look as if it could be a knitted one, has many names. I have found it also called Spider Lace and Ring Lace. It is quite tricky to knit, so I recommend copying this chart and crossing through each worked row line with a pencil or felt tip pen; or use a row counter, so that you can keep track of where you are. It is especially important to leave a casting on "tail" of wool (or a stitch marker) to identify the odd and even rows – see "How to Read a Chart". This advice applies to all complex lace patterns. **This is an 8 row repeat pattern**.

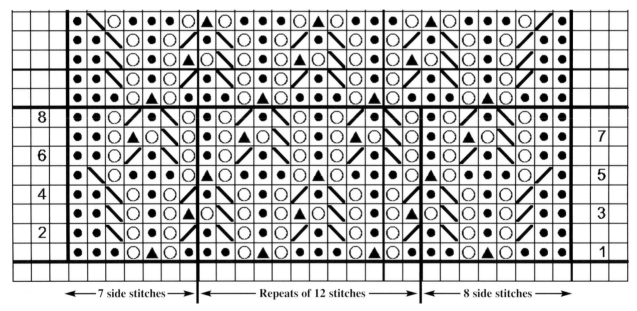

Experience *****

Cast on multiples of 12 stitches + 15 (7 + 8 extra stitches on each side)
e.g. (12 x 12) + 15 = 159 stitches.

N.B. You may if needed, cast on extra stitches for each side. Include these in the above sum.

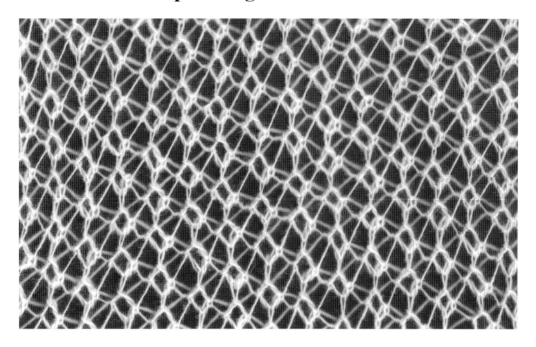

I made this variation of a Spider lace by omitting the even rows of the Bird's Eye Pattern. This makes a useful *fill-in* pattern or background to other elements in Shetland lace knitting; in "Project 6", this is a centre pattern in one of the Unst Stole's Border diamonds. A larger version could be obtained by alternating the pattern rows, as given below, with plain knitting rows.

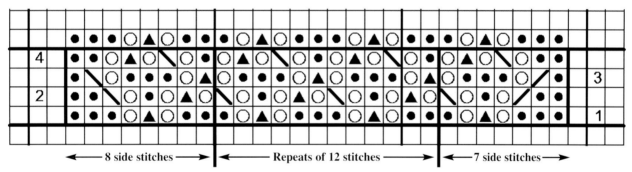

Experience *****

Cast on multiples of 12 stitches + 15 (8 + 7 extra stitches on each side)
e.g. (12 x 12) + 15 = 159 stitches.

N.B. You may if needed, cast on extra stitches for each side. Include these in the above sum.

Rose Diamond Lace is a *close-worked* version of the traditional Shetland pattern Rose Lace. Again, it is quite tricky to knit because it needs a good, loose but even tension and final careful dressing, to get the best results. I made the above in a Shetland 1 ply with British size 11 needles (3mm, American 2).

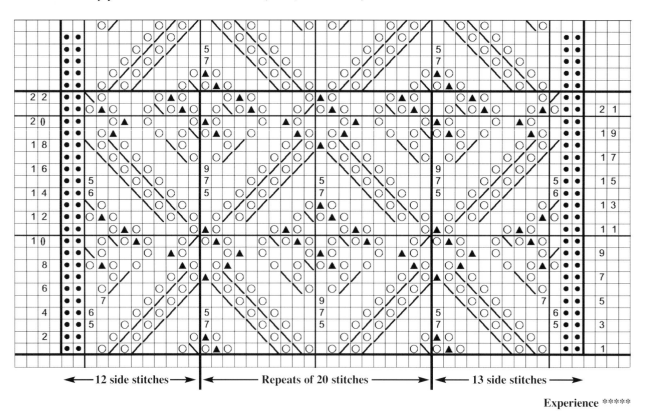

←—— 12 side stitches ——→ **←—— Repeats of 20 stitches ——→** **←—— 13 side stitches ——→**

Experience *****

Cast on multiples of 20 stitches + 25 (12 + 13 extra stitches on each side)
e.g. (20 x 6) + 25 = 145 stitches.

N.B. If needed, cast on extra stitches for each side. Include these in the above sum.

Spider Webs, Spiders and Diamonds Pattern

This most beautiful allover pattern I believe originates from the remote Isle of Unst in the Shetland Islands, where reputedly the best and most intricate Shetland lace patterns were worked. I believe the Spider Webs are also known as a Puzzle Pattern – they are formed from two small tree motifs, one mirroring the other. This gives a plain diamond shape between them. The spiders are in each hexagon motif and the diamonds divide the hexagons from the webs. This pattern really should be worked on the finest needles with finest one ply yarn, ideally Shetland 1 ply, and dressed carefully for the best effects. A variation for this is Spiders Web, Spiders And Diamonds II. Another very similar design is the centre pattern for the "Unst Lace Stole – Project 6".

This is a traditional lace dating from at least the middle of the nineteenth century, I have seen a very fine shawl of the period with this as the centre pattern – excepting that the mirrored trees were larger, so making the webs between them bigger.

Spider Webs, Spiders and Diamonds Chart

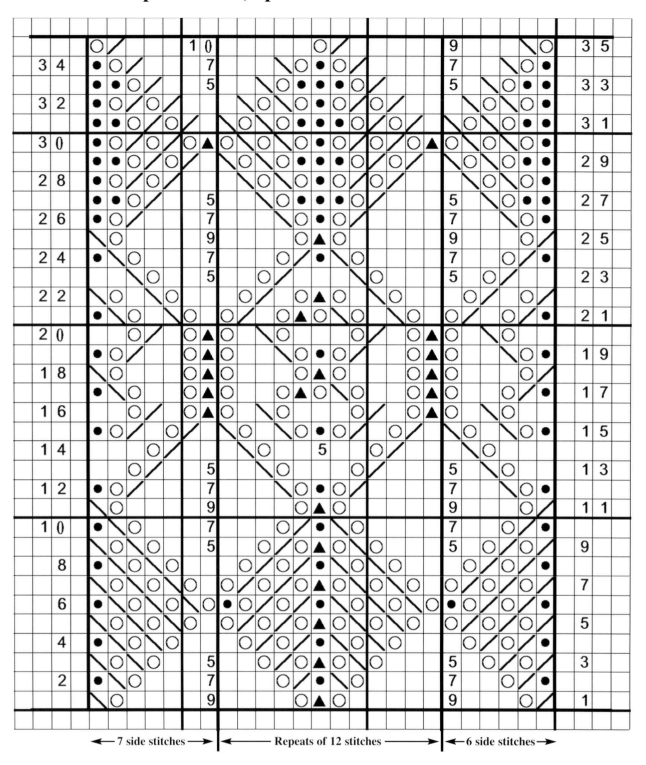

←— 7 side stitches —→ ←——— Repeats of 12 stitches ———→ ←— 6 side stitches —→

Experience *****

Cast on multiples of 12 stitches + 13 (7 + 6 extra stitches on each side)
e.g. (12 x 10) + 13 = 133 stitches.

N.B. You may if needed, cast on extra stitches for each side. Include these in the above sum.

This could be a useful variation on the previous, very delicate pattern giving more solid "dumb-bell" shapes between the spider hexagon shapes. It could be used where a more dense ground is required to balance areas with solid plain knitting in the borders. I created this variation simply by adding in two extra stitches to the Spider Webs, Spiders and Diamonds Pattern.

Spider Webs, Spiders and Diamonds II Chart

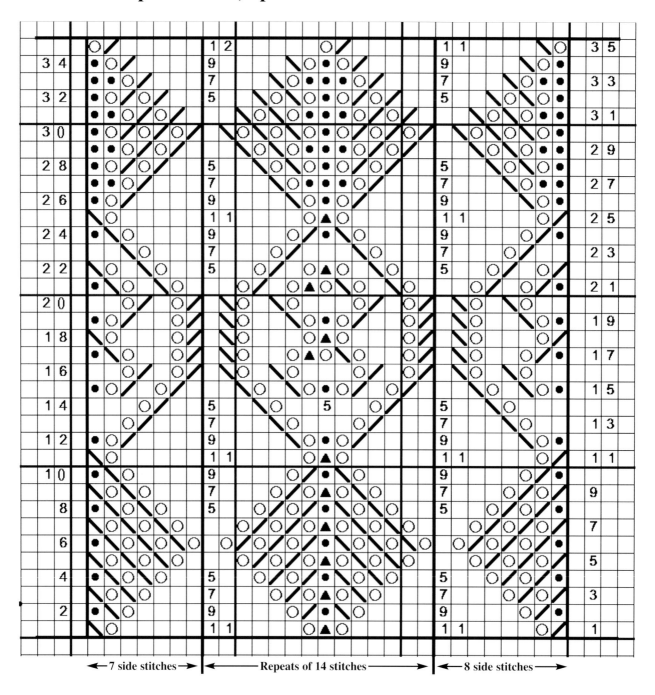

←— 7 side stitches —→ ←————— Repeats of 14 stitches —————→ ←— 8 side stitches —→

Experience *****

Cast on multiples of 14 stitches + 15 (7 + 8 extra stitches on each side)
e.g. (14 x 10) + 15 = 155 stitches.

N.B. You may if needed, cast on extra stitches for each side. Include these in the above sum.

Shetland Twins with Lace Hole Diamonds Pattern

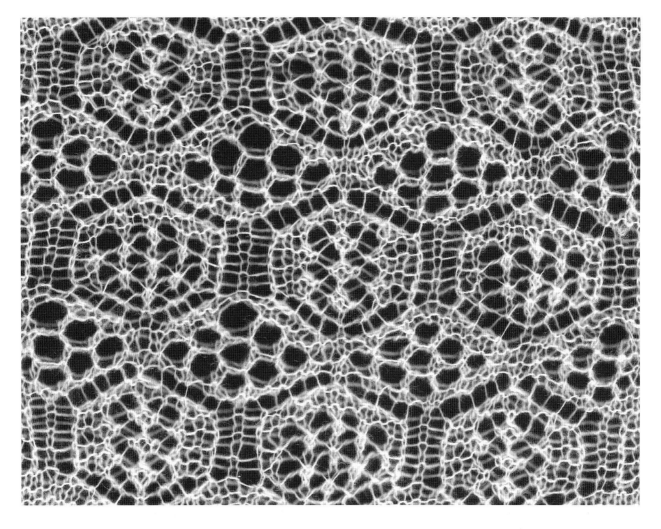

This lovely, traditional pattern deserves to be done in the finest yarns so that its beautiful structure is best displayed. It isn't as hard as it looks to knit, because of its regular geometric elements.

Remember: The lace hole diamonds are asymmetrically placed – it doesn't show in the finished piece. **The pattern repeat block is 28 stitches by 48 rows**. I have given 9 stitches each side as a suggested start and finish. **Cast on multiples of 28 + 18 sts, e.g. (5 x 28) + 18 = 158 sts.**

N.B. Each blank square should be plain knitted in garter stitch.

The Shetland Twins are a famous pattern, but basically are just two hexagons (one a "brother" and one a "sister" – see "Design Library", Section Four) with alternating fine bead mesh stitch and bead motif centres. It's easy to see how this pattern could be experimented with:

• Knitted without the lace hole diamonds – or with a single centre bead in a plain diamond or a bead diamond instead;

• Put spiders instead of beads;

• Make all the hexagonal in-fills the same.

Experience *****

This version is slightly different to that pictured on page 139 because I have put plain diamonds in (rows 21-26); to recreate pattern on page 139, simply work rows 41 to 50 instead afer row 20, then resume at row 27.

Spider, Tree and Diamond Lace Pattern

This beautiful traditional allover pattern was another also collected by **James Norbury** (1904 – 72). This charismatic man, the son of a Cheshire blacksmith, was taught to knit by his grandmother. He was a gifted designer who worked prolifically after World War II; he presented some of the first television programmes about knitting and was also one of the first of his time to try to attempt some of the history of knitting. To record Shetland lace, Norbury used a version of knitting charts, with a looped tadpole-like symbol to represent "make one and knit two together". Another of the traditional patterns collected by him is Shetland Twins with Lace Hole Diamonds – he didn't name these; but just called them Shetland Shawl Centre (above) and Traditional Allover Pattern respectively. Norbury suggested this one would be "perfect" for the centre of a shawl, with a garter stitch border all round.

Spider, Tree and Diamond Lace Chart

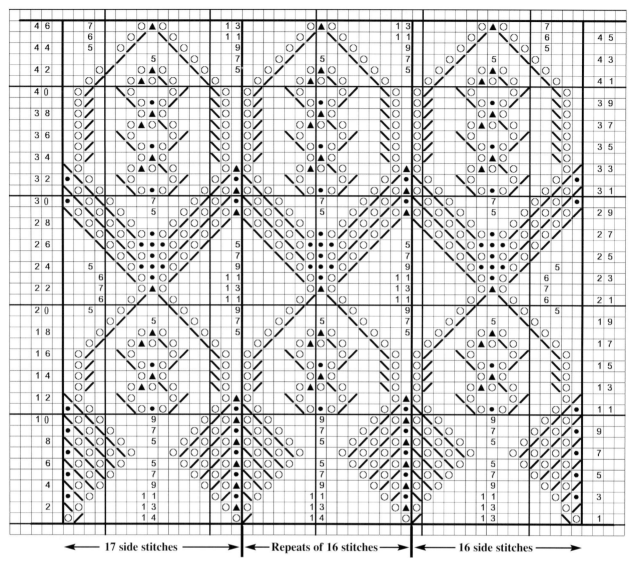

← 17 side stitches → ← Repeats of 16 stitches → ← 16 side stitches →

Cast on multiples of 16 stitches + 33 (17 + 16 extra stitches on each side)
e.g. (16 x 9) + 33 = 177 stitches.

N.B. If needed, cast on extra stitches for each side. Include these in the above sum.

Diamond, Tree and Lace Hole Diamond Pattern

This traditional pattern gave me quite a lot of trouble to knit – and to chart – but none the less, I can see it is a graceful lace and relatively easy to knit, once one's understood that there are extra pairs of stitches created and used in the lower halves of the plain diamonds (e.g. from rows 12 to 18 inclusive, row 19 gives the compensating decreases). For clarity of charting, I have doubled stitches into the squares affected to keep the rest of the pattern in alignment (see the final notes of "How to Read a Chart").

A beautiful variation of this pattern is made by placing a small bead motif in the centre of the plain diamond, another idea would be to make the trees point upwards (see "How to Adapt a Pattern") or exchange them for fern motifs.

N.B. Row 1 is starred; this is because it is different from row 37 (also starred). On row 37 and each subsequent full repeat of the pattern at this point, (i.e. the repeat row 1s), there are extra stitches to be taken in at the start of the lace holes diamond which are not present on the first row (row 1).

Diamond, Tree and Lace Hole Diamond Chart

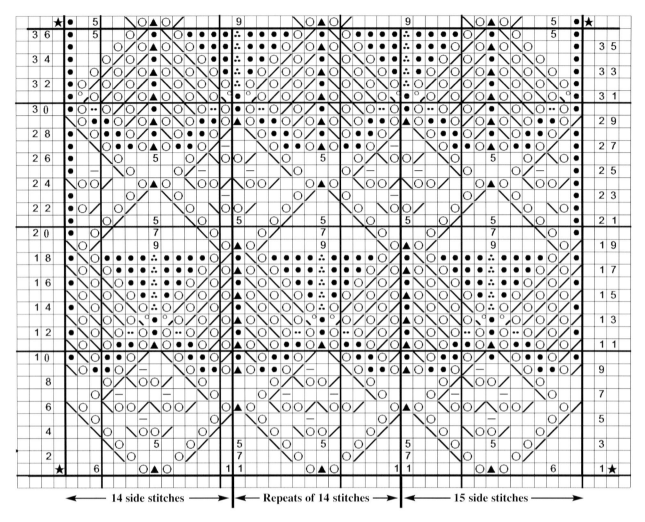

← 14 side stitches → ← Repeats of 14 stitches → ← 15 side stitches →

Experience *****

Cast on multiples of 14 stitches + 29 (14 + 15 extra stitches on each side)
e.g. (14 x 10) + 29 = 169 stitches.

N.B. If needed, cast on extra stitches for each side. Include these in the above sum.

144

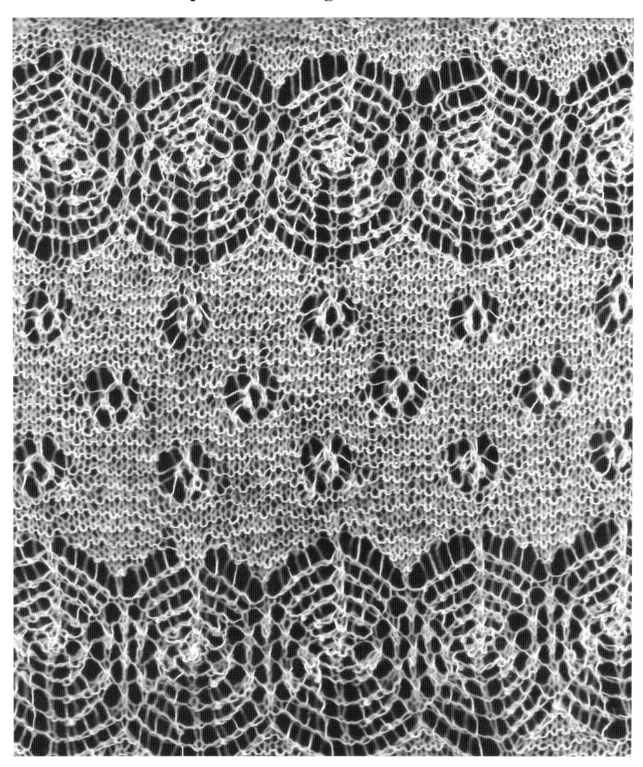

This large centre* pattern is my recreation of one from a nineteenth century fine lace shawl originally made in Unst. This is one of the largest centre patterns I have found, although it is made up from only two main pattern motifs. It is best that this is worked on the finest needles with the finest yarn to achieve the full effects. Experienced knitters could replace the tiny bead or Small Leaf Pattern in the webs with plain stitches.

N.B. The starred webs section (rows 1 – 26) must be repeated after the final full repeat of the pattern so the piece begins and ends with lines of webs and looks balanced. **This is a 56 row repeat block.**

* And it is so large, it could be a border design in its own right.

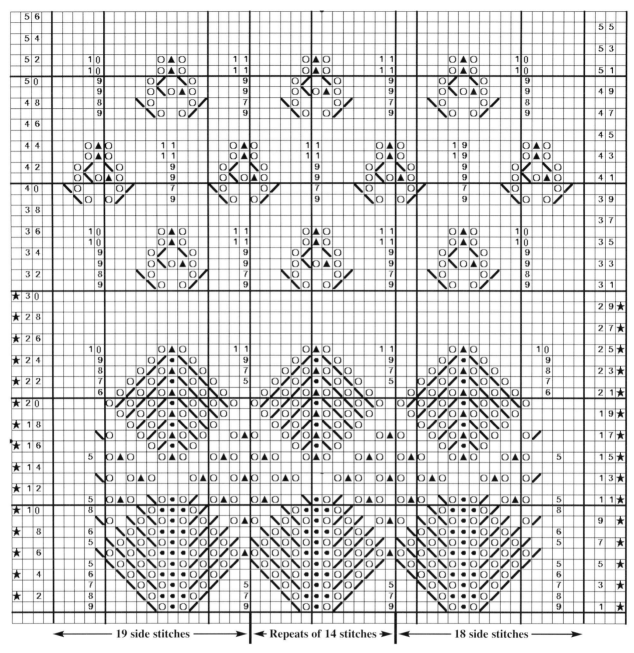

← 19 side stitches → ← Repeats of 14 stitches → ← 18 side stitches →

Experience *****

Cast on multiples of 14 stitches + 37 (19 + 18 extra stitches on each side)
e.g. (14 x 10) + 37 = 177 stitches.

N.B. If needed, cast on extra stitches for each side. Include these in the above sum.

This unusual pattern gave me a bit of trouble to recreate because I was working from an old photocopy. It has interesting arrowhead shapes in and was popular in the mid 1800s, similar ones are on a lot of very fine Shetland lace. I have seen a version of it on an antique tray cloth worked in a framed border of cat's paws, then surrounded by Alpine Edging II. That had been worked in fine thread and had the tree motifs set closer – as with this chart detail, **right** – also the cigar shapes between the arrowheads were two stitches wider. A close look at the arrowheads bottom and top in the photograph will show that I decreased the number of repeat rows with the ones at the top to get shorter cigars as an experiment.

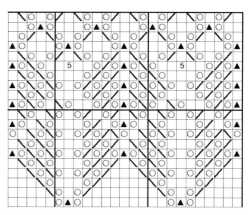

Antique Centre Pattern Chart

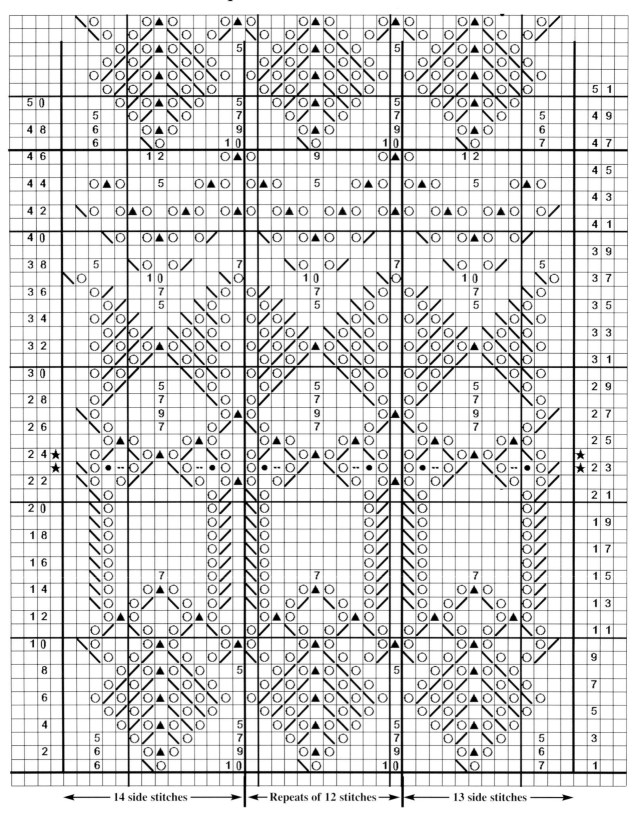

← 14 side stitches → ← Repeats of 12 stitches → ← 13 side stitches →

Starred Rows 23 and 24: Extra stitches are made and cast off with these rows.

Experience *****

Cast on multiples of 12 stitches + 27 (14 + 13 extra stitches on each side)
e.g. (12 x 9) + 27 = 135 stitches.

N.B. If needed, cast on extra stitches for each side. Include these in the above sum.

Bead Column, Tree, Spider and Diamond Pattern

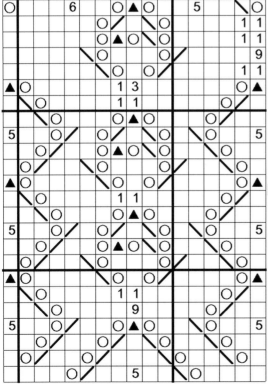

This centre pattern is from the Framed Shawl shown on page 215 and demonstrates just how pleasing and effective a simple linear arrangement of motifs can be. It could be adapted by increasing the number of spiders from one to three as shown by the chart, **left**. Notice the different "diamond point" start of the tree (rows 27 to 31) – this could be experimented with elsewhere.

Bead Column, Tree, Spider and Diamond Pattern

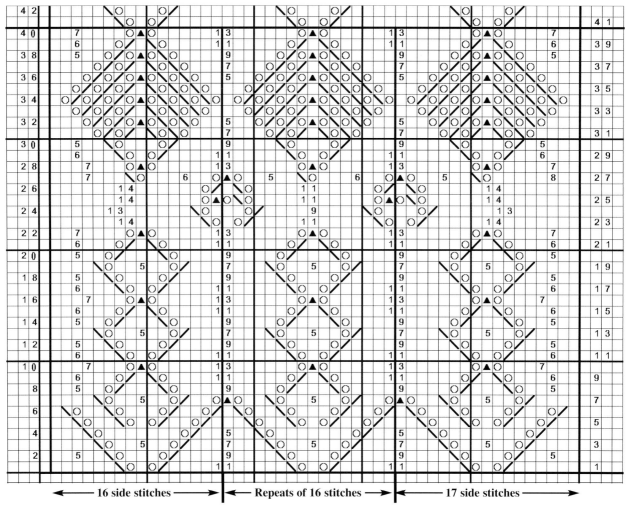

←— 16 side stitches —→ ←— Repeats of 16 stitches —→ ←— 17 side stitches —→

Experience *****

Cast on multiples of 16 stitches + 33 (16 + 17 extra stitches on each side)
e.g. (16 x 10) + 33 = 193 stitches.

N.B. If needed, cast on extra stitches for each side. Include these in the above sum.

This large pattern is from one of the very first knitting pattern manuals of the 1840s. This is a strikingly effective pattern which could be used as an alternative centre to Elaborated Print O' the Wave, or as a border pattern. Easy to alter, the large diamonds could be left plain, or filled with other small motifs. I believe this pattern is named by Mrs Gaugain after Queen Victoria's second daughter Princess Alice Maud Mary (1843 – 78); a direct ancestor of H.R.H. Prince Philip, the Duke of Edinburgh.

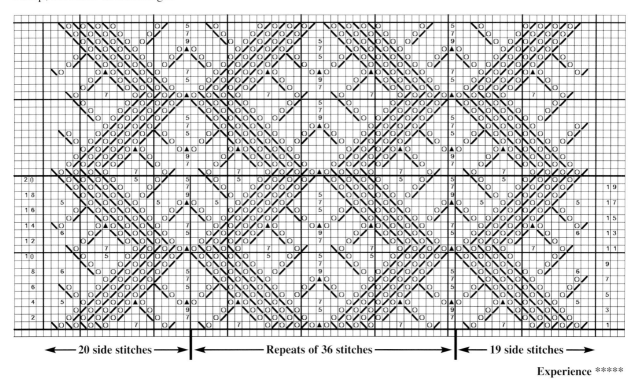

◄——— **20 side stitches** ———►   ◄——— **Repeats of 36 stitches** ———►   ◄——— **19 side stitches** ———►

Experience *****

Cast on multiples of 36 stitches + 39 (20 + 19 extra stitches on each side)
e.g. (36 x 3) + 39 = 147 stitches.

N.B. If needed, cast on extra stitches for each side. Include these in the above sum.

Bead and Peerie Flea Diamonds Border Design

This makes a suitable stole/shawl border for the Allover Tree and Diamond Pattern, see page 201 for advice on forming the mitred corners. **N.B.** On even rows – not charted – knit and purl into the *double increases* formed on the previous rows.

Experience * * * * *

Cast on multiples of 18 stitches + 42 (21 extra stitches on each side)
e.g. (18 x 3) + 42 = 96 stitches.

Bead and Peerie Flea Diamonds Border Design

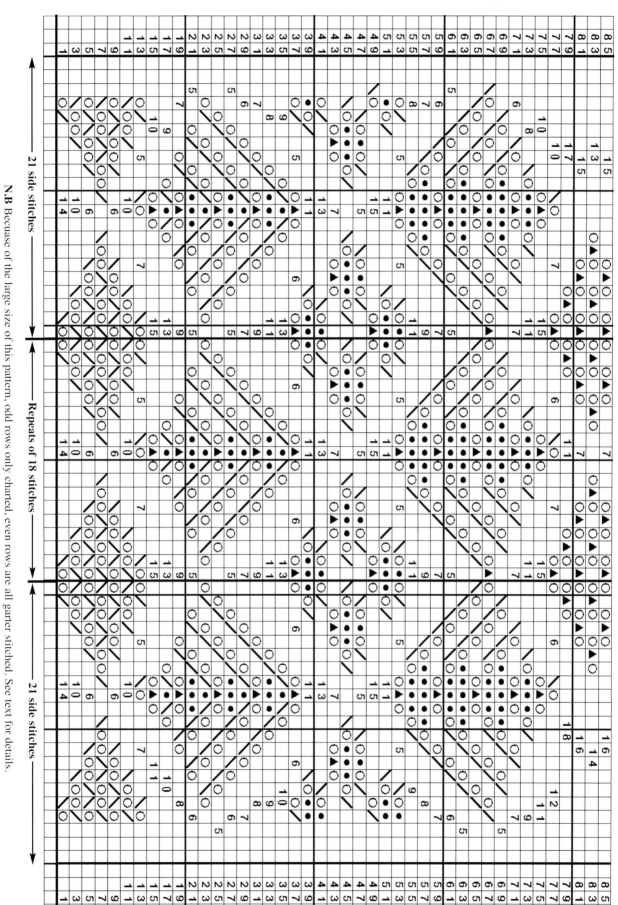

N.B Becuase of the large size of this pattern, odd rows only charted, even rows are all garter stiched. See text for details.

21 side stitches

Repeats of 18 stitches

21 side stitches

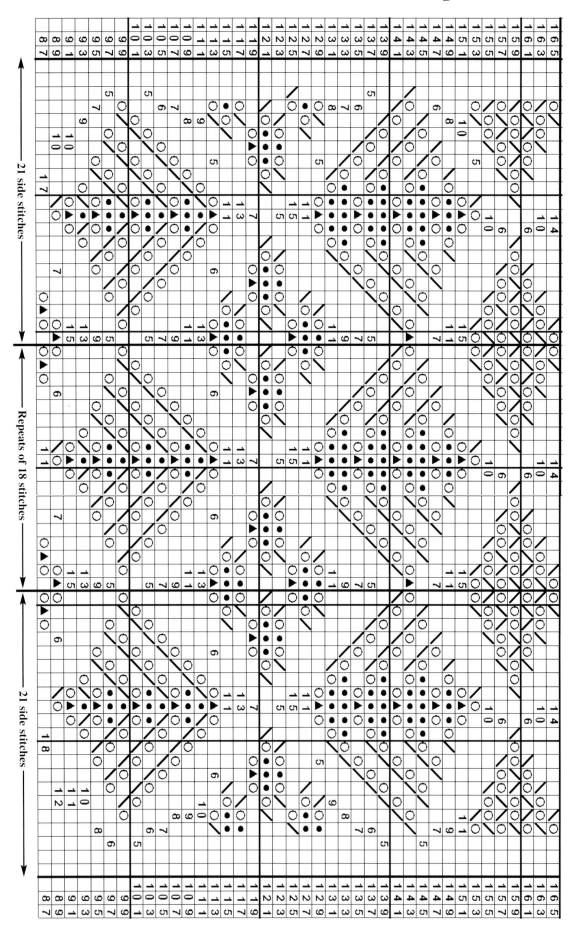

Pineapple Pattern Border

This is an interesting border pattern, worth studying to "unpick" its elements for use in your own designs. Apart from the unusual pineapple shape, notice there is an intriguing coral-like motif and a mesh pattern similar to the Cat's Eye Pattern. I also like the possibilities of the zigzag line of small tree motifs. Again, although this originally bordered a fine one ply stole, I think it would make an attractive shawl border. Knitters will see I have modified the main chart slightly by knitting in a small bead diamond in the top plain triangle. The little chart shows how I did this.

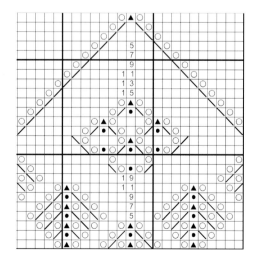

Pineapple Pattern Border Chart

← 18 side stitches → ← Repeats of 28 stitches → ← 18 side stitches →

Experience *****

Cast on multiples of 28 stitches + 36 (18 + 18 extra stitches on each side)
e.g. (28 x 4) + 36 = 148 stitches.

N.B. If needed, cast on extra stitches for each side. Include these in the above sum.

Even row numbers only given here. Row 1 is a simple *break pattern*. Row 3 starts the border pattern, but extra pairs of rows can be worked before row 3 if desired.

Snail Shell with Cable Border Design

I like this border design for its snail shell or "sprouting seed" motif, which I have seen many times in traditional Shetland designs.

I put personal elements in it too with the spider web diamond motif – as far as I know, this is not a traditional one but composed of traditional elements. Nor is the jellyfish-like shape between the shells, again this came from playing with Shetland motifs. This is a large pattern that I believe should be treated as directional – the "sprouting seed" should always point upwards in the finished item.

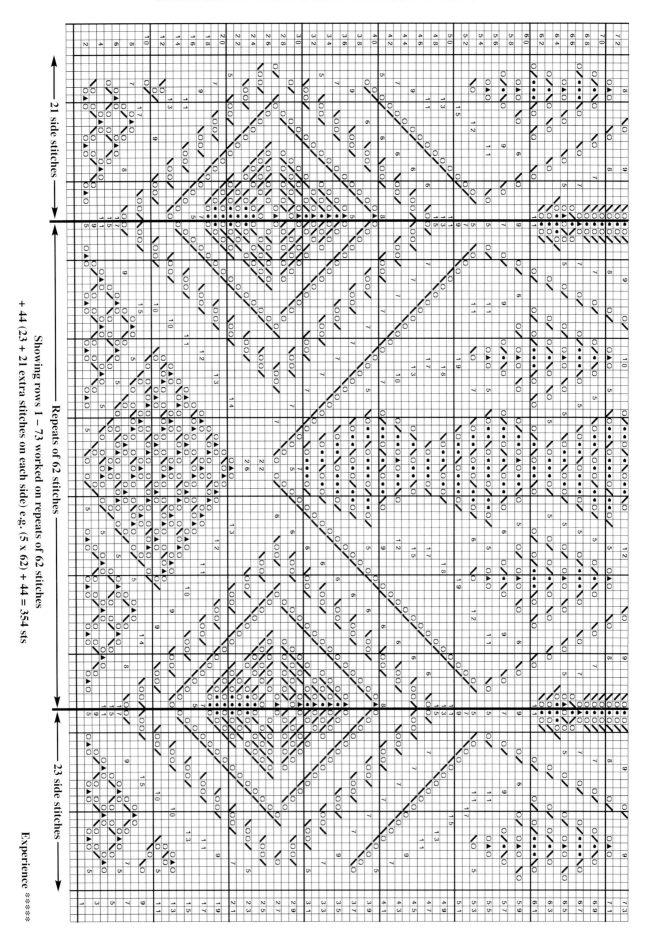

21 side stitches

Showing rows 1 – 73 worked on repeats of 62 stitches
+ 44 (23 + 21 extra stitches on each side) e.g. (5 x 62) + 44 = 354 sts

Repeats of 62 stitches

23 side stitches

Experience *****

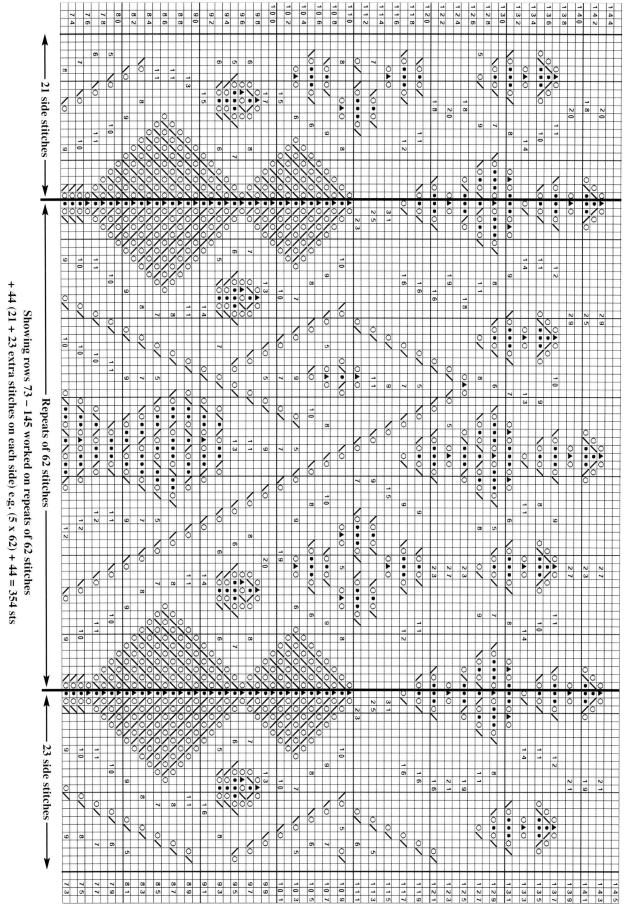

NB: Row 73 given here again for reference – knit it only once!

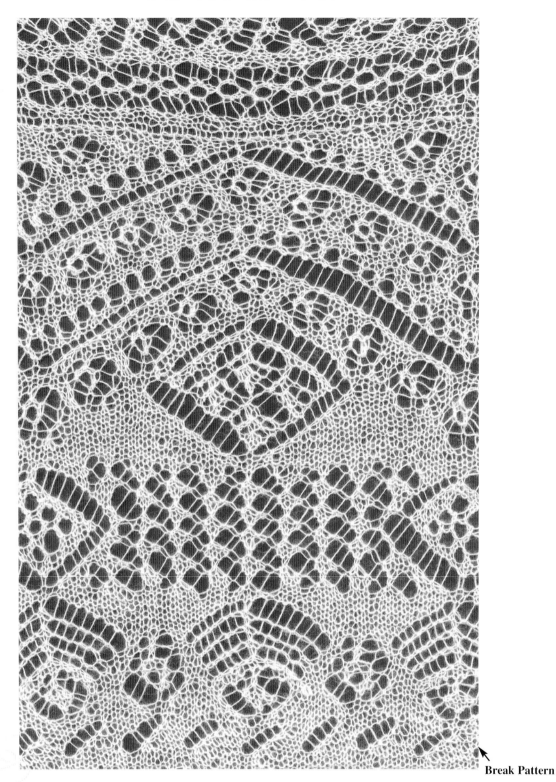

Break Pattern

This border design is composed of traditional Shetland designs that can be re-used by experienced knitters. I used this for the Framed Shawl pictured on page 215 and worked it using the "borders outwards" method of construction. To finish, I knitted an edging round the borders' stitches – the insertion part of this can be seen crossing the top of the photograph.

Extra stitches are created in this pattern with the parts involving the double increases; again they are corrected later. I found that a good way of working the ＼, was to do it as shown in "Stitch Advice". The pattern rows below the pattern outline show a repeating 6-stitch *break pattern* design that gives slanting "sticks" in the knitting.

Framed Shawl Border Chart 1

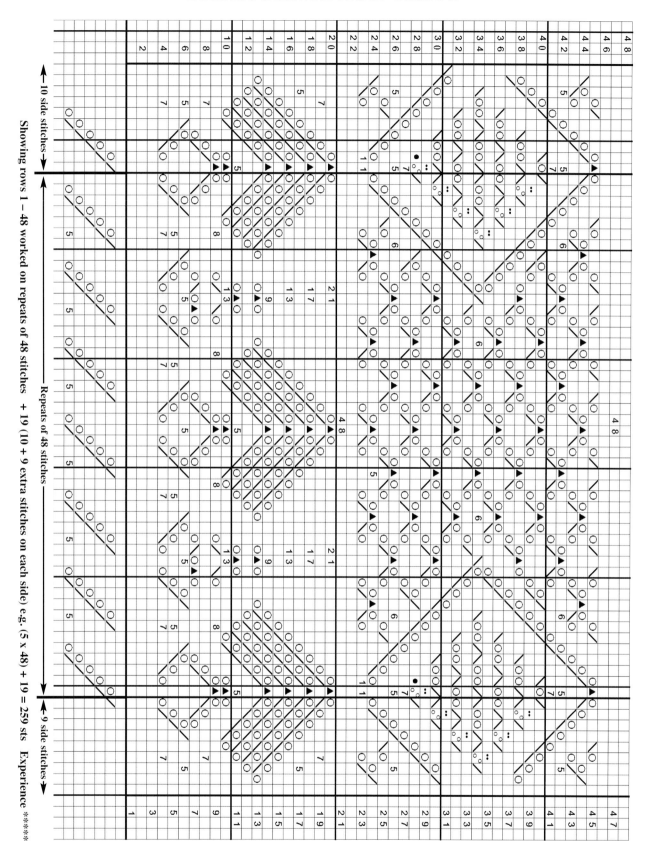

Framed Shawl Border Chart 2

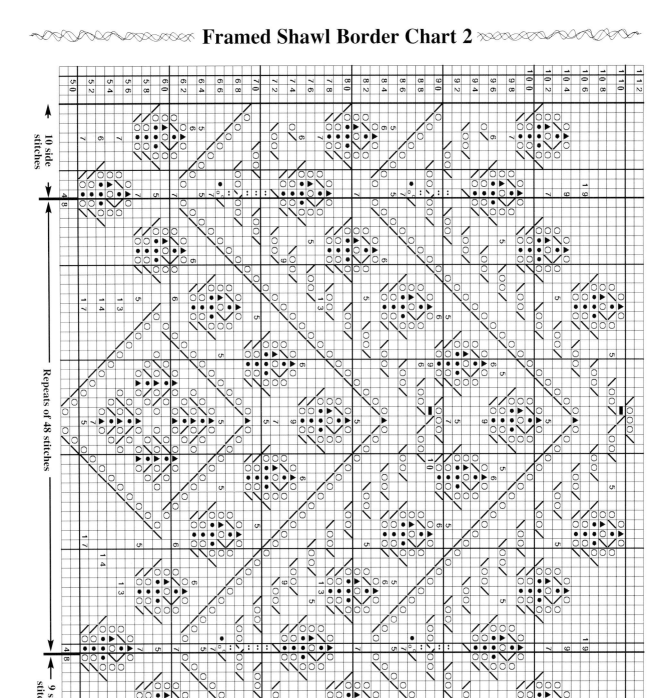

Showing rows 49 – 112 worked on repeats of 48 stitches + 19
(10 + 9 extra stitches on each side) eg. (5 x 48) + 19 = 259 sts

N.B. The minus symbol on the centre stitch of rows 89 and 110 indicate a "non stitch" due to the decrease by it.
The stitch is recreated by an increase directly above on the next row.

Tree of Life Border Chart II

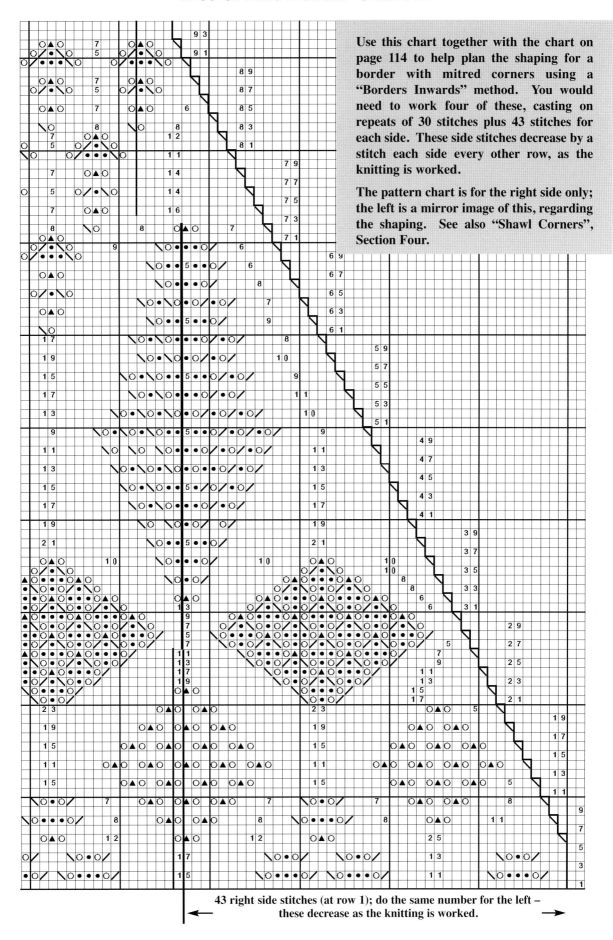

Use this chart together with the chart on page 114 to help plan the shaping for a border with mitred corners using a "Borders Inwards" method. You would need to work four of these, casting on repeats of 30 stitches plus 43 stitches for each side. These side stitches decrease by a stitch each side every other row, as the knitting is worked.

The pattern chart is for the right side only; the left is a mirror image of this, regarding the shaping. See also "Shawl Corners", Section Four.

**43 right side stitches (at row 1); do the same number for the left –
these decrease as the knitting is worked.**

Feathered Border Pattern

I wanted to make this large and beautiful border design as a tribute to the lace knitters of the nineteenth century. It is based on a fine, large, triangular shawl that was a duplicate of one made for Alexandra, Princess of Wales in 1863, the replica is in the collection of the National Museums of Scotland. A close look at this design shows how the overall complex arrangement is made up of much simpler patterns and motifs. The pattern charts which follow show the placing of the motifs (which could easily be rearranged or substituted). The feather may originally have been taken from Paisley shawls – the small "sprouting seed" at the top of the sword-like pattern certainly resembles a Paisley one. I used this pattern for a triangular shawl made in DMC Cordonnet Special 70 cotton and a circular needle British size 12, metric 2.75mm. I began by knitting a long edging strip, then picked up 938 stitches for 11 feathers and two half-sword designs for the sides; the original had sixteen feathers – I needed less because I was working with thicker thread. Lastly, by changing the curl to point to the right, I made half the "sprouting seeds" curl inward towards the central feather. This pattern should be regarded as directional and therefore worked using the "borders inwards" method.

Cast on repeats of 78 stitches + 80 side stitches.

N.B. Side stitches for the R.H. side only are shown because this is such a large pattern. **Charts Advice**: complete the L.H. side to mirror the R.H. side by changing the final stitches on the L.H. to ones that mirror the R.H. where needed. When knitting the Right Hand side stitches, ignore the chart numerals at stitches 2 and 3, on rows 1 and 50 – just plain knit these. Remember to knit and purl into all the *double increases*.

Experience * * * * *

164

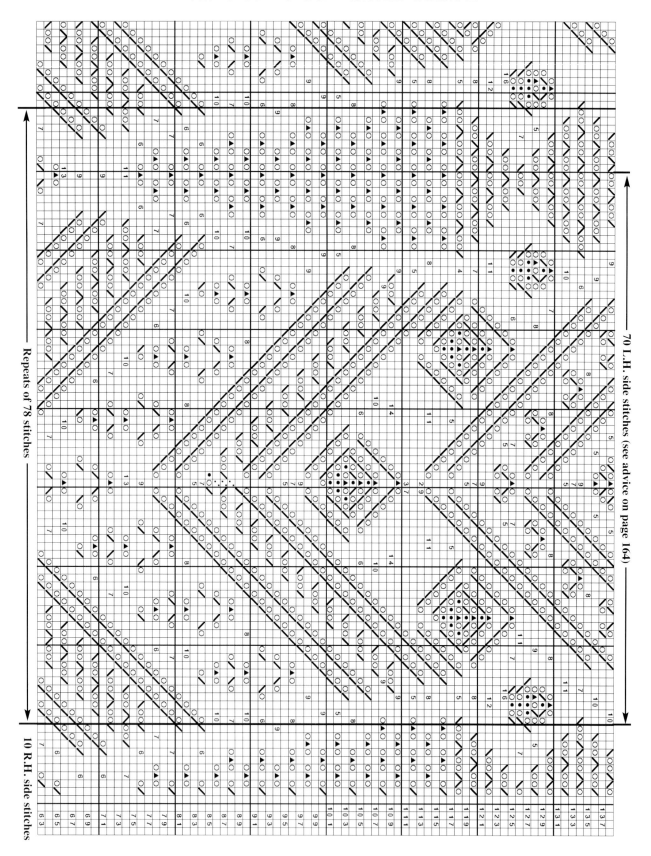

166

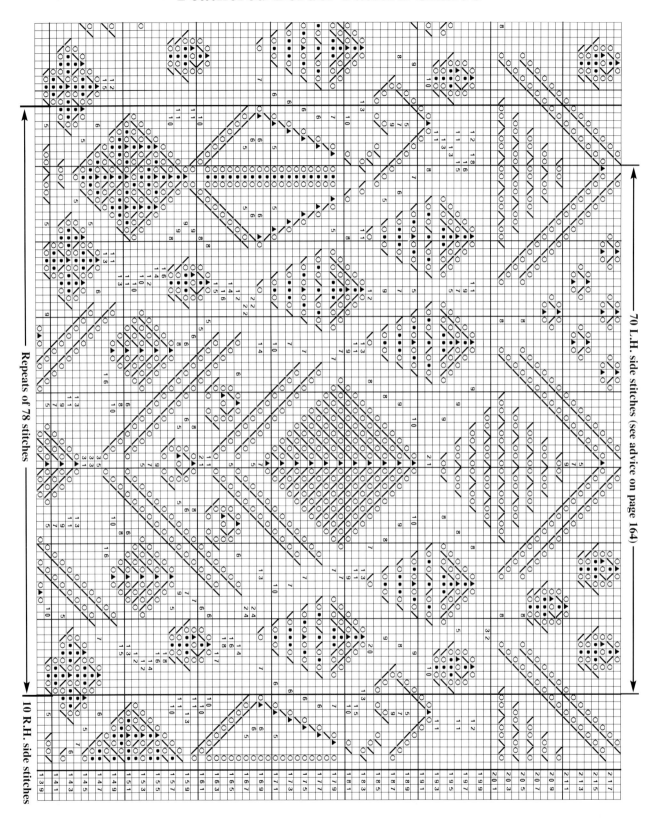

Snail Shell Edging with Bead Insertion

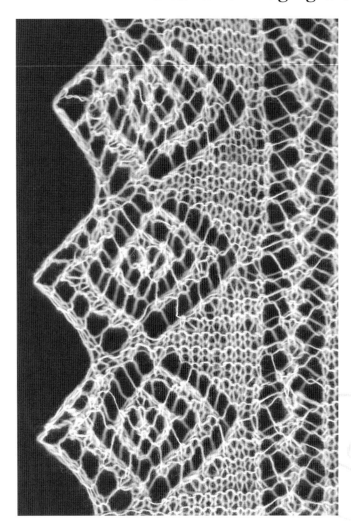

This pattern is quite a complicated looking design that seems to have been popular about a hundred years ago in Shetland lace. In a much larger form, the "sprouting seed", it enclosed other pattern elements (such as a lace cable motif) in border sections – see Snail Shell with Cable Border Pattern. I give it here with a bead insertion worked on the first ten stitches. Experienced knitters could change this insertion for another.

A modification would be to alternate the patterned rows with plain knitted rows, modifying the stitches as necessary. It could also be a narrower edging, i.e. worked from stitch 10 on the odd rows outwards. The first stitch on the odd rows could be slipped if a tighter straight edge is required.

N.B. The stitches on the decrease outside edge need careful working. Stitch 10 on row 11 needs to be replaced by a knit stitch if the insertion element is re-used.

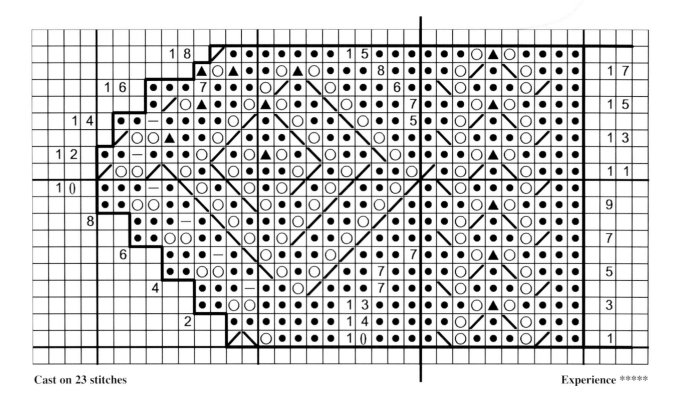

Cast on 23 stitches

Experience *****

168

Ring Shawl Lace Edging with Spider Insertion

I made this from an old photograph of a nineteenth century Shetland Ring Shawl. The original shawl had a Spiders Webs, Spiders and Diamonds Pattern as the centre with an Unst Lace Stole Border. The first 10 stitches worked up, make a pretty spider-like ringed insertion (with stitch 10 on row 1 replaced with a knit). The remaining Lace Holes or Drops Edging is a traditional edging in itself.

A relative of this is the Lace Holes Edging pattern. Experienced knitters will be able to re-use the Spider Insertion or exchange this element with another insertion.

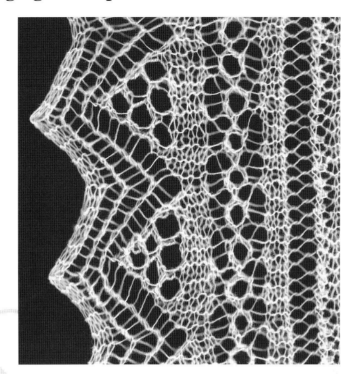

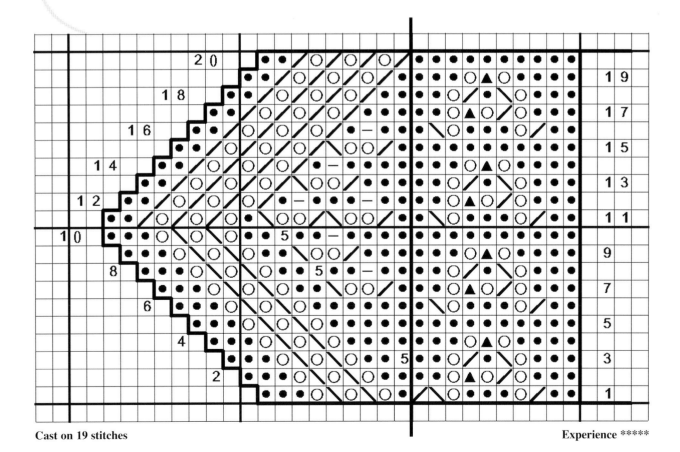

Cast on 19 stitches

Experience ***

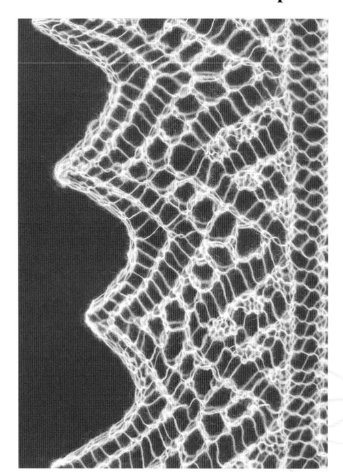

This combination of a lace hole zigzag and a bead group in an edging was very popular in white knitting a hundred years ago. There are several versions of "Alpine Edgings" as they were called, I have seen one very similar to this but with a plain knitted outside edge worked on three stitches. Mrs Sutherland's Fine Lace is obviously related too.

This edging would work well with the finer knitted lace shawls/stoles and looks best made up in the finest yarn on the finer sized needles.

I give it here with the narrowest of straight edge sides, two or three more plain knitted stitches could be put in after stitch 5 – a dividing bar marks the place – remember to include them in the casting on.

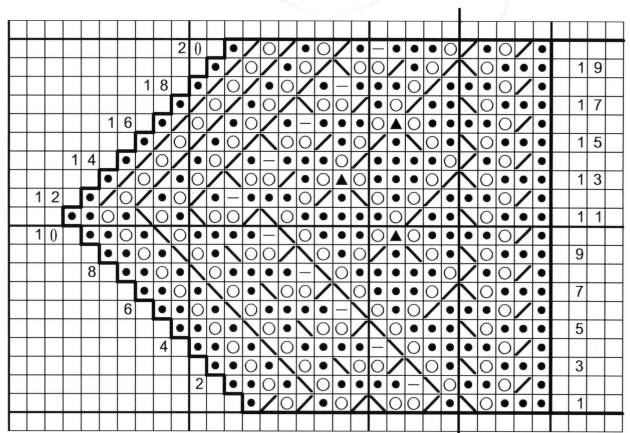

Cast on 18 stitches

Experience ***

Alpine Edging II

This very pretty Alpine Edging is very similar to one on an antique tray cloth in the Lerwick Museum and Library, Shetland. That one has another line of faggot zigzag on the inside of the lace hole zigzag (to match the one on the outside, before the last four stitches).

The photograph left, shows the edging knitted with the *Lacy Edge Stitch* worked on the first two stitches of every even row.

Experienced knitters will be interested to notice that instead of the usual *double increase* in the lace hole zigzag element, there is just a single increase and on the following row, a knit and a purl is worked into that particular stitch; this gives a neater hole. It will also be noted that a simple bead insertion is worked at the inside on the first ten odd row stitches. Obviously, this can be easily omitted or exchanged for another insertion, should the knitter wish.

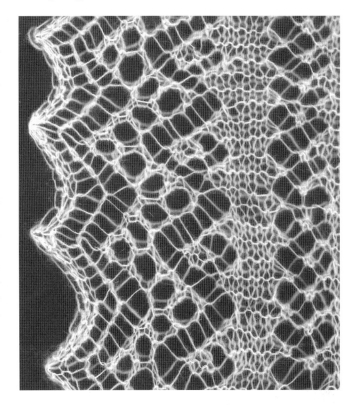

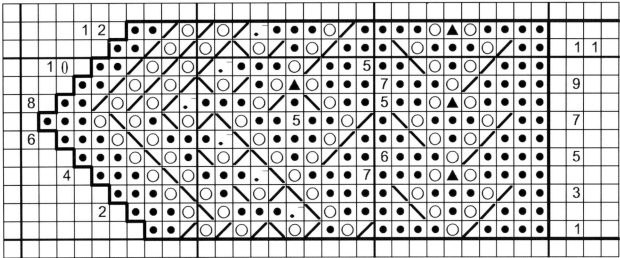

Cast on 25 stitches   **Experience *******

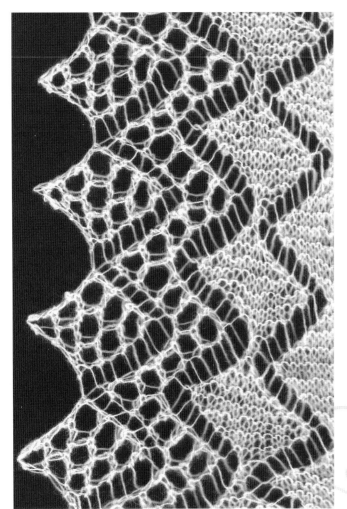

Edgings are called laces in Shetland. This unusual 16 row repeat pattern is a direct recreation from a photograph of an exhibit in the Lerwick Museum. The information with the photograph, gives it as being "Fine Lace Knitted By Mrs Sutherland, Unst, in 1900". It is unusual in its trapezoidal element, whereas the lace hole diamond and lace hole zigzag occur in other contemporary patterns. It was made in a very fine yarn and on the finest of needles. I have made it here in Shetland 1 ply with 2.25 mm (British 13s) needles.

This edge is very suitable for the finest and most complex of shawls and should only be attempted by the confident! It could be combined with an insertion such as Bead Insertion to make a wider and more intricate edge. A variation I give of this pattern is Fine Lace Hole Diamond and Zigzag Edging.

N.B. It begins with **•**. finishing the increase rows on rows 1 and 3. This indicates that you must knit into the front and back of the final stitch – making an increase of one stitch.

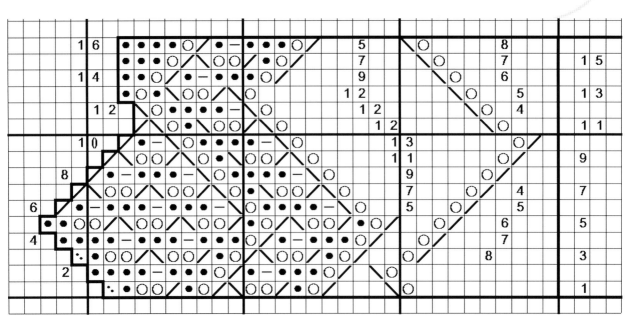

Cast on 28 stitches   **Experience** *****

Fine Lace Hole Diamond and Zigzag Edging

This is a regular, symmetrical form of Mrs Sutherland's Fine Lace and to all intents is exactly the same, apart from the straight edge side. Compare the two and you will see how this has been created.

Again, this is one of the "Alpine" edgings that were very popular a hundred years ago. I believe the name refers to the peaks occurring in the pattern.

I recommend this as a matching lace edging for the finest one-ply shawls with diamond and lace hole elements e.g. Diamond, Tree and Lace Hole Diamonds.

A narrower edging can be obtained by omitting the first ten-stitch block (marked by dividing bar cutting between stitches 10 and 11).

N.B. It begins with • • finishing the increase rows on rows 1, 3 and 5. This indicates that you must knit into the front and back of the final stitch – making an increase of one stitch.

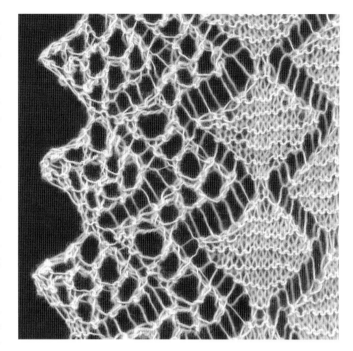

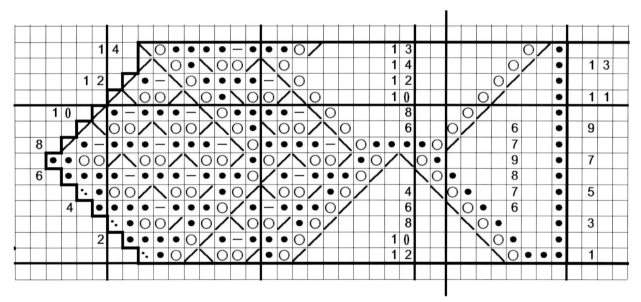

Cast on 28 stitches

Experience ✳✳✳✳✳

Rose Diamond Lace Edging

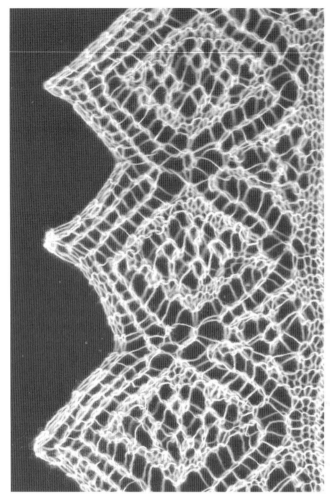

This pretty lace edging I created by experimenting with the Rose Diamond Lace centre pattern. It is quite a complicated edging to knit but goes very well with that pattern. Both would be suited as a stole or *un-bordered* evening shawl. Certainly, this type of sophisticated lace really has to be worked in the finer yarns.

Experienced knitters will see that quite a few *allover* patterns with an underlying diamond structure could be adapted in this manner and this is why I show this lace.

The pattern is given with a very narrow straight edge side, I think a Spider Insertion might be tried – there is one with the Ring Shawl Edging – this could be worked directly paired with the chart below.

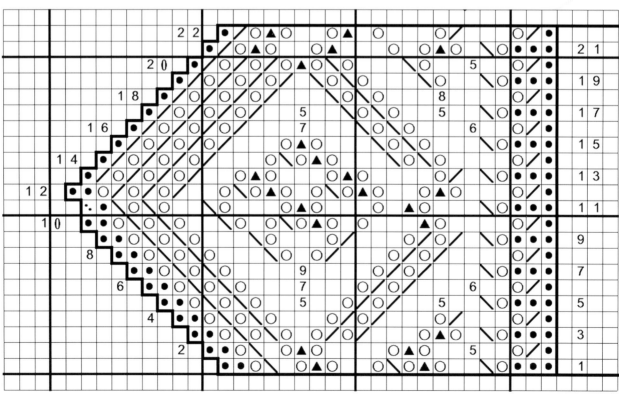

Cast on 22 stitches   · . = increase by "knitting into front and back of stitch"   **Experience *****

The Clematis Edging

This very pretty edging is not a known Shetland lace as such; but arguably, apart from the *picot* outside, the elements of the pattern are recognisable Shetland forms. The pattern (as given here) is a slightly modified version of a doyley design dating from before World War I. I used this to edge the Cobweb Crepe Shawl – see "Projects Section".

Experience * * * * Knitters: The **stars** at the end of each even row mean you can do either of two things throughout: Either knit each last stitch plain, for an edging strip **or** knit the last stitch together with a picked up stitch from the border of an item (with the shawl in the project, I did the last option). Traditionally, Shetland shawls were made from the outside in; this means the edging was cast on first. For "modern" or "imitation" Shetland shawls (for want of a better term), the edging is worked last. See "Shetland Shawls" for advice about this.

N.B. The picot element is identified by the last "make 2s" only, on the patterned rows. The picots may be omitted.

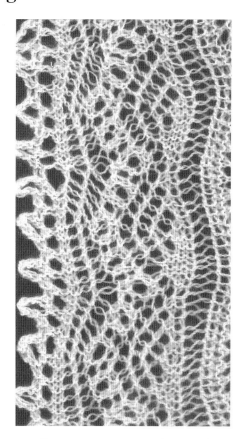

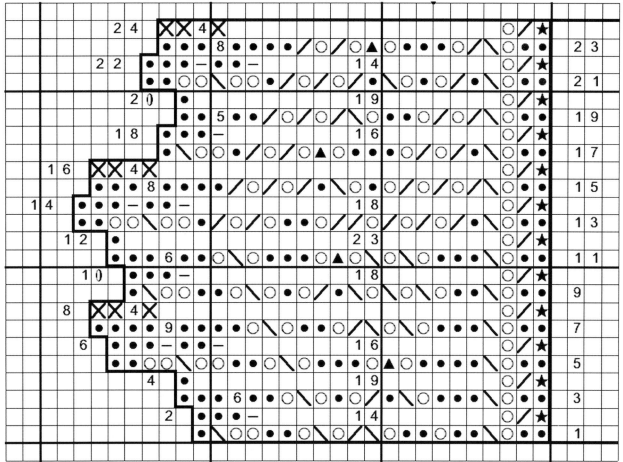

Cast on 19 stitches

Experience *****

175

1851 Wedding Veil Lace

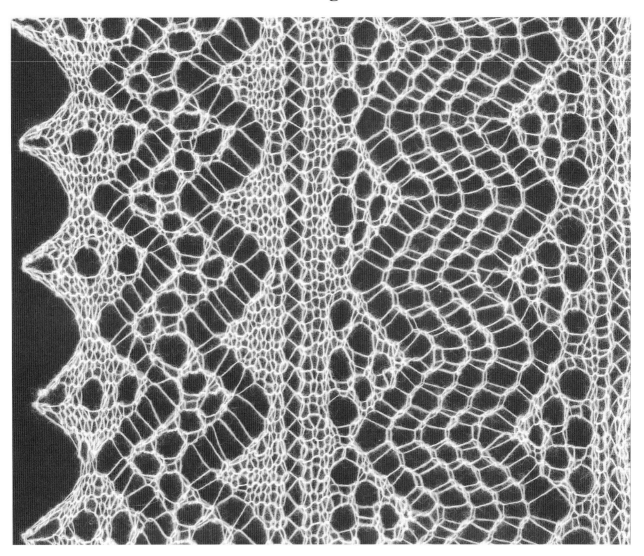

This very beautiful lace is from the Madder and Ivory Wedding Veil that was exhibited by Edward Standen at the Great Exhibition. It is made up of a wide insertion (14 row repeat) and a matching edging (12 row repeat). This means that both combined have a **84 row repeat** – 6 repeats of the insertion to 7 repeats of the edging – and this consideration has to be born in mind when calculating what length, and therefore stitch count, one needs. It easily divides back into a separate insertion and edging and I give these pattern charts on the following page. I would like to thank the excellent Shetland Guild of Spinners, Weavers and Dyers (based at the Shetland Textile Working Museum, Weisdale Mill, Shetland ZE2 9LW) for supplying the picture from which I recreated this pattern.

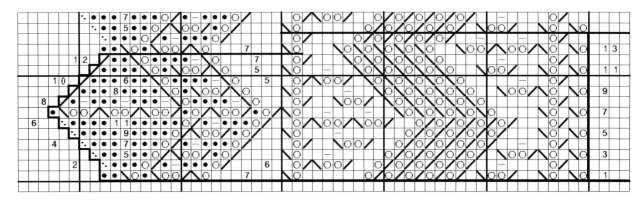

Cast on 48 stitches   **Experience *******

Insertion

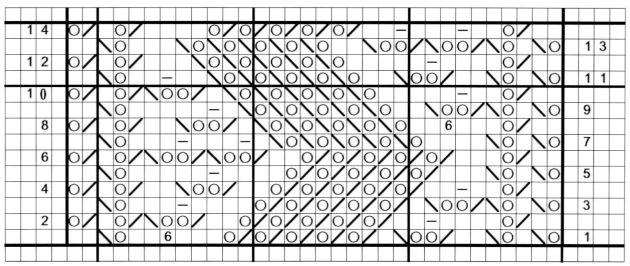

Cast on 32 stitches

Experience *****

Edging

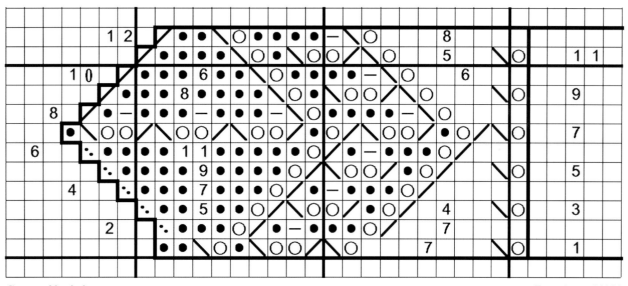

Cast on 20 stitches

Experience *****

Heirloom Knitting

Section Four – Design

Yarn – Production & Suitability

If you want to get the very best results from your knitting, it helps to understand the properties of the materials you are going to use and to know something of how they were produced. A lot of words that we regularly use when knitting are interchangeable or ambiguous – wool, for example, should actually refer to sheep's hair, but we often use it to describe anything we knit with. For the purposes of clearly understanding what we are talking about here, I intend to use the following words with these simple definitions:

> **Yarn** – Anything that can be knitted with, natural or synthetic.
> **Wool** – The hairy yarn that comes from sheep only.
> **Thread** – A yarn that is non-hairy, natural or synthetic – e.g. cotton.

Wool

All **wool** has in-built warmth, elasticity and durability. Looked at under a microscope, an individual hair of wool has a circular cross-section and is a thin, springy shaft (about an inch to eight inches long/2.5 – 20cm), covered in fine, overlapping scales; these help provide the insulating qualities wool is noted for. Additionally, all wool yarns have tiny air spaces between the spun hairs that trap and hold warmth. When wool is wound too tightly, rubbed repeatedly, exposed to harsh chemicals or extremes of temperature during cleaning, these hair strands get easily tangled and damaged; such treatment spoils the appearance of the knitting, even causing shrinking and felting. To prevent this and to preserve their qualities, it's very important to care for woollens in the right way – and this more than repays the extra trouble. As well as the classic wool yarns such as double knit, 4 ply, 2 ply and single ply; modern yarns include **lightweight wools** for summer which make lighter and cooler knitwear, and **baby yarns** which are designed to be non-irritating. Modern **"shrink–proof" wools** are chemically treated to lessen the likelihood of shrinking, but need to be knitted with a firmer tension to ensure that they don't, in fact, stretch when washed.

Generally, *worsted* **yarns** are made of the longer hairs which have been combed* and make into more durable fabrics, less prone to felting, and *woollen* **yarns** are made from carded* blends of various lengths and mixes (the fibres can be 'brothered' or made alike, by cutting up longer hairs for inclusion; in pre-industrial times this was done with an axe and chopping block). **Icelandic wool** is a bulky 1 ply yarn which knits into extra warm items, it's very similar to roving* and is sold loosely coiled in boxes. It has the least possible twist spun into it – extra twist being given by the knitting process. **Heavyweight wools** include those which are naturally waterproofed by having more of the lanolin left in – not scoured* out. These are normally used for skiers' and fishermen's jerseys – such as those from the Aran Islands, Ireland. **Lambs wool** is made of wool from the first shearing.

Today, **Shetland lace** is normally made using Shetland mill spun worsted for the Lace-weight 2 ply wool (classic 4 ply), and the Cobweb 1 ply wool (classic 2 ply). These give the famous airy, warm and light qualities to the lace; that with suitable needles, allow that wool's innate elasticity to dress into gossamer patterns. Another good, soft, quality wool comes from Merino sheep; on its own though, this is less suited for lace knitting as it is fluffier, and like all softly spun yarns, it can *pill* and is more likely to felt.

---

* These terms are explained later on in the chapter.

The Shetland Sheep

The Shetland sheep of today are a pure hill breed, with characteristic medium-sized heads, short ears and straight noses. They are one of the Northern short-tailed breeds, whose hornless ewes weigh in the range of 27 – 32 kilograms; and are similar to the Faroese sheep of Iceland, and the Scandinavian and Manx Sheep. The Shetland sheep still retain many characteristics of their wild ancestors, being small-bodied, agile and hardy. They are usually white in colour, but there are coloured sheep, whose fleeces are named in the dialect as follows:

Shaela steel grey, **emskit** blue grey, **moorit** red brown, **midget** light moorit, **black** dark grey, **fleckit** white, with large patches of black/brown and **katmollet** light coloured nose and jaws.

Shetland sheep are perfectly adapted to the exposed conditions and poor vegetation of the islands and graze on moorland heather and ebb-tide seaweed. It seems that their restricted diet is important to the fineness of the fleece quality, park fed Shetland sheep give wool that's not as good.

The weight of each individual fleece normally ranges from 1.1 – 1.5 kg. Apart from its special softness and longish staple length of approximately four inches (10 cm), another important distinguishing feature of the fleece is its tight crimp (the natural waviness). This means that spun woollen yarns have just the right elasticity to dress perfectly the knitted lace patterns, (the Merino's higher crimp in comparison, is too springy; so the patterns made with this wool are held not to display as well).

Today, the Shetland "clip" of fleeces is sent to the wool brokers to be sorted. Whilst some fleece is dispatched to hand spinners, the majority is commercially spun, either in Shetland; or in Brora, in the North of Scotland, then returned for retailing from the Shetland Islands.

Shetland ram lambs have very fine wool, especially suited to being spun into fine lace worsted yarn.

Photograph courtesy of Mr Oliver Henry.

Other Hair Yarns

Broadly speaking, these expensive fuzzy yarns and yarn mixtures are more attractive than wool, but are much less elastic. They come from animals that are not sheep, and include **mohair** (from the goats of Angora now Ankara, Turkey) and **cashmere** (from the goats of Kashmir or the Himalayas). Both mohair and cashmere are highly desired for their long, soft fibres that take readily to the spinning and dyeing processes. However, these are luxury yarns because of their high production and transportation costs (e.g. for premium cashmere – the Pashmina, only the downy undercoats and chin hair of the Asian cashmere goat is combed out in the Spring, and a large part of that is rejected). Cashmere is especially soft; its wavy fibres seen in cross-section are both smooth and round, and of a finer diameter than wool – under 18.5 microns.

Lace knitters should note that cashmere alone is not as durable as wool but can be mixed with wool for warmth and elasticity; or with silk, for lustre and clearer stitch definition. Because there is wide variability in the pure cashmere yarns available (and some yarns are more prone to *bobbling*), it is always wise to buy and test knit a sample skein to see how it washes and dresses. Avoid cashmere with the stiff, coarse, straight "guard hairs" of the outer coat included – this may indicate a poorer quality yarn. Good cashmere is an investment and has more natural drape and loft (lightness) than wool. It makes lovely lightweight scarves and stoles as well as quality baby wear. Mohair in comparison, is much coarser and thicker, and the often irritant hairs make it unsuitable for clothing worn next to the skin or for infant wear. However, knitted with the larger sized needles, stunningly attractive lacy scarves and stoles can be made.

Alpaca and **vicuna** come from different breeds of South American llamas – which are mountain dwelling animals – and are distant cousins of the African camel. The Alpaca fleece that is most desired comes from the Suri breed because it is denser, finer and silkier. Alpaca, from Peru, are traditionally sheared every two years; each fleece can weigh up to eleven pounds/5kg. Vicuna fleece comes from the smallest breed of llama (now a protected species) and gives one of the most prized yarns. Historically, Vicuna was only for Royal Incan use, again because of its *loft* and silkiness.

Angora can still be goat hair (mohair), but now is usually the name for the hair from the Angora rabbit that was originally commercially bred in France, Belgium and The Netherlands. The main "harvesting" of the fluffy hair is during the cold months, when each animal can give up to sixteen ounces (450g) of fur. Because it is so short (usually under three inches long) and fluffy, the valued angora hair is usually mixed with yarns such as silk to "hold" the fibres in place; despite this, angora yarn is well known for "shedding" or dropping soft loose hairs; and angora knitwear is more prone to *pill* or *bobble*. Not usually recommended for durable clothing or baby wear.

These along with wool are the principle hair yarns but there are spinners who custom spin hair from other animals (e.g. from their pet dogs), usually for their own use. It is important that all hair yarns are washed very carefully and stored without flattening to maintain their good looks over time. Always follow the spinners' care directions.

Natural Threads

Silk floss comes from unwinding the long monofilaments from the cocoons of the silk moth (Latin: *Bombyx Mori*). The reeling begins when each inch (2.5cm) long cocoon is dropped into warm water and its unravelled silk – of about one mile in length – is wound onto a spool. This makes (when 5 – 8 filaments are spun together – termed "throwing"), a smooth thread that is strong, very lustrous and readily dyed. **Spun silk** is made from the shorter lengths of silk drawn from the hatched out cocoons of moths required for future breeding. **Dupion silk** occurs when two silkworms make a cocoon together, the result is a slightly "slubbed" thread.

Under a microscope, a non-elastic silk strand has a triangular cross-section, which allows a closer density of fibres in yarn (they can "pack" together more than wool can, with its circular cross-section). The result is the glossy handle and drape of silk, and a cooler fabric to touch and wear. Pure silk's shine and drape is unmatched, and since its earliest days in Indo-China, silk has been a luxury item – once more prized than gold. In a knitting yarn, non-hairy silk gives clarity to stitch definition in lace patterns, but its surface can be spoiled by "*bobbling*" or "*pilling*" when over rubbed. Some problems with surface flattening of the knitting are also known.

Cotton, linen and **ramin** come from plants, usually grown in temperate climates. Cotton (native to South America, as well as India and North Africa) comes from fluffy, mature seedpods and has to be teased and separated from the seeds by a machine called a "gin". Linen normally comes from the blue flowered flax plant – probably introduced to Britain by the Romans. The woody fibre is extracted by splitting and soaking flax stems for weeks, to "unglue" them from their resin. The fibres (called "tow") can vary in length from six inches (15cm) to over three (90cm) feet in length. Linen can also be made from other plants – Mary Queen of Scots, a lace knitter herself, is reputed to have had fine linen sheets made from stinging nettles. A strand of cotton has a fine but irregular cross section; that of linen is much thicker and coarser. Easily washed, these plant fibres (like silk) make into a smooth fabric that is cool next to the skin. Linen especially, makes a strong, hardwearing thread and fabric, but can be easily crumpled and also can be scratchy. These are all non-elastic fibres but when knitted, can produce a stretchy fabric. Lace knitting with these can dress well if executed with the correct size needles; again, there is very clear stitch definition. All these durable threads are available as mixes with other natural and man-made fibres.

Man-Made Yarns

Man-made fibres are almost too numerous to mention in detail, but popular knitting man-mades (nylon, rayon and polyester) are all industrially made artificial imitators of natural fibres; their main period of invention dates from around the middle years of the twentieth century. **Rayon** is a semi-synthetic silk made from chemically regenerated cellulose. **Nylon** is a plastic (first made in 1934 by American chemist W. H. Carothers), and is a synthetic filament made from a drawn polyamide of benzene and butadiene. It has lightness, strength and elasticity. **Polyesters** are plastics made from a reaction of organic acids with alcohols. Synthetics can either be "wet spun" where fibres are immediately set by being streamed into a cool bath; or dry spun, where they harden naturally.

The man-mades are often made into the cheapest available knitting yarns, but apart from when they are made as quality yarns or blends with natural fibres, I personally don't like using any of these, as I don't find they wash and wear well for a period of time. In all cases, I strongly advise against using a cheap yarn, unless you have made a sample and subjected it to lots of "wash and handle" tests; *bobbling* or *pilling*, flattening and over-stretching are common problems with these cheaper synthetics.

Making Fibres Into Yarn

Once sufficient quantities of a fibre have been gathered, the next process is to spin them into yarn of a useable "grist" or diameter. Spinning is the process of drawing out and twisting fibres together to make them into a strong, continuous thread (usually for weaving) or yarn. With slight exceptions, the mechanised process is in essence, the same as when it was first done by hand thousands of years ago. I shall explain in detail how wool is spun.

Wool Preparation and Spinning

It is thought that wool was the first fibre to have been made into a fabric during the New Stone Age, over seven thousand years ago. Possibly, "felting"– which, in its simplest form is the making of a thick, waterproof fabric by boiling loose layers of wool, preceded spinning and weaving. Once the wool has been collected by shearing, gathering or plucking ("rooing" is the Shetland name for the traditional plucking of the soft neck wool at moulting time), the next job is to **sort** it – by grading it into qualities ranging from that suitable for the premium yarns for fine woollen clothing, to that used for carpets. The governing factors in determining quality are its "handle" (softness), density, length and "crimp"– the natural waviness of hair. Where the hairs come from on the body strongly affects their final usage – the premium wool comes from the neck, sides and shoulders is usually longer and finer than the coarser fleece of the flanks and back.

After sorting, the fleeces are **opened** or pulled apart, and the unusable wool is removed – to do this today, fleece is fed into a machine that beats it over an open screen allowing dirt to drop through.

Next the "stock" is thoroughly cleaned by repeated washing – **scouring**. This removes remaining dust and dirt and also takes out most of the greasy wax called lanolin, which naturally waterproofs the animal's coat. Interestingly, the finer the fleece, the higher the grease content – which can be between 20% – 50% weight of the fleece. Scouring continues breaking open the lumps of wool. Most of the shrinkage of the fleece occurs during the cleaning, a fleece will shrink between 10% – 70% depending on the breed and how the fleece is handled. Up to 50% of a hill Shetland fleece's initial weight can be lost at scouring as the moor peat and heather is washed out.

Afterwards, the wool is rinsed and part dried, and then put through a **de-burring** process, which picks out seeds and any twigs that are still caught in the wool. Then, the scoured stock is ready to be combed or carded and if necessary, carded and combed.

Carding is a very important process that straightens the curled and knotted wool and teases out the tangles. It also continues to remove any remaining small impurities. Once, children commonly did this with "hand cards" (similar to

Scotch Hands used by butter makers, see photograph on page 12; or like square table tennis bats finely nailed with angled sharp pins on one side of each bat). A tuft of wool was placed on the pins, then teased and pulled by the hand cards being stroked together, so the interlacing pins could draw out the individual hairs. When done by hand, the finished carding rolls were about twelve inches by one inch (30cm x 2.5cm), the wool in thin, uniformly layered strands called **slivers**. For very fine yarns, such as those used for Shetland lace knitting, the wool was usually combed.

Combing is done with the finest, long stapled wools to make the hairs lie parallel. Sometimes, combing is an extra process for slivers as it removes the shortest hairs, and the remaining hairs are smoothed and more lustrous. Combed slivers are then loosely twisted together to form **roving**.

Spinning By Hand

In pre-industrial times, the slivers were passed to women for spinning. These were held ready in place on a *yard* long, cleft stick called a distaff; which was held securely under the crook of the standing woman's left arm. Initially, fibres were drawn from this, spun between the finger and thumb of the right hand and then knotted to a spindle, dangling from the right hand. As the weighted spindle was freely spun, it gradually took more loose strands of wool from the distaff and twisted them into a continuous yarn. From time to time, the spinster* halted the spinning to wind up the newly created yarn to store on the notched spindle before resuming. Typically, a woman could spin about 550 yards of wool in a day.

Spinning wheels were early wooden machines for making finer thread or yarn more quickly, and most probably were introduced into Europe from India in the early 1300s. With the earliest spinning wheels, a spindle was mounted horizontally and rotated via a cord looped round a large, hand driven wheel. These made the spinster's job easier because she could now sit down to do her work.

The 1400s saw the simple addition of a wooden spool called a bobbin to the spinning wheel, onto which the new yarn was wound, and a foot treadle now rotated the wheel itself. Over the years, there have been many refinements made to the spinning wheel. From the 1700s, the Shetland women traditionally used the old lint or upright Scotch and Norwegian-type spinning wheels, whose small sizes best suited crofting life. A modern "Shetland" wheel is shown below.

Incidentally, the hand spinning process is essentially the same for other natural fibres, such as cotton – excepting that cotton is usually spun into a 3-ply yarn today:

> The spinner took short fleecy rolls in which the cotton was stripped off the hand-cards, applied them successfully to the spindle, and, whilst with one hand she turned the wheel, and thus made the spindle revolve, with the other she drew out the cardings, which, receiving a slight twist from the spindle so as to form cops. In the second process, the roving was spun into yarn: the operation was similar, but the thread was drawn out finer, and received much more twist.
>
> Edward Baines: *History of the Cotton Manufacture in Great Britain*, 1835.

Handspinning is still done today for the finest wool yarns – see below. The lightest weight yarns have to be hand spun, as they then can be as fine as 30,000 to 50,000 yards to the pound (450g) of wool. At one time, the spinning record for a pound of wool was 168,000 yards (over 95 miles!) and the spinner thought she could have done better had she used Shetland wool. Incidentally, this single ply yarn – as fine as human hair – was too fragile for knitting but perfect for weaving.

* Spinning wool was traditionally a woman's job; hence the word spinster for an unmarried woman, and the term "distaff" applied to the woman's side of the family.

Handspun Gossamer Today

Handspun Gossamer (a fine 2 ply yarn) is still made today by only a handful of expert spinners world-wide. Because of the time needed to produce it, this wool is usually for the spinner's own use. Handspun Gossamer is customarily much finer than commercially spun wool as the information below shows:

A Commercially spun Shetland 2 ply Lace-weight: has approximately 230 yards an ounce, 210m per 28g.

A Commercially spun Shetland 1 ply Cobweb: has approximately 430 yards an ounce, 393m per 28g.

A Handspun Gossamer: has up to 1,400 yards an ounce (1280 per 28g), and is made up of a doubled ply (2 ply) – so actually contains 2,800 yards (2560m) of yarn, (a single ply this fine would be too fine to knit into a useable fabric). Each ply may have as few as five to ten hairs twisted together.

For a typical Shetland lace shawl of today measuring 45" square, 4,600 yards (4206m) of ply have to be spun to make the necessary 2,300 yards (2103m) of finished Gossamer 2 ply. To do this, the spinner begins with a small quantity of fleece taken straight from the animal. After soaking it in tepid water for a short period, the fleece is hung up to dry. Then, taking a few "locks" at a time, these are first *combed* before being spun into lace *worsted*. Such fine yarns require extremely careful handling and must not be spun with work-roughened hands that might snag them. A high amount of twist is needed to prevent the ply breaking, and it is also essential that as it is spun, it is not put under too much tension. An ideal spinning wheel for this is a small, upright wheel with a spinning ratio of 11:1, which can put 66 twists into each inch of ply (this means that the spinner actually treadles six times for each inch (2.5cm) of single ply – so it takes almost a million treadles to make enough Gossamer 2 ply for a shawl). Because it can take as long as nine months to spin enough of this supremely fine and delicate yarn to make a Shetland shawl – as opposed to only six weeks to knit it, the commercial production of these shawls is uneconomic; but they are a testament to the skill, patience and dedication of their makers and their Shetland predecessors.

Very fine staple wool ready to be handspun for use in lace knitting.   Photograph courtesy of Mr Oliver Henry.

Spinning By Machine

Today, large drafting rollers refine the slivers or rovings by drawing them to their maximum, before a spindle begins to twist them around each other in a *ply*. Twisting by spinning crucially imparts strength to the yarn fibres, by interlocking the individual fibres in a spiral. Extra twists are given as the forming yarn is gradually drawn thinner and thinner still until it is a fine ply of yarn. These plies can themselves be twisted together to make 2 ply, 3 ply and so on, or if lace-weight wool, made as the slightly thicker Cobweb one ply. **"Crepe" yarns** are intensively twisted to introduce a kink into the plies so they are stronger still, and less hairy in appearance. Depending on how they are to be sold, the finished yarns are then wound into hanks, balls or onto bobbins ready for sale.

With the **synthetics**, spinning is easier and simpler because these don't require extensive preparation to clean and de-grease them. The tiny filaments are simply twisted together as they stream out of the "pin-like" spinnerets of the extruder, or, more often though (for knitting yarns), the filaments are first cut into short staple lengths to better imitate wool before they are spun.

Dyeing

Adding colour to yarn and thread can be done either before or after the roving is spun. Before the discovery of chemical dyes in the 1800s, only natural dyes made from minerals or plants were used. Birch and acorns for example, gave tannin for dyeing; oxalic acid (from rhubarb) was used for dyeing and bleaching. Brilliant natural dyes used in Shetland included madder root for red and indigo for blue – these were imported from the 1600s onwards; but natural island produced dyes were made, usually from lichens: purples from *Lichen tartereus* called in dialect "korkelit"; yellow-browns and reds from "old man's beard" (*L. saxitilis*); orange from "scroita" (*L. parietinus*); browny-purples from *L. omphaloides*. Yellows could be made from grass and 'doken' leaves; and black made from "yuleburse" and meadowsweet, or from a type of peat. Chemical dyes were first distilled from naphthalene and from coal tar; acid green was made in 1835, and a pure purple, one of the hardest colours to obtain naturally, was discovered in the 1850s. Most dyes need fixing in place by a mordant (which make the dye less soluble or likely to wash out); typical mordants are alum, tin oxide and iron sulphate.

An 1882 *Dictionary of Needlework* described the wool and listed the colours available:

Shetland Wool.—As sold in the shops, this is a yarn much employed for the knitting of shawls, and the weaving of stockings of the finest quality. The yarn is exceedingly soft, and has only two threads. It is to be had in oleander (a new pink), white, black, slate, brown, azurine, scarlet, violet, buff, coral, purple, partridge, gas blues and greens, and ingrain, and is sold by the pound or ounce. Wool of this kind is not produced in England proper. It is thicker than Pyrenean wool, and softer than both it and the Andalusian, not being so tightly twisted. It is employed for the knitting of shawls, hoods, jackets, and shoes for infants. The sheep producing it are of small size, and run wild all the year over the hills until—the ground being covered with snow—they descend to the sea shore and feed on weed. The staple of these sheep is longer than that of the Merino, and their skins are much employed as Furs.

which pin down to the Pillow out of the way of the Bobbins. To avoid constant shifting when working very narrow lace, prick two pieces of PASSAMENT at the same time with the same design, and fasten them on to the Pillow so that no break intervenes, or prick as long a pattern as the Pillow will allow, taking care that the ends will correspond and allow of the design being continued.

Ship Ladder Stitch.—See *Ladder Stitch*, EMBROIDERY STITCHES.

Shirred.—A word employed by Americans, derived by them from the old German *Schirren*, and employed to signify an irregular GAUGING. Shirrings are close Runnings, or cords inserted between two pieces of cloth, as the lines of indiarubber in Shirred Braces or Garters, or the drawing and puckering up any material. See French

Today, Shetland wools, like most yarns and threads, come in a colour range of natural and artificial dyes – you can write to the suppliers to obtain a shade card to choose from. If you are unsure which colours to blend together for a piece of knitting (and I think for most of us this does take practice), find a piece of material whose colours you like and try to match them. Another useful tip is to select shades from only three of the four primary colours (red, green, blue and yellow) to use together with or without shades ranging from white through grey to black, or beige to brown.

Conclusion

As will be found, there is an enormous choice of available materials for knitting with, and it can be rewarding to explore the different yarns in their variety of colours, and discover their tensions and characteristics with differently sized knitting needles. But, as I have written many times, beware when trying a new yarn or thread for a large project such as a shawl; it really is essential to have (at least!) knitted one small item such as a baby coat or scarf, and satisfied yourself by frequent handling and laundering, that it is suitable before you use it for something bigger.

As a last piece of advice, always **buy sufficient yarn of the same dye lot** for an item (normally noted on the label together with tension advice and washing instructions), and allow for an extra ball or two for mending/altering the pattern. If necessary, store and wash the extra yarn or thread at the same time as the article itself, so that they "age" at a similar rate.

Feathery Border detail from a shawl in the collection of the Lerwick Museum.

Needles, Tension & Lace Design

Since the invention of knitting, possibly by Arabs during the second to fourth centuries, knitting has had to be produced on fine, usually straight, smoothed implements. The earliest of these knitting tools were very likely made of wood or bone, and most probably had hooked points – similar to crochet hooks or the Arabian knitting needles of today. By the 1300s in Europe, it appears that these early needles had evolved to sets of four or five unhooked, straight double pointed pins; and by the late Middle Ages, it was possible for wire drawers to reliably draw fine enough steel needles to knit with, but they were uncommon and expensive. The difficulty in making long enough, strong enough, needles in quantity, governed what could be made and with what, and it wasn't until the late 1500s that the process of steel needle drawing was perfected – it seems no coincidence that the rapid popularity of fine lace knitting dates from then. By the 1700s, very small diameter needles (as fine as sewing needles) were used for the then fashionable "white knitting" and by the middle of the 1800s, the standardising of needle sizes was underway, initiated by individual suppliers, such as Mrs Cornelia Mee; one of the earliest authors of knitting manuals.

By the 1900s, the British size needles we are familiar with today were uniformly identifiable, but it's interesting to see that they once went down to a size 26 (!) – like a tapestry needle of today in diameter – instead of the British size 14 (2.00 mm) that's the smallest size commonly available to buy now. I'm pleased to say specialist handmade, very fine needles are still available, see "Suppliers List, Appendix 6".

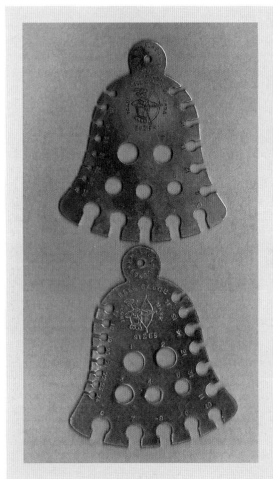

Warning!

It's wise to treat early British knitting pattern information (pre c.1930) regarding needle size as suspect. I have a small collection of early gauges and they rarely agree; the biggest surprise came from these two Archer brand gauges – to all appearances apparently identical. These are early, undated "bell" knitting needle gauges and though made by the same company at about the same time, each show different gauges for needles ranging from sizes 1 – 24. My British size 14 needle (2.00 mm) of today is a size 17 with the top one and a size 24 with the other!

A truer guide is stated tension, where given; then you can experiment with needles and reproduce the size. Other than that, take the overall dimensions and calculate back from them how many "stitches per inch (2.5cm)" there should be and again, try matching needles to your wool to reproduce that.

Some mid-Victorian knitting equipment: a wooden yarn holder, a thimble case, a pin-cushioned sewing box and a needle case with sets of double pointed needles. These would originally have been purchased as souvenirs for ladies.

In the 1800s, Shetland lace knitters continued using wooden needles but soon used imported needles which they called "*wires*"; ideally these were made from brass (in preference to steel ones that would rust).

Mary Thomas writing in the 1930s, noted the most popular size for Shetland lace knitting was the British size 12 needles, in sets of up to five double-pointed pins, each about 14" (35cm) long; these were employed with a knitting pouch* worn with a belt to enable the knitter to reach the incredible knitting speeds of 200 plus stitches a minute.

Nineteenth Century Fancy Knitting.

* The knitting pouch is a horsehair stuffed little pad studded with holes, worn on a belt on the right hip. The knitter inserted the point not in active use (of the R.H. needle) and so could use the hand freed from holding this needle for quicker stitch work. Forerunners of this were first, a simple twist of straw stuffed into the apron's belt and then, a "maakin whisp" of bound feathers etc.

Tension and Lace Design

Knowing about tension is not only essential when you design garments that need to fit, it is also crucial to the laciness effect in the design of non-fitting things such as shawls.

After mastering the principles outlined in this book, I have found that for most lace knitting, I don't need to worry about tension except for the necessity of matching needles and yarn to *dressed* laciness*. As I have said with the advice with shawls etc., the odd discrepancy of a few inches (cm) over the dimensions of a shawl doesn't matter as it would if it were a jumper – the display of the lace pattern does. So, if you intend to knit lace shawls and stoles it will be useful to know that with an average tension, the **usual recommended ranges of needles to wools are:**

Cobweb 1 ply:
British size 11/ 3 mm / U.S. 2 – 12 / 2.75 mm / U.S. 1;
For the denser areas (much less lacy, such as garter stitch centres) – British size 12 / 2.75 mm / U.S. 1.

Lace-weight 2 ply:
British size 9 /3.5 mm / U.S. 4 – 11/ 3 mm / U.S. 2;
For the denser areas – British size 10 / 3.25 mm / U.S. 3.

It is up to you to find out which combinations with yarn you prefer and there is no alternative but to knit a small test sample for each new lace design you make (cast on sufficient stitches to display repeats of the pattern or a minimum of 30 stitches). Dress the sample* (but do not overstretch); when dry, judge the effect as explained below. Remember for lace, the desired effect is normally for "lightness" or "fragility" and clarity of lace pattern.

Factors to be Considered with Lace Knitting

So, with lace knitting of any kind, there are three primary factors to consider, the **medium** – by which I mean the wool or thread and the appropriate needles and tension; the **design**, that is the harmony of individual patterns and/or the composition of patterns in groups called elements; and much more intangibly, the **background** – what can be seen through the finished knitting or, the effects of light and shadow. This last is purely aesthetic, yet can make or mar the final result.

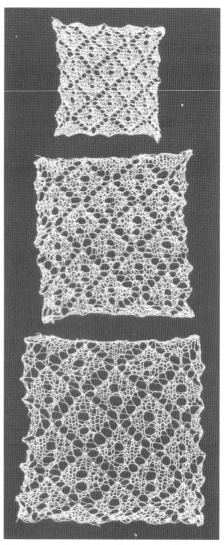

These samples are knitted using the same pattern with the same number of stitches and rows in each case (30 stitches x 60 rows) and a Shetland 1 ply.

The top example is knitted with a British size 14 needles, the middle with a size 12 and the bottom with a size 10. Note how simply changing the needle size affects the dimensions, the density, drape and clarity of pattern.

*Dressing lace knitting: It is very important to remember that dressing lace knitting can have a dramatic effect on the result's dimensions, the same piece of knitting can be dressed to produce a square or a long narrow rectangle, depending on how you stretch it with the pins and leave to dry. The ruling factor must be the appearance of the lace patterns in the design.

N.B. With ultra lacy *knitted lace*, the stitch and row count can sometimes be the same e.g. 6 sts x 6 rows per sq. inch (2.5cm). Normally, with *lace knitting* it is double the number of rows to stitches when garter-stitched.

Lace Test Samples – Decisions, Decisions

Always hold your finished lace test samples up to the light; against clothing; view them from across the room, or reflected in a mirror. As you judge the effects, ask yourself:

Would this look better worked with larger sized needles or smaller? In another yarn? (e.g. wool stretches more than silk, but silk has a greater stitch clarity). With another pattern?

Is it going to be unsuitable for what I'm going to use this for? (See "Design Considerations", page 203).

If the answer to any of these is "maybe" or "yes"; adjust accordingly and make another test sample and judge again. More questions:

If the item is a shawl, etc. needing to "drape" when worn: will there be enough pliability in the fabric to do this? – If the chosen yarn is bulky, try larger sized needles, or choose a lacier pattern.

Has the lace pattern "disappeared" because the stocking stitch or garter stitch *ground* is too open? If so, switch to smaller sized needles.

Although evaluation can be an extremely frustrating process to go through at a time when what you really want to do is get on with the project, this preliminary work is very important and you'll gain valuable experience as you discover what works and what doesn't. You could keep a small box file with notes of needles, yarn and sizes that relate to the samples. Or, if madly dedicated to variety of pattern, you can knit your own reference sampler and for my sins, I have three of my own of these – one that goes on for yards!

Test Samples and Calculations

When you are happy that the test sample is what you want and fit for the purpose, you next have to match the "number of stitches and rows per inch (2.5cm)" information you get from the test sample to the actual dimensions of the piece you intend to make.

My "test sample" for a lace coat for a baby made from Cobweb 1 ply and on a British size 11 (3mm) needle. Once this piece was dressed, I could work out how many stitches and rows per inch (2.5cm) it had.

Calculations and Finished Sizes

If the test sample is for a **fitted item**, such as a jacket, you will be able to use it to calculate how many stitches you will need to cast on for the back. For example, you have a dressed test swatch with a tension of 8 stitches and 11 rows per inch/2.5cm. If you want to make a coat with a finished chest measurement of 20 inches/50cm – the coat's back would have to measure 10 inches/25cm, therefore needing 8 x 10 = 80 stitches to be cast on. From then on, and using the information given with the "Children's Sizing Chart" (Appendix 3), the rest of the calculations can be made as demonstrated below:

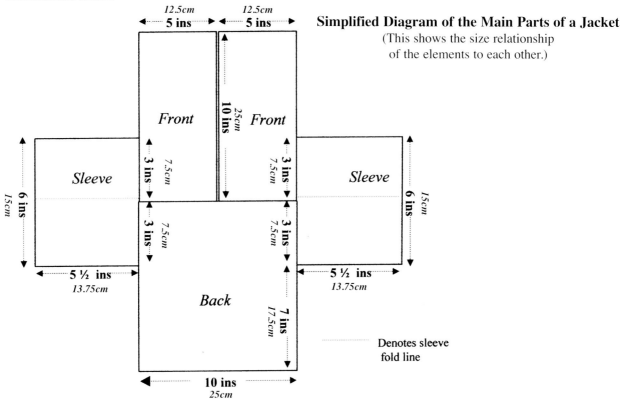

Simplified Diagram of the Main Parts of a Jacket
(This shows the size relationship of the elements to each other.)

Basic instructions for a first size unshaped jacket with a lace tension of 8 sts and 11 rows per square inch/2.5cm: (made with Cobweb 1 ply on a British size 11 needle/3mm).

Back: cast on 80 sts., knit in pattern for (11 rows x 10 inches/25cm =) 110 rows (when dressed, back measures 10 inches square/25cm²) cast off.

Fronts: (both alike): cast on 40 sts., knit in pattern for (11 x 10/25cm =) 110 rows (when dressed, 10 inches/25cm) cast off.

Sleeves: (both alike): cast on 48 sts., knit in pattern for (11 x 5½ inches/13.75cm =) 60 rows (when dressed, 5½ inches/13.75cm) cast off.

This will make a jacket to fit a baby with an actual chest measurement of 18 inches/45cm, about 0 – 6 months old.

It doesn't matter that there's no garment shaping at all; this simple, unfussy design works well with lace patterning. As you gain in experience, you can add on some extra stitches for the back and fronts to be cast off at the underarms; shape the front necklines; try ribbing for the cuffs; try raglan sleeves; etc. (Use the information from a favourite, basic, published knitting pattern as a reference to plan them.)

If the lace is for a **non-fitted item**, e.g. a shawl, you can begin by calculating how many stitches you will need to cast on for the centre or for the border. If you plan to start with the **centre,** remember these can customarily range in size from 24 to 36 inches square (60 to 90 cm square). For a very lacy pattern, the stitch and row count **can** sometimes coincide, e.g. 8 sts and 8 rows per inch (2.5 cm) so the centre could be cast on as:

8 x 24 (inches/2.5cm) = 192 sts and knit for 192 rows to make a 24" square (60cm²).

If the pattern is not as lacy, or is to be *plain knitted*, it is easier to follow the simple two rows for every stitch rule for dressed tension, so for 196 stitches, knit 392 rows. As said before, the ruling factor here is the dressed appearance of tension/pattern test sample – that in turn, can be greatly influenced by the "medium" (whether it is an elastic yarn such as wool, or not) and needle size. Another widely used formula is to knit three rows for every two stitches – so for 196 stitches you would knit 294 rows. Again, experimenting is the only way to find which will be the best for a particular project.

If you are going to start by casting on a **border**, begin by deciding how long each border should be at its maximum and calculate accordingly: for a border measuring 48 inches or 120 cm, the result from an 8 stitches per inch (2.5 cm) dressed tension would be 384 stitches.

Remember, you have considerable leeway with non-fitting dimensions, but it's always a good plan to refer to the pattern information given under each pattern to find the multiples needed for a full repeat of the pattern, and cast on accordingly – e.g. the border design of Spiders and Large Webs (page 145) has a pattern repeat of 14 stitches (+ 19 and 18 stitches for each side) so the calculations to match it to a 48 inch (120cm) shawl border with the tension of "8 stitches per square inch (2.5cm)" would be:

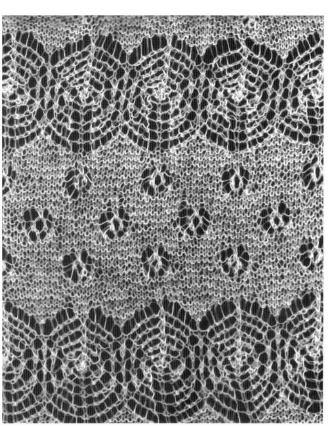

19 + 18 side stitches = 37 sts

this leaves (384 –37) = 347 stitches.

347 divided by 14 (for each pattern repeat) is 24 whole pattern repeats and 11 stitches remaining.

This is so close to another full repeat (only 3 stitches short), that it is best to increase the overall cast on by 3 to get 384 + 3 = 387 stitches.

This will give 19 side stitches + (25 x 14 sts repeats) + 18 side stitches = 387 stitches. So cast on that number or make a suitable edging strip and work from there – see page 196.

The border design of Spiders and Large Webs.

Tip

My best advice for you is to work with a dressed tension of "double the number of rows to stitches" for pieces to start with; later, you can experiment with a "3 rows to 2 stitches" or even the much rarer "1 row to 1 stitch" dressed tension.

Calculating Yarn Quantities

Method for Yardage:
1. Calculate the number of square inches you are going to make, e.g. a shawl measuring 60" square, has 60" x 60" = 3,600 square inches.

2. Using the information from the dressed sample for the number of stitches and rows per square inch, knit a 4" x 4" sample of the pattern with intended yarn and needles. Then, undo this sample and wind the yarn around a piece of card 18" wide – each full wind will equal a yard, or 36". Now, divide the yardage by 16 to find how much is needed to knit a square inch.

3. Finally, multiply that by the total number of square inches to find the amount of yarn needed – e.g. 1 yard per square inch x 3,600 = 3,600 yards needed for the project; 18ins per sq. in. = 1,800 yards, (18ins = ½yd). To be on the safe side, add 10% to the figure to allow for changes of mind etc.

Method for Metres:
As above, but multiply the final figure by 0.9144 (use a calculator!) to find metres: e.g. 1,800 yards = 1,646 metres.

N.B. if ever you need to convert metres to yards, multiply by 1.09359: e.g. 3,292metres = 3,600 yds.

Shetland Stoles & Scarves

Stoles

Stoles, originally known in Victorian times as "veils", could be unbordered or knitted with borders as well as centres and edgings. With one traditional method, the stitches for a border were invisibly cast on or picked up from an edging strip. This border was knitted **inwards**, then **half** the centre. The process was repeated and the two halves were *grafted* together exactly in the middle. Lastly, the edging was knitted/completed. Another traditional method like this ("borders inwards"), used a Waste Wool Cast On, then the first border and the entire centre was knitted and reserved; a matching border was knitted separately and was *grafted* to this (**dotted arrows** show the directions for this knitting). Lastly, an edging was made.

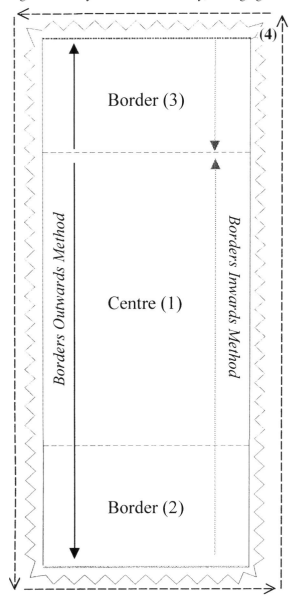

The **solid arrows** on the diagram show a modified and simpler way of working Shetland stoles that eliminates the *grafting* that was traditionally necessary. First, cast on the stitches for the centre using the Waste Wool Cast On. Next, knit the centre (1) right through and then continue by knitting the first border **outwards** (2). The **solid arrows** show the direction of knitting. Leave these stitches on a holder, rotate the knitting so that it's upside down, but be careful **not** to turn it back to front as well. Now pick up the required loops through the Waste Wool Cast On, carefully snipping out the waste wool as you go. Using these new loops as foundation stitches, knit the second border (3), again **outwards**, so it mirrors the first. This finishes the main body of knitting and an edging needs to be worked for completion*. I call this a "borders outwards" construction. I use this method for the "Unst Lace Stole – Project 7".

Edging (method for this is the same for all stoles).

Cast on the required number of stitches for the edging using the Waste Wool or Loop Cast On method. Following the direction of the dashed outer arrows first knit the edging to the reserved stitches/cast on from the second border (3). Take care with the deeper edgings to ease the fullness around the corners. Working down the first long side, pick up a *side loop* from the main body to knit together with the final edging stitch on the returns (see "Attaching an Edging"). Again, use the reserved stitches or cast on from the first border to attach the edging to the main knitting. Finish by knitting the edging on to the final long side and *graft* the edging ends to each other (4).

* Some border designs must be worked in one of the traditional ways. Experienced knitters wil be able to invert other "borders inwards" patterns if necessary, to make them suitable for the modified "borders outwards" way.

Stoles were also made by knitting just one lace pattern throughout to the desired length, then an edging made all round as previously described above, e.g. Madeira and Diamond Pattern + Irish Lace Edging (see diagram below).

Typically, a stole measured 60 inches by 24 inches (150 cm x 60 cm approximately) and was knitted on British size 8/9 (4.00-3.75mm) needles for the Lace-weight 2 ply (approximately 90 stitches)* **or** British size 10/11 (3.25 – 3.00mm) for the Cobweb 1 ply (approximately 125 stitches)*. A brief guide to choosing centre and border patterns is in the "Suggested Pattern Combinations", Design Section.

Scarves

Scarves were made in exactly the same manner as stoles but were approximately three quarters the size. As well as being made as smaller versions of the bordered and edged stoles described above, they had other forms. They could be the simplest of all Shetland lace knitted items to make, in that one lace pattern only could be chosen and made to the required length – with no edging needed. Feather and Fan, Razor Shell, Horseshoe and Old Shell were frequently used patterns and can still be made into lovely scarves today. These are especially suited to be made in a coloured yarn throughout but can be even more effective when knitted in differently coloured bands – See "Project 2 New Shell Scarf".

It is important to note that traditionally, the method of construction for this latter form of scarf is as follows:

Begin with the Knitting Cast On or similar elastic casting on. Knit one half of the scarf but do not cast off. Now, knit another to match exactly and graft the two halves together. This is done so that the coloured shapes of undulation formed by the pattern's knitting, mirror each other. Again, scarves made like this did not need to be edged.

Typically, a scarf measured 45 inches by 18 inches (115cm x 45cm approximately), and was knitted on British size 8/9 (4.00-3.75mm) needles for the Shetland 2 ply (approximately 70 – 85 stitches)* **or** British size 10/11 (3.25-3.00mm) for the Cobweb Shetland 1 ply (approximately 85 – 100 stitches)*.

Reserved Stitches
(Used Up As Edging Is Knitted)

Lace Pattern Panel

Direction of Knitting

Invisible Cast On

*These figures are for guidance only, an indication of what was traditionally made. *Dressing* increases the overall finished size of an item by up to 30%. Don't worry about this, actual overall sizes for stoles, scarves and shawls **can** vary a few inches here or there; it doesn't matter so long as the knitter is happy; after all, these are not garments designed to fit.

Shetland Shawls

Traditional Method (borders inwards)

Traditionally, the edging was first cast on and knitted in a long strip for each mitred border (**solid outer arrows**). Stitches were picked up from each edging's straight side which were then used for that border's first row. The border was then knitted; its mitred corners were formed by decreases to each side of the border at regular intervals. When it was finished the stitches were not cast off but reserved. This was repeated until there were four completed trapezoidal borders that were then *herringbone stitched* together. Using the reserved stitches from the first border (1), the centre square was made, including the stitches from the two side borders (2 and 3) as it was knitted up. Finally, the last border's (4) stitches were *grafted* to the centre's stitches (**dotted arrows** show the direction of each border's knitting). "The Shetland Lace Shawl, Project 4", is made this way.

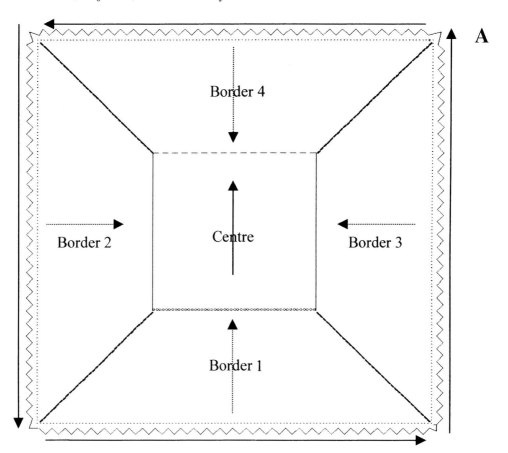

Modern Method 1 (borders inwards)

Taking advantage of today's circular needles, this is very similar to the above, but the edging for the entire shawl is knitted first. The corner positions are established and stitches for all four borders are picked up from the edging's straight side. Then, all four mitred borders are knitted at once, possibly with **purled** even rows to replicate the garter stitch traditionally used. (**N.B. with circular needles, plain knitting each row or "round", produces stocking stitch**). Again, the borders' stitches are not cast off but the centre is worked on them and the shawl finished as above.

Modern Method 2 (borders outwards)

This method starts with the entire centre knitted first by using an invisible cast on. The final row's stitches are used for border 1; then **using circular needles**, the stitches for the three other borders are picked up. The corner stitches positions are marked – one marker being different from the other three to indicate that this is the starting point of each new round (set of four rows). Now the border pattern is knitted – but instead of the trapezoidal shapes being formed by decreases on each alternate row, they are formed by increases – compare the two diagrams A and B. Finally, the edging stitches are cast on with a Loop Cast On and an edging is worked round the border stitches by knitting the last stitch of each even row of the edging together with a stitch left over from the border, (see also page 213).

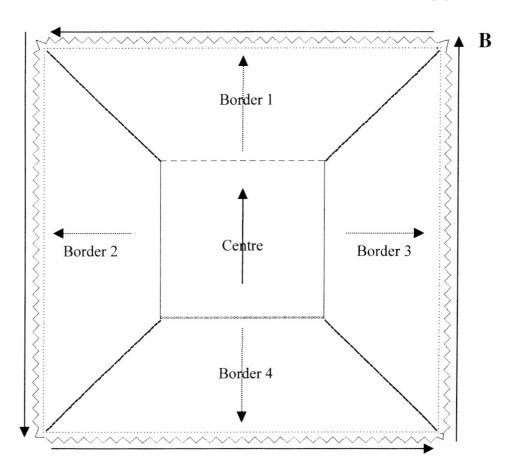

This method can be used for *Hap* Shawls, which traditionally have Old Shell borders, and I use this for the "Cobweb Crepe Shawl, Project 5". Very experienced knitters will be able to convert other border patterns and work them like this but **remember some lace designs of a border are directional** and may need inverting to be successfully worked – see "How to Adapt a Pattern". (The **dotted arrows** above show the direction for this method of construction).

The major advantage to all the modern methods detailed above is that they virtually eliminate the need for matching and sewing together borders and/or *grafting*, which has to be one of the most difficult processes of knitting. The major disadvantage is that each round can have several hundred stitches and a serious mistake in one row could entail several thousand stitches needing to be undone. This is why I only recommend these methods for experienced knitters. Less experienced knitters could still work them in a modified way, e.g. "borders outwards" by just picking up and knitting each border separately, then sewing them together before edging.

The typical sizes of these shawls are 54 inches (138 cm square) and 72 inches (180 cm square). They are usually knitted on British size 8/9 (4.00-3.75mm) needles for the Shetland 2 ply (approximately 160/210 stitches per longest side)* **or** British size 10/11 (3.25-3.00mm) for the Cobweb Shetland 1 ply (approximately 240/320 stitches per longest side)*.

* These figures are for guidance only, an indication of what was traditionally made. *Dressing* increases the overall finished size of an item by up to 30%; don't worry about this, actual overall sizes for stoles, scarves and shawls **can** vary a few inches here or there; it doesn't matter so long as the knitter is happy; after all, these are not garments designed to fit.

Triangular Shawl

The triangular shawl could be started with the centre being made first – by casting on one stitch and then increasing a stitch each row until the desired size of triangle is made:

e.g. Cast on 1 stitch, turn. *Put wool around the needle once and knit to end** (2sts). Repeat last row from *to** adding one stitch each row until the triangle of knitting has 158 stitches on the needle. Pattern stitches could be incorporated. Then, two borders were made in one of the manners described above and the edging was knitted all round the **three** sides. Alternatively, it could be made from the start, using a "borders inwards" method.

Because these are like square shawls folded in half diagonally, the dimensions of these are again 54 or 72 inches (138 or 180cm) along the two shorter sides and they are made in the same range of needles and wool as above. I demonstrate how to make a shawl like this with "Project 5, the Cobweb Crepe Shawl", excepting that this is a square shawl; it starts in the same way.

Traditionally in Shetland, the centres had little peaks to them, to be worn over the head – see John Bruce's Christening Shawl in "What Is Shetland Lace?" To do this, the knitter either worked extra pattern rows on the centre, or had sewn on a separately made triangle of knitting.

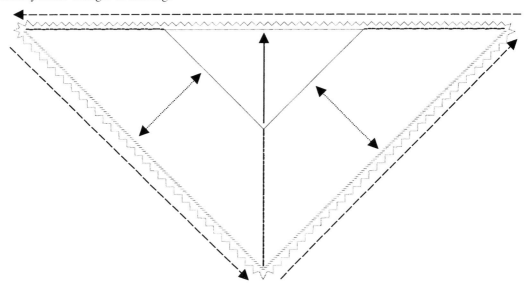

The coloured arrows show the different directions of knitting for each element – the centre, (solid arrow); the borders, (dotted arrows) – could be made "outwards" or "inwards"; and the edging, (dashed outer arrows).

*These figures are for guidance only, an indication of what was traditionally made. *Dressing* increases the overall finished size of an item by up to 30%. Don't worry about this, actual overall sizes for stoles, scarves and shawls **can** vary a few inches here or there; it doesn't matter so long as the knitter is happy; after all, these are not garments designed to fit.

Circular Shawl

The circular shawl is a bit of a misnomer. Commonly it was made with a hexagonal centre (based on triangles, the **dotted arrows** show one direction of knitting – see diagram below). Using the stitches reserved from the centre, the border is knitted outwards in one piece (**solid arrows**) with increases typically made in the pattern every alternate round or row. As described previously, the chosen edging is knitted around to finish, using up the borders stitches as it is made (**circular arrow**). I demonstrate how to make a circular shawl like this, in the "Projects" section, "Project 3, Black Hap Shawl".

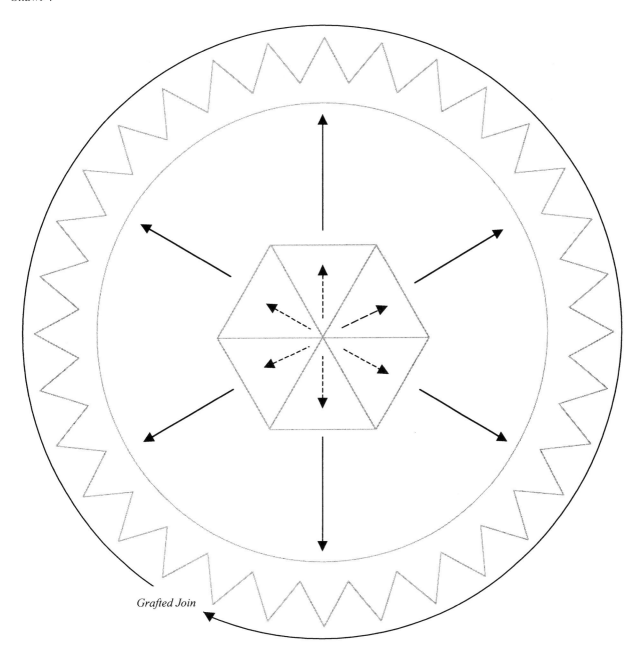

Grafted Join

Sizes are usually 54 inches (138 cm), 60 inches (150 cm) or 72 inches (180 cm), in diameter, with wool and needles as outlined above.

Shawl Centres

Most commonly, shawl centres are basically knitted squares, but as a shawl when worn in the traditional manner is usually folded across the diagonal, the knitted square then appears diagonally knitted (see photograph). It is for this reason that diamond or bias centres can be made instead for 'Borders Outwards' shawls, so when the finished shawl is again folded on the diagonal, this centre's rows appear horizontally knitted. Either type of centre can have pattern stitches worked in.

Tip

When knitting the last stitch of each diamond centre row, knit into the back strand of that stitch to "open" the loop created by the "wool around the needle" of the previous row.

The Diamond Centre

Cast on 1 stitch, turn. *Put wool around the needle once and knit to end** **(2sts).**

Repeat last row from * to ** adding one stitch each row until the triangle of knitting has the desired number of stitches (see example, below right); see also tip above. Now, decrease each row until there is one stitch again by doing the following – *put wool round the needle once and knit 3 together, knit to end**. Repeat this row from * to ** decreasing one stitch each row until one stitch remains. You should now have a **diamond shape** of garter stitch knitting with loops on each side. These loops can be picked up and used as foundation stitches for the shawl borders; this method is used in "Project 5, The Cobweb Crepe Shawl".

The Square Centre

Alternatively, the knitter could make a simple garter stitch **square** by casting on a number of stitches invisibly and knitting for exactly double that number of rows – see example below. Do not cast off the final row's stitches, these leftover stitches will be used as the foundation row for one of the borders. The examples below contrasts the two methods for identically sized finished centres.

A square centre: eg. cast on 180 stitches and knit exactly twice as many rows (360 rows) to make a square, do not cast off. See details above.

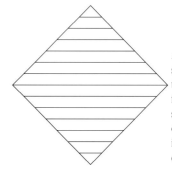

A diamond centre: eg. cast on a stitch and increase one stitch at the beginning of each row to form a knitted triangle 180 stitches wide; then, decrease by one stitch each row, until there is one stitch again. Cast off. See details above.

Shawl Corners

I note here how to make straight border charts expand sideways to become useable charts for knitting the mitred corners for shawls. Normally, shawl borders have triangular corners shaped by gradual increases ("borders outwards" method) **or** decreases ("borders inwards" method). I show one of the most common ways of forming these, which is to work the increases **or** decreases each side of every other row – usually the knit row of garter stitch – as the first and last stitches of that border row.

The charts below example the R.H. corner, the L.H. corner should be an exact mirror image of the R.H. one. **See also the sections on "Shetland Shawls" and "Shawl Borders".**

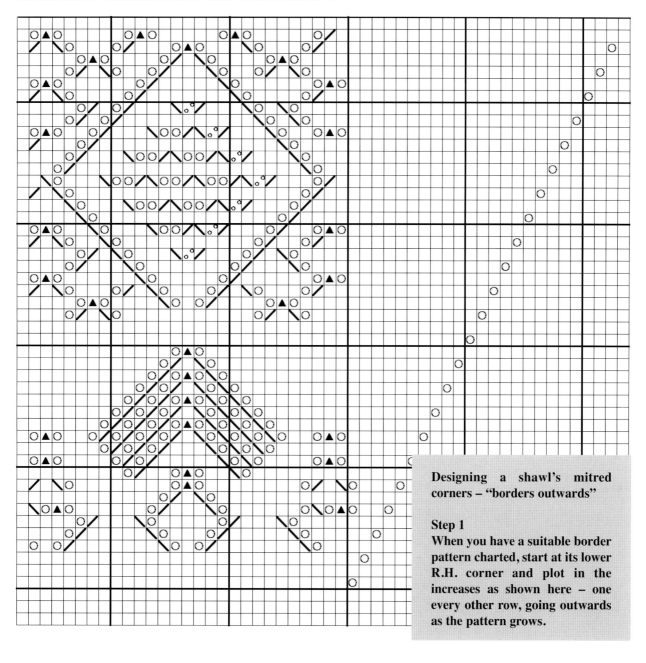

Designing a shawl's mitred corners – "borders outwards"

Step 1
When you have a suitable border pattern charted, start at its lower R.H. corner and plot in the increases as shown here – one every other row, going outwards as the pattern grows.

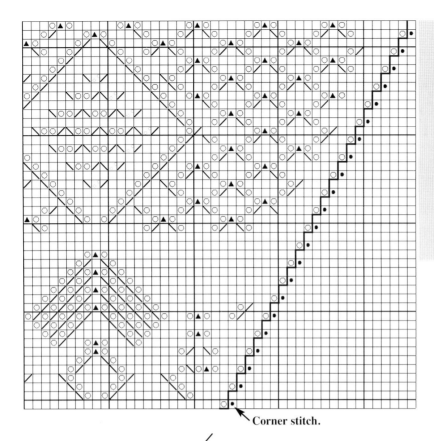

Designing a shawl's mitred corners – "borders outwards"

Step 2
Extend the patterning row by row towards the corner, stopping two or three plain stitches before each row's Corner Stitch.* Tip: As you put in the pattern stitches, make sure there are pairs of increases and decreases to keep the correct number of stitches per row.

Corner stitch.

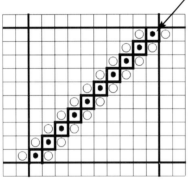

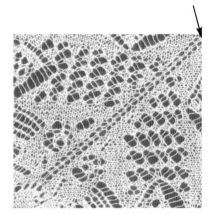

* The corner stitch (arrowed on the small chart left and in the photograph right) is the knit stitch between the increases. It is an extra stitch and marks the end of one border and the start of the next.

Small Chart: In practice, the corner stitch looks like this on odd rows (even rows are not charted here so that you can see the 45 degree angle to corners made by this rate of increase).

Designing a Shawl's Mitred Corners – "borders inwards"

With this method of construction, the mitred corners for borders are slightly easier, because you start with the maximum of stitches per border and then decrease a stitch* each side of each border every other row, towards the centre. The result is identical to the method above, but it's simpler because you have to work less pattern stitches as the border grows and decreases inwards. Again, it's recommended to have a couple of plain stitches just before and after the shaping stitches.

* by knitting "2 together"; or better, by making an increase after the corner stitch as above, then immediately "knitting 3 together" at the start of each border row. End each border row with this in reverse order immediately before the next corner stitch.

See page 163, which shows a "borders inwards" pattern chart.

202

Consideration & Elements

When you are feeling inspired to try going it alone without commercially produced knitting patterns, you are left with the exciting (if mildly scary at first) possibility of designing for yourself. Surprisingly with Shetland lace, this is not as daunting as it might seem, because there is a simple step-by-step procedure which you need to think through beforehand: The first decisions are about what I call the **considerations – intended use, size, materials, tension, style and patterns** – most of these are interrelated; altering just one, can have a radical effect on the others.

Usage

What are you making and who for? Is lace in the design appropriate? Baby clothes or shawls are traditionally made with finer yarn and needles for many reasons, not least so that the variety of lace pattern fits the smaller scale of the item. Obviously, items of clothing that need to be durable or waterproof are not suitable for lace knitting.

If it is for a baby, is the pattern chosen so lacy that it is a danger to small fingers and toes being trapped or entangled? Not a good idea if the baby to be left alone with it, but suitable if the jacket or shawl is removed before baby is left untended. Again, **mohair/angora type yarns are extremely dangerous for babies and small children** because of a real possibility of the fluffy fibres being inhaled – **do not use them for children**. Lastly, think where suitable fastening are to be, if buttons, are they small and secure enough, or in sites on the garment where they aren't going to be uncomfortable? Remember, lace doesn't have to be confined to clothing – curtains, tablecloths, and cushions have also been traditionally made in knitted lace.

Is the individual you are making for allergic to the yarn you intend to use? Ask, or place something already worked in the intended yarn against their skin for a period and see if there is redness, itchiness etc. With shawls, this is less of a problem as the wearer is likely to be clothed and actual contact with a suspect yarn is less likely; as a safeguard, a pretty fabric liner made to match the size could be used effectively.

Will the yarn stand up to the intended wear? Obviously, a very fine one ply woollen scarf, shawl or stole will not stand daily wear and weekly washing for long (but will last generations if used "for best" and washed with care). Edgings and other items knitted in crochet cotton are quite robust.

Finally, if it is to be a present, is it wanted and will it be looked after? Be wary, it can be upsetting to say the least, if you spend hours and hours making a delicate, intricate one ply woollen that gets boil washed by a heedless recipient and they end up with a misshapen, shrunken doyley instead of the airy circular shawl you gave – perhaps it would be wiser to use a slightly less agreeable, machine-washable double knit yarn and a simpler design if you have reservations; or imitate the original Shetland knitters and offer a laundry service! (If you detect the sour note of bitter experience in this paragraph, you're right!) In all events, give details for dressing and warn that the article will revert to a shrivelled state when wet, this doesn't mean it's ruined!

Size

How big is the piece to be? What looks dainty in one yarn can look awful in another, try a test sample, even if it's just a stocking stitch square, and get the feel of how the intended yarn works with the intended needles. Then, when you are happy with the tension and pattern, calculate exactly how many stitches per inch you will need to get the size of the item you need. The advice in the section "Knitting Needles and Tension", helps with this, as does the "Ready Reckoner" and the "Children's Size Chart" (Appendices 1 & 3).

Remember the advice given with "Shetland Shawls and Stoles" – often the finished item doesn't have to fit exactly; for example, the good thing about designing a shawl yourself, is that no one else need know or care that it actually came out six inches (15cm) shorter than you had thought, the size range of these items is so broad! In the mid-twentieth century, there were "Head Shawls" only about 28 inches (70cm) square for babies, as well as the standard sized "Carrying Shawls" (as they were then termed) of about 42 to 58 inches (105-145cm) square.

Materials

This is a crucial deciding factor and worth spending time on. I hope I have convinced you that it is a good idea to **use the traditional, natural yarns where possible** – re-read the sections on yarns and yarn production (page 180) if need be, before thinking about use and size again. Try to choose from a selection of possible yarns – again, **knit test tension squares** if you are not very familiar with their properties. If in real doubt about what to use, have a look at what "proper" (published) knitting patterns suggest you use for similar items and try them.

If you are thinking of designing for yourself, then it is likely that like me, you already have a preference for working with a certain yarn, wool or thread – you know how it responds to use and laundering. Usually, it will come in a family of plies or "thicknesses" so experiment with the close relations if need be, if you are branching out into a new size (or "grist"– technical term for diameter) of yarn for the first time.

Tension

This must be considered in close conjunction with materials; the size of the needle used greatly affects the finished appearance of the knitted item. Again, one can rely on a preferred set of needles (mine is a circular needle, about 16 inches long, British size 11 (3.00 x 40cm), for most things in Cobweb 1 ply) or one can work with others. As explained in "Needles and Tension", what you use affects the airiness of the knitting, as well as dramatically affecting the stitch count per inch (2.5cm). Re-read that chapter if you are trying your own designs, as it explains some important reference calculations and considerations.

Style

This means the actual final form the piece takes i.e. in the case of a baby jacket: the shape, the neckline, whether it has buttons or not, overall length, patterned or plain (with baby clothes it is customary to base all the stitches in a garter stitch as this produces a more stretchy fabric which can allow for substantial infant growth).

Also to be considered is tradition is the item going to take the customary form, or are you going to try something slightly different? – This is also considered with "Patterns", below.

Patterns

By this, I mean not only the actual lace patterns alone and in combination in each piece, but commercially produced knitting patterns themselves. Although you may be going to design for yourself, it would be unwise to totally ignore the successful designs of generations before. I have a large reference of old knitting patterns and often pass an hour going through them, mentally noting what I particularly appreciate in them; and occasionally using their suggestions for yarn, needle, tension and size as jumping off points in my own work. Doing this, one develops not only preferences but inspiration for future projects as well, by "mixing and matching" – using the sleeve style from one with the neckline of another in a pattern of your choice.

As for the selection and grouping of the actual lace patterns, I find it a good rule to have a motif (say, a tree, in different sizes) common to all the elements – centre, border and edging – for me, this gives unity; but I have read that the more pattern variety in a piece, the better.

Design Elements

"Elements" here means the building blocks of a piece; usually these are as set out below – brackets show optional elements:

Scarves and Stoles – centre, edging (borders).

Shawls – centre, edging and usually a border; though there was a fashion in the 1950s and 1960s for shawls to be simply large rectangles of centre patterns with narrow edgings e.g. a 48 inch (120cm) square of Cat's Paw Pattern worked on a stocking stitch ground edged with a Brand Iron Edging, again worked on a ground of stocking stitch. Rarely, a centre pattern alone, or a centre pattern with a wide, garter stitched frame, these were fashionable in the early 1900s.

Christening Robes – as described by diagram in "Project 8", edging, a deep, intricate bordered skirt graduating to smaller patterns by the chest, sleeved or un-sleeved (an under-dress).

Clothing – the "body" of the piece: the fronts, back and sleeves (edging).

After deciding which elements to use for a piece, the next consideration is their relative size to one another: e.g. for shawls: large or small centre pattern with wide or narrow border and edging. I find it helpful to try a quick trial sketch for this, and luckily as the shapes involved are usually so simple, this doesn't call for much artistry.

Once a pleasing balance of elements has been arrived at, the next and most satisfying part of designing is the selection of the lace patterns. I often find I have a choice of at least one already in mind, but logically, it is best to let the most dominant element dictate the overall choice. With shawls, for example, the border is often the piece that allows for the most individual creative input and I usually plan the patterns for this first, as it is the biggest, and therefore the most potentially complex element. Once the lace pattern(s) for that have been chosen, it is normally a matter of settling the choice of patterns that "go with" or harmonize with it. With a border featuring large diamonds of beads, for example, I think it is worth considering a bead centre and edging.

A good starting exercise is to take a basic old favourite knitting pattern and knit it again and again, changing one thing or another each time,– the form of the sleeves, the lace pattern, the yarn, the needle size etc. Many surprisingly pleasant variations can be achieved by doing this, and as you gain confidence, you take further steps towards designing for yourself.

Remember, knitting patterns weren't handed down on tablets of stone; they are the product of evolving experiment. Take one of the shawl knitting patterns in the "Projects" section, substitute another edging for the one I've used – it's easy and it's a beginning. Some Shetland knitters never reproduced a pattern and I'm convinced that once you grow accustomed to the variety of pattern and style available, you too, will be reluctant to produce two items exactly the same.

These two jackets are based on the pattern given as "Project 1", the first one is worked on British size 10 (3.25mm) needles with double knitting wool; the second is worked in bead scale pattern* with a DMC Crochet Cotton 60 and British size 11 (3.00mm) needles. Both fit an average toddler, despite them starting with the "cast on 61 stitches" formula that I give for the newborn sized jackets.

* Page 88.

How to Adapt a Pattern

Using knitting charts makes it remarkably easy to identify, use and change lace motifs for your own designs. **The following information for experienced knitters** outlines some basic activities that can be done with charted motifs. Once these principles are understood, it is easy and rewarding to adapt patterns to your satisfaction.

Adapting pattern charts commonly involves doing one or more of the following: **adding or taking away plain knitted rows** (*close-working* a pattern or not, see Madeira and Diamond Pattern, pages 97 and 99). **Changing the spacing** between motifs, or **rotating a motif** through 90 or 180 degrees, – the tree motifs below demonstrate this. You can easily make the trees point outwards (**A**) not inwards (**B**) by exchanging their places; or you can increase their sizes to make, for example, a much larger diamond pattern element. Rotating motifs 90 degrees is only a little more complex. A good tip is to plan where the "holes" – circle symbols, should be on graph paper and put in neighbouring single or double decreases next as needed. I experimented a lot with both the tree and fern motifs in the pattern collection and it may be useful to refer to these.

When knitting borders, it is sometimes necessary to **invert a motif or a design**. The top and bottom trees in chart A demonstrate how this can be done, where the central knit stitch and single decreases are exchanged for a double decrease. Be aware that some things shouldn't conventionally be inverted – such as the Tree of Life – so consider another motif instead.

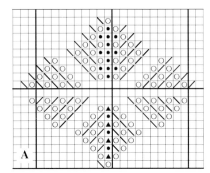 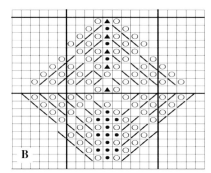 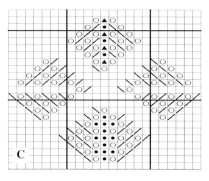

Changing the spacing between motifs is quite easy, but it is important to allow for the motifs to "expand" upwards as well as outwards; I find it useful to keep an odd number of stitches between them: compare charts B and C. The same motifs are now 5 squares/stitches or rows apart (incidentally, this meant I had to alter the centred *double decrease* of B). Have a look at page 101, where I do this with the Allover Tree and Bead Diamond Pattern.

Sometimes you have to create a **half-motif** to finish the sides of items. Again, remember that for the stitch count for each row to remain the same, each increase must be matched with a decrease. With a large tree motif as an example (right), see how the whole motif's central *double decrease* is exchanged for a single one in both the L.H. and R.H. side half-motifs. Notice too, how the position of the single decrease at the base of the L.H. half-motif is switched.

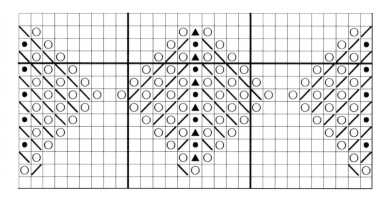

The next useful thing to consider is the **arrangement of motifs** within a design. Obviously, the same motif can be used in lines, (vertical or horizontal) or in simple pattern grids. Look at Fern Straight Repeat and Fern Staggered Repeat – pages 82 and 83, which use the same motif in different alignments. Finally, look at this photograph of a small tree pattern that demonstrates the use of half-motifs and rotated motifs in a half staggered pattern.

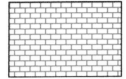

A half staggered arrangement of the small tree motif – above, and photograph. If the motifs were further apart they would be in a chequered arrangement below.

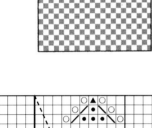

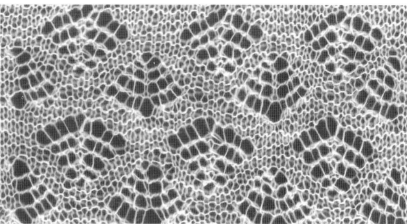

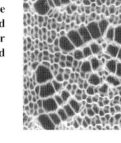

As a final thought, get into the habit of looking for **motifs to use as separate groupings** on their own, such as with these Madeiras, where there are upwards and downwards triangular groupings of motifs. These could be useful as the first or last design line in a border or could be used by overlapping two together to make diamond shapes (below):

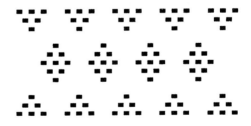

Or they could be composed in larger border designs with other motifs.

It is essential when charting lace motifs to have squared paper, pencils, rulers and a calculator – even scissors and a photocopier can help with copying, cutting and pasting together designs for your own use. I can heartily recommend doing all this on a suitable computer with a needlework design programme, using needle font symbols, which makes all this many times easier.

Adapting an Edging Pattern

I needed to create a narrower version of The Elaborated Print O' the Wave Edging for a black evening stole. To do this, I decided to ignore the first ten-stitch block (see A below, – stitches to be ignored are shaded light blue) and then I had to further amend the pattern by changing some stitches.

The golden rule to remember is, in a straight panel of knitting, if there is an increase/decrease, it must be matched with another decrease/increase to keep the number of stitches for that row.*

So, if, in the adapted pattern there are unaccompanied increases/decreases – shaded dark grey in A, alter a nearby stitch to compensate – see example B, where the newly amended stitches are also shaded dark grey. To complete the new pattern, I needed a "finish" to the straight edge side, so I added a simple three stitch *faggot* insertion – the small strip of pattern stitches, shaded light pink in B.

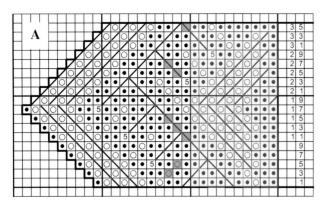
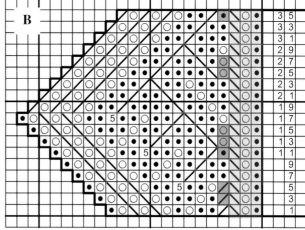

Doing this gave me the narrow edging (cast on 13 sts. instead of 20 sts.) I wanted.

Within reason, this process works in reverse:
If a wider edging is required, extra pattern "blocks" (e.g. one of the insertions), can be similarly "pasted" directly on to the straight side of an edging to make it wider – I do this with the Baby's Christening Robe, see "Projects" and pages 210-211.

Chart B (slightly enlarged) shows the narrowed edging, with a new faggoted straight edge (shaded light pink) and a few altered stitches (shaded grey, see text above) so the stitch count is maintained. The photograph shows the finished edging worked in a Black Cobweb 1 Ply.

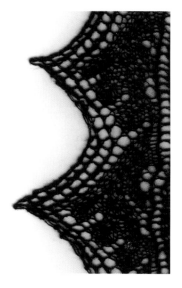

* Obviously, this does not apply to the outside or pointed edge, where first, rows with single increases, then rows with single decreases shape the triangles.

Design:
A Practical Demonstration

This section is for very experienced knitters interested in designing for themselves.

Designs for shawls, stoles and scarves are relatively straightforward because with them, you are dealing with regular rectangles of one sort or another, or other simple geometric shapes. For practical demonstration purposes, I show here how I designed the Christening Robe, step by step, because with this, there are slightly more complex decisions to make, most of which apply to the above in simpler forms.

Materials: size 2 mm (British size 14) circular needle (40 cm); 5 oz (10 x ½ oz [14g] hanks) cobweb 1 ply white. Dressed garter stitch tension = 32 sts to 64 rows per 4"/10cm square.

Because the robe was to be in effect a "masterpiece" for this book, I decided to make it in the finest sized needles and wool. Obviously, I began by thinking of the governing factors – intended use; size; materials; tension; the traditional style and patterns.

I went through the collection of knitting patterns I liked and broadly decided that I wanted to make a longish robe with a double skirt – the underdress being plain knitted (this would stop little toes being caught in the *eyelets*). For the overskirt – a sort of elaborate pinafore, I envisaged a lacy edging and border coming up onto quite a plain, fitted bodice with long sleeves – this certainly wasn't finalised at the start – something in the style of a *matinee coat* worn back-to-front was in my mind. I also liked an *insertion* I'd found and thought that it could have a place as a waistband or as part of the bodice design as well as being part of the edging.

It was important to consider what the baby would wear underneath, because with lacy patterns, underclothing shows through. I thought that the baby would wear one of those useful, basic, white baby vests – sleeveless and with popper fastenings at the crotch.

Skirt Edging

As usual with Shetland lace, the edging is one of the first things to be thought about, as it's from the edging that you pick up stitches to knit the piece.

I wanted to do a **Bead Stitch Edging**, I designed this based on the Bead Diamond Pattern (page 80) coupled to the Victorian Insertion, taken from the design on page 125. I knitted this up as a sample, on a size 2 mm (British size 14) needle in Cobweb 1 ply and decided it was too large in scale for my purpose, so I resized both the edging and the insertion to make them smaller and more "dainty" when using the same needles and wool (see also "Adapting an Edging").

How the edging was adapted: With a pencil and squared paper, any charted knitting pattern can be experimented with by simply using the symbols to represent the stitches and always obeying the simple rule that:

each increase must be accounted for with a corresponding decrease and vice versa.

The first edging I tried was too large in scale (chart A, next page) so to make it smaller, I decided that each bead would only need to be 5 stitches wide instead of 7 stitches. I narrowed the insertion as well, so that the new edging was only 18 rows per point, instead of the original 24 (Chart B).

Next, I knitted this new edging up for five repeats and then keeping the stitches on the needle (bottom of photogrpah on next page), I dressed it to see if I liked it – which I did. I could now knit the edging, and as I knew that each dressed point was 1¾" (4.5cm) long, I could calculate how many I needed to make to give me a wide enough hem. I decided that 28 points would be ideal: 28 x 1¾" (4.5cm) = 49" (126cm), which meant that when folded in two, the skirt width would be 24" (60cm).

Chart A

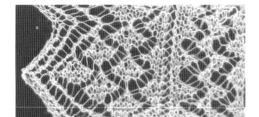

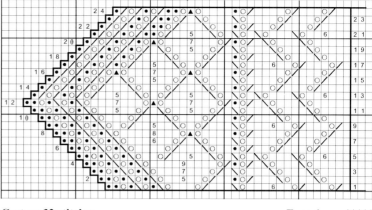

Cast on 32 stitches   Experience *****

Chart B

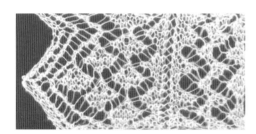

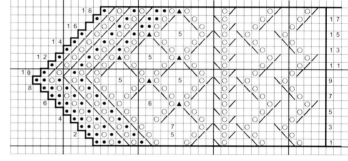

Cast on 30 stitches   Experience *****

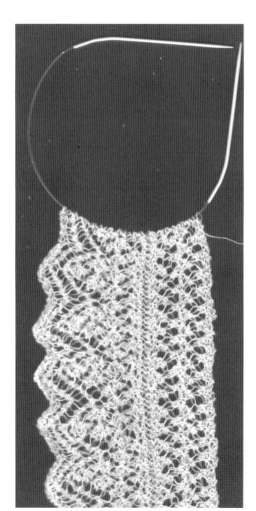

The edging I was using had an 18 *row repeat block* which, following the simple rule of picking up one stitch for each *ridge*, meant that it would give 9 border hemline stitches per point. This meant I would pick up (9 x 28) + 4 = 256 stitches for the skirt hem. I needed the extra 4 stitches for fullness.

Once the 28 points had been knitted, I transferred the edging's stitches onto an odd length of contrast thread to graft later and then picked up the skirt's **256 stitches**, from along the insertion's straight side – 252 stitches from each ridge and 4 extra picked up evenly spaced from the sides.

The Underdress

I decided to make the plain underdress first, so I first knitted 4 rows of garter stitch and then I transferred the stitches to a size 10 (3.25mm) circular needle to make it quicker to knit and more gauzy. Then I knitted these stitches up in stocking stitch to make a separate underskirt about 24 inches (60cm) long. Now it was time to return to the overskirt, so I left the under skirt stitches on a stitch holder.

It was at this point I became slightly unhappy with the edging itself and decided to modify it further for the lace overskirt by adding a matching 3 stitch faggot pattern to the inside or straight edge. I then got involved in making the overdress or apron, so put the underdress aside for the moment.

Overdress Edging and Skirt

The chart below shows the edging I worked for the overskirt, again 28 points long – the shaded stitches are the added faggot stitch panel.

210

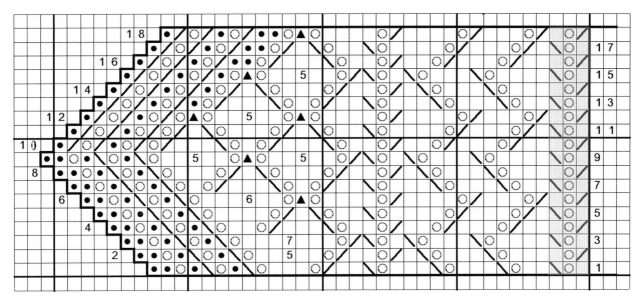

Cast on 32 stitches

Now I was reasonably happy with the apron edging; the next important element to decide on was the border for the skirt. I very much liked a traditional border that was on an Unst lace stole pattern in my collection and decided that if I played with it a bit, it would make the large element I wanted. In the "Design Library", I show the Shell Grid (page 231) that is the basis of the border. It has a 32 stitch by a 37 *row repeat block*. All I did then was to fill it with a combination of small motifs – also from the "Design Library". I envisaged the skirt border to be 8 full repeats of 32 stitches as a suitable size, giving an overall stitch count for the border of 8 x 32 = 256 stitches, + 3 side stitches.

After picking up the 259 stitches as described above, I knitted 4 rows of garter stitch and then worked the border lace as shown on Border Lace Chart with "Project 8". When this was completed I had a large rectangle of knitting, I slipped its stitches onto a thread and dressed it so that I could study it to decide on the bodice.

Bodice

I then further modified the insertion element of the edging to produce a matching tiny insertion for the bodice. After completing the overskirt as charted, I halved the number of stitches by doing a row of "knit 2 together" to end. Then I cast on 15 stitches for the bodice insertion, worked 2 rows plain, and then proceeded to work the insertion.

For the insertion – see page 272, I found that it was a good idea to slip the first stitch of each row to get a tight, chain effect; also, it was necessary to attach the insertion to the skirt's stitches by working a *double decrease*. When this was finished, I cast off the insertion's stitches loosely – effectively, I now had a large skirt rectangle gathered onto a waistband.

As I had taken care to centre a tree motif in the middle of the skirt I knew exactly where the centre front was. Using this as a guide, I picked up fifty stitches from the insertion's straight edge (25 from each side of the midline) and worked these up for the fifty rows of the bodice. Next, I cast off the 10 stitches for the neck and decreased for the neck for one side before completing the other side to match. As it was traditional to have a triangular design element in the bodice, I worked three strawberry motifs there. I cast off both sides of the bodice as I finished knitting them. As can be seen from the picture page 271, the apron is simply a square worked on top of a rectangle.

The Apron's Cap Sleeves

By now I decided that the overdress would be an apron; sleeves were for the underdress. On each side of the bodice I had 50 *ridges* or side loops to attach my arm edging. I decided that an odd number of points per side (preferably 5 or 7) would look best because the centre point would then lie on the top of the shoulder. Fives into fifty go 9 times,* so using 5 repeats of the edging's 18 row repeat pattern would work. I modified the skirt edging so that it was just the outside points, and knitted this to fit each side, being careful to mirror the casting off join to the body so that the chain of stitches matched left to right side.

Then I cast off and sewed the entire piece together and sewed in all the ends. To finish, I crocheted a picot edging around the neck and back opening; this provided the fastening loops for the three tiny buttons I sewed on. Then I washed and dressed the robe, smoothing it to dry over a pillow. As it dried, I gave it a light spraying of starch.

* Yes, I know it's actually 10, but I wanted an odd number! I lost the extra 5 in the making – see page 280.

The Underdress

Now it was time to return to the underskirt I had put aside. By this point, I decided a plain-sleeved dress would suit the apron best, so I completed a simple one as explained from (3) waistband on page 283. I knitted the under-dress and dressed that *inside* the overskirt – I put my hands inside both dresses from underneath to shape and get fullness and alignment, then left them to dry flat.

This details some of the decisions and planning that went into quite a big project. Next, we shall look at those encountered with designing shawl borders.

Design:
Shawl Borders

This section is for very experienced knitters interested in designing. Once you have decided to make a shawl and have planned through who it's for, what it's to be made with, size, etc., as explained earlier on page 203, you next have to decide its construction. You will use either the "borders inwards" or "borders outwards" method and this has to be an early choice, as it crucially affects the orientation of the designs and motifs in the border.

Because I particularly hate sewing knitting together and grafting, I normally prefer to construct shawls using the **"borders outwards"** method, page 197. This is easier as, using a circular needle, you knit the centre, then pick up stitches for the borders and knit them at one go. Normally, I chose a centre pattern I like, calculate how big I'd like it to be and how many stitches per inch (2.5cm) that will need, and cast on enough stitches to suit. Then, it's usually a case of knitting approximately twice as many rows in pattern as there are stitches. e.g. a centre with 260 stitches for 520 rows or thereabouts; making sure the final pattern line of motifs balances the first. (Don't forget to allow a few stitches each side and a few rows top and bottom to be plain knitted – as the "frame" – page 48). This ratio of 2 rows to 1 stitch* means you can more easily pick up the same + 1 as a centre stitch for an odd number of stitches for each side – e.g. 261 x 4 = 1044 sts. Now, mark** the centre stitch of each side and knit the borders outwards as suggested in Shawl Corners, till they are deep enough.

For a **"borders inwards"** method – page 196, the mitred corners are bigger to start with and then diminish as the knitting is done. With this, you need to design the border first – although an edging strip could be made as this is done. This method is most suited for directional designs such as feathers, hearts and crowns that are not easily knitted the "borders outwards" way. Start by casting on or picking up from an edging, the calculated number of stitches and knit about six plain rows as a foundation to the border, then mark its centre stitch.

Snail Shell with Trees Border Design, a "borders inwards" pattern

*There are other ratios you could use, e.g. 4 rows to 3 stitches, it depends on the dressed laciness of the centre pattern – see page 190.
**By wrapping contrast wool around it, to be removed later.

With either method, you will soon need firm ideas about what is to go in the border and I find it useful as a preliminary to have looked through my reference collection of Shetland borders and chosen which motifs and pattern groups to use. Then it's time to plan on graph paper how these work together, see pages 206 and 207 for some tips with this.

For the Framed Shawl Border – (**"borders outwards"**) page 160 and shown below, I felt I needed strong horizontal bands of pattern to complement the centre's frame. I chose a bead and lace hole diamond panel for this and a lace hole zigzag band; I settled on these being repeats of 48 stitches. Then, I placed other motifs large and small between and around these at regularly spaced intervals.

I decided the **centre stitch*** of this design would be through the third of five large lace hole diamonds and I matched this centre stitch to the centre stitch of the first side of the border. When it came to knitting this, I cheated, and didn't start patterning the stitches of this row until I reached this centre stitch; doing this saved a lot of counting back. By the time I reached the end of the first side, I knew how the pattern finished the row, with six plain stitches to finish.

The second side began with an exact reflection of this part of the pattern…six plain stitches…and by the time I had patterned to the centre stitch of this new side, it coincided again with the border chart's centre stitch. The rest of the *round* was completed and at the start of the second round, I put in the first half row's pattern stitches for the first side by correcting their plain stitches (by reworking with pattern where necessary before working the pattern stitches of round 2 of this design). Then it was a case of working the pattern stitches into the extra stitches as the mitred corners grew. Details of the centre for this shawl, which was knitted first, are given on page 216 onwards.

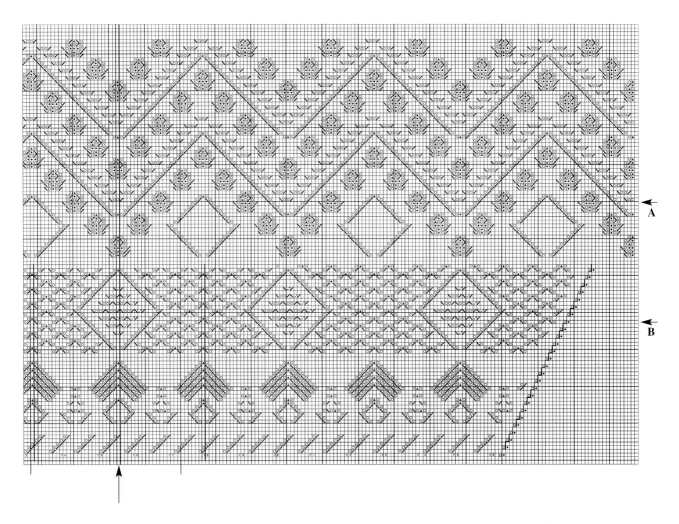

* The arrow points to the centre stitch of this border pattern, the left hand side of the border would reflect the right mitring. There are 48 stitches in each pattern repeat. I picked up 259 stitches for each side and knitted the pattern up including extra stitches into the pattern as I went. A is the lace hole zigzag, B is the bead and lace hole diamond panel.

For a **"borders inwards"** design, again start with composing the patterns and allocating the centre stitch and pattern repeats but this time, count back from the centre stitch of your plain foundation rows and identify exactly how the start of the first row is patterned.

As you gain in experience in designing borders you will be able to take a straight border pattern and work it for a mitred border without charting. The most important thing is to centre the pattern first, so that both sides of the design balance.

I hope you can see that how you make your borders and what you put in them, is up to you. I always find this part of Shetland lace knitting the most challenging, yet the most satisfying and hope you will too. As a last word of advice, if in doubt, knit up (with separate needles), a few stitch-repeats of the proposed border pattern from start to end. This can be treated as a test swatch to be dressed and evaluated before using the pattern for the shawl.

Fine Lace Framed Shawl – see pages 216 – 218.
The centre stitch for this version is through the sixth flower of the border (circled).

Frames

The following information is for experienced knitters interested in design. While studying Shetland lace shawls in museums, I noticed that some of them had centre patterns that were attractively "framed" with repeat motifs, as shown below. With a little careful forethought and planning out on squared paper before knitting, this effective detail is possible for knitters to reproduce in their own designs.

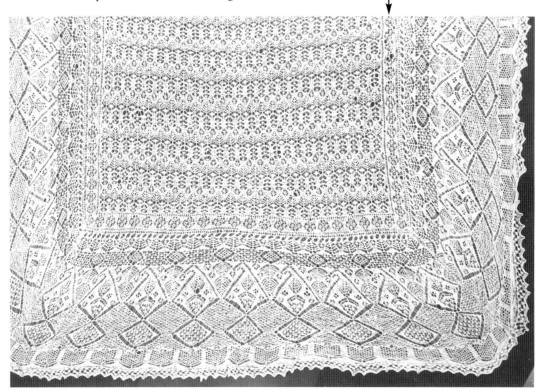

A detail of an antique lace shawl from the collection of the Lerwick Museum and Library, The Shetland Isles. As well as an exquisite border, this shows a frame of Spider Lace Diamonds around the centre pattern (arrowed) – the details of this centre pattern are on page 149.

Start by choosing a repeating motif for the frame. For demonstration purposes, I used a spider lace diamond – there are other motifs to select from in the "Design Library". Calculate how many stitches each motif needs and add on an odd number of "spacer stitches". In my example, there are 13 sts per motif and three spacer stitches between each diamond. Next, multiply this total (e.g.16 sts.) till you have a number that fits in the range of a suitable shawl centre pattern size*. In the photograph, there are 24 repeats of 16 stitches, which produces an enormous centre width of 384 plus stitches – this probably means the shawl was made in an ultra fine hand-spun.

*This will depend on two related things: how big you want the shawl to be and what you are going to make it with. As a broad guide, for a Lace-weight 2 ply – between 200 and 300 stitches with an British size 11 (3mm) needle; for a Shetland Cobweb 1 ply – between 250 and 400 stitches with an British size 13 (2.25mm) needle; the above shawl could be as much as 72" (180cm) square.

Experiment with wool and differently sized needles to find a density effect (or *tension*) you like, then calculate how many stitches this requires per inch (2.5cm). A shawl centre is generally from 24 to 36 inches (60-90cm) but remember, this is your shawl and any element (the centre – framed or unframed, the border or the edging), can be as big or as small as you like.

Frame Width: For my framed shawl (pictured on page 215, dressed size 72 inches/180cm), I planned on 16 repeats of spider lace diamonds (A) and so needed 16 x 16 plus a final lot of three spacer stitches (256 + 3) = 259 stitches. This gave the base line of diamonds in the frame.

It is usual to have a simple two-stitch *break pattern* (C) between the inner centre pattern (B) and outer frame (A) to give definition. To find where to put (C) and to find the overall number left for (B) deduct 20 stitches (2 + 16 + 2) from each side of the frame. This leaves 219 stitches for (B) the centre design, to fit into.

It is useful to mark the finished chart's centre stitches and rows (D). This helps balance the patterns together and also helps later when centring the border's elements. For reference, tie contrast wool in the knitting to mark these stitches and rows.

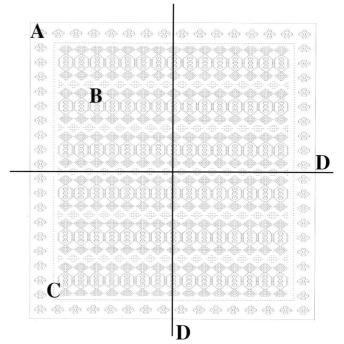

 (A) **Frame of Spider Lace Diamonds**
 (B) **Centre of Spiders, Diamonds and Beads**
 (C) **Break Pattern**

Frame Height: Because the motif isn't a square, I judged the frame's height would need to be between 18 to 22 motifs high. As the spider lace diamond is only 11 rows high, a number of spacing rows needed to be worked between motifs. This number had to be decided along with the selection and arrangement of the chosen centre pattern (B), as it was necessary to work out how to place that symmetrically within the frame. After a bit of fiddling about, I got my two patterns' heights and widths to correlate nicely together; and by using 7 spacing rows between motifs, the frame's height was 20 diamonds high (see above and following chart). Obviously, the framed pattern (B) could only be 18 frame motifs high; as it was a narrow design, 15 repeats fitted into the width. That was as far as careful planning and maths could get me. This gave a 36 inch (90cm) square.

The shawl was to be with 1 ply Shetland Cobweb wool (17 x ½ oz/14g) and a British size 12/2.75mm circular needle. Using the Loop Cast On I cast on 259 stitches, and knitted six rows plain before working the rows for a line of 16 spider lace diamonds. Next, I knitted four more rows plain, then a line of "knit 2 together, make 1" on the central 219 stitches only, to make the base *break pattern* (C) of the frame.

Now, keeping the patterning of the two vertical sides of the frame constant with spider lace diamonds by working them **and** working their break patterns as charted every 3 rows each side, I worked the framed centre pattern of spiders, diamonds and beads as charted next page. This was not a knitted square when finished but a rectangle of only about 350 rows – a tension ratio of "3 rows to every 2 stitches" – I chose this as I knew that this lacy centre (B) easily stretched to a square when dressed and displayed well at this tension, **see diagrams 1 and 2 below**. If this hadn't been

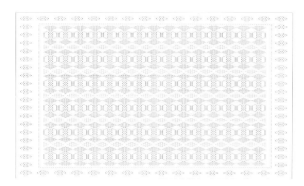

Diagram 1 represents the knitted rectangle of the finished but undressed, framed centre.

Dressed tension: 28sts x 56 rows to 4"/10cm.

Diagram 2 shows the chart of the knitting that is actually a vertical rectangle approx 1½ times taller than its width – 360 rows x 260 stitches. The large diagram at the top of this page represents the framed centre dressed to a square.

such a lacy centre I would have followed the more usual "two rows for every stitch" tension ratio – see page 193.

When I had knitted six whole repeats of the main centre pattern (B) motifs, I worked 3 plain rows and another break pattern row, then patterned the top line of spider lace diamonds to mirror the bottom and so completed the frame. As this centre was so large I originally thought that it could **either** be a small un-bordered, un-edged shawl in its own right – these were fashionable around the 1940s; **or** the centre of a large bordered shawl. If this was to have been the small shawl, I would have cast off using the Sewing Cast Off to make it ultra stretchy. But I wanted to make this a bordered shawl, so I reserved the final row's stitches for one of the sides (using the "borders outwards" method, see page 197).

After picking up 259 stitches for each side, I matched the centre stitch of each with contrast wool to indicate the centre of the border chart (so the patterns would balance) and made the borders using the Framed Shawl Border, page 160. This was interesting because for the first time, I had to incorporate pattern stitches in the purl rows as well – "purl 2 together" etc., – but the result proved it could be done successfully.* The mitred corners' extra stitches had the pattern worked into them as the knitting grew. To finish, after slightly decreasing the overall stitch count by a sixth (by doing a row of "knit 2 together, knit 4"), I knitted an edging round.

* I was purling even rows because I was knitting "in the round", see page 197.

This chart is unnumbered – no row numbers or plain stitches counted – this is how I originally work them, and do the counting later. Experienced knitters could work this, remember to make the L.H. frame side reflect the charted R.H. side.

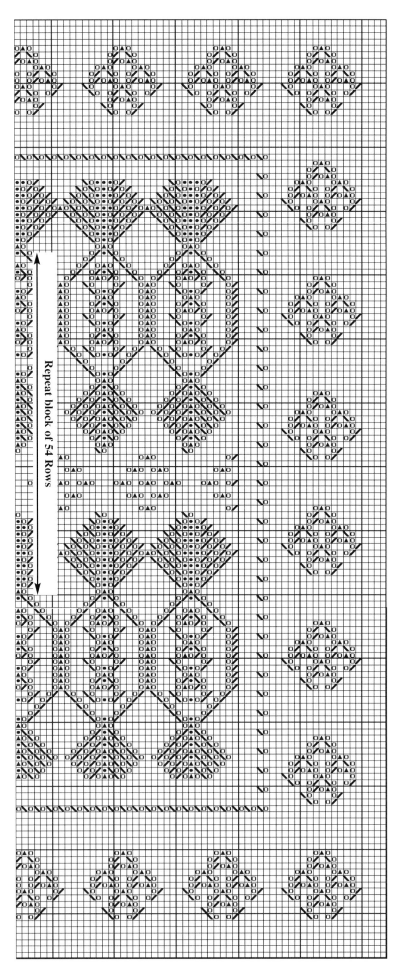

Repeat block of 54 Rows

Some Suggested Shawl Pattern Combinations

The following are just ideas of patterns I think would look well together to get you started:

Mrs Montague's Pattern as a Fine Lace + Diamond, Tree and Lace Hole Diamond Pattern + Queen's Lace Edging

Small Trees Alternating and Staggered + Border Design of Bead And Peerie Flea Diamonds + Traditional Scalloped Edging

Bead Column, Tree, Spider and Diamond Pattern + Snail Shell with Cable Border + Snail Shell Edging with Bead Insertion

Again, try working from an existing pattern and change something of that – an edging or a different centre pattern – till you gain experience and confidence. I have seen this done many times by knitter designers in their published work and it seems a necessary first step in progressing to completely designing on your own.

Final Word

In this section on design, I have tried to get on paper some of the "tricks of the trade" I use. I have tried hard to explain these as simply as possible, but I do not expect they will make a lot of sense to beginner knitters. If this is the case with you, have patience and re-read these pages again when you have tried a few of the "Projects" – they should be more understandable!

This book explains how I have tackled some common problems encountered with Shetland lace knitting and pattern making. Every knitter develops his or her own solutions so may well not need to precisely follow my methods and ways but I believe it's always interesting to read how others deal with things, even if you don't adopt them.

I hope Heirloom Knitting has explained the basics and will encourage you to try this sort of knitting for your own and others pleasure. There is plenty left for you to investigate on your own – try making stars and other geometric shapes, I'm very inspired by the patterns of Fair Isle knitting and think these would readily make interesting lace knitting – try metallic thread – try bands of colour – above all, enjoy the possibilities.

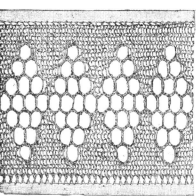

OPEN DIAMOND INSERTION.

This insertion will be useful for a variety of purposes, and may be knitted with any cotton and needles to suit the article for which it is required. Cast on 24 stitches, and knit 1 plain row. 1st Pattern row—Slip 1, knit 9, knit 2 together make 2, knit 2 together, knit 10. 2nd row—Slip 1, knit 11, purl 1, knit 11. 3rd row—Slip 1, knit 7, knit 2 together, make 2, knit 2 together, knit 2 together, make 2, knit 2 together, k 8. 4th row—Slip 1, knit 9, purl 1, knit 3, purl 1, knit 9. 5th row—Slip 1, knit 5, knit 2 together, make 2, knit 2 together, knit 2 together, make 2, knit 2 together, knit 2 together, make 2, knit 2 together, knit 6. 6th row—Slip 1, knit 7, purl 1, knit 3, purl 1, knit 3, purl 1, knit 7. 7th row—Slip 1, knit 3, knit 2 together, make 2, knit 2 together, knit 2 together, make 2, knit 2 together, knit 2 together, make 2, knit 2 together, knit 2 together, make 2, knit 2 together, knit 4. 8th row—Slip 1, knit 5, purl 1, knit 3, purl 1, knit 3, purl 1, knit 3, purl 1, knit 5. 9th row—Same as the fifth. 10th row—Same as the sixth. 11th row—Same as the third. 12th row—Same as the fourth. 13th row—Same as the first. 14th row—Same as the second. 15th row—Plain. 16th row—Plain. Repeat from the first row for the length required.

OPEN DIAMOND INSERTION.

A nineteenth century magazine's knitting pattern saved in a 1940s exercise book that belonged to a knitter.

Design Library

This section is a small assembly of traditional Shetland motifs and designs that I have put together for experienced knitters to select from for use in their own work. They are usually featured together in combinations on borders and I will refer in the text that accompanies each entry where the knitter will see them pictured elsewhere in this book. I will also give the actual *row repeat block* size of each motif as it is given here, but by now I do hope that readers will understand that if they like a particular pattern/motif and it isn't quite the right size, it can easily be modified by re-charting – see "How To Adapt a Pattern" for an explanation of how to do this.

These motifs/designs can be used in lines, or groups or inside larger geometric grids – some grids are included here as well; this all enables true creativity for the individual experienced knitter, the scope of possible design is limited only by imagination. This library isn't complete, but intended to be a "jumping off" or "departure point"; there are other compositions and motifs in this book that keen knitters can readily identify and take from the relevant charts for their use.

The Shetland Twins

This is one of the most well known of the Shetland lace pattern motifs, usually always used as shown – in brother and sister pairs. These can be spaced at more than a stitch apart; the "shield" outline can be enlarged. Pictured on page 139.

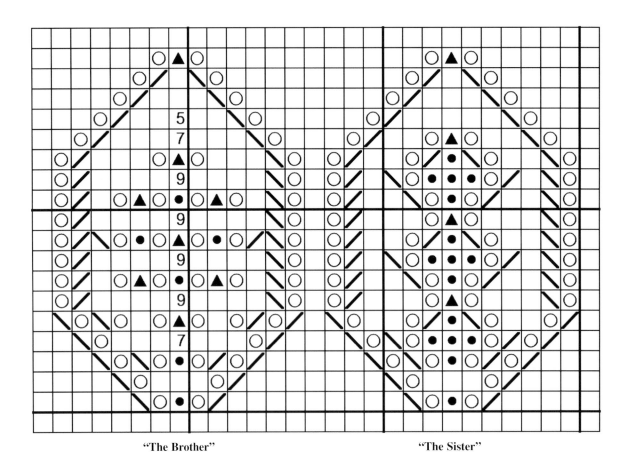

"The Brother"   "The Sister"

The row repeat block is 28 stitches by 18 rows

Can be made in various sizes, see below.

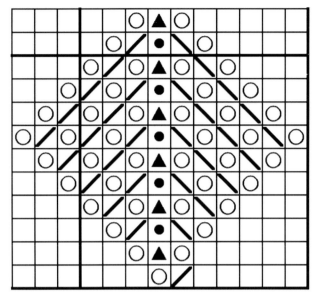

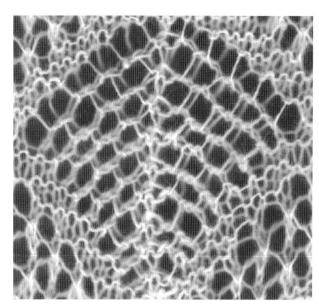

Small – 13 sts wide x 12 rows high.

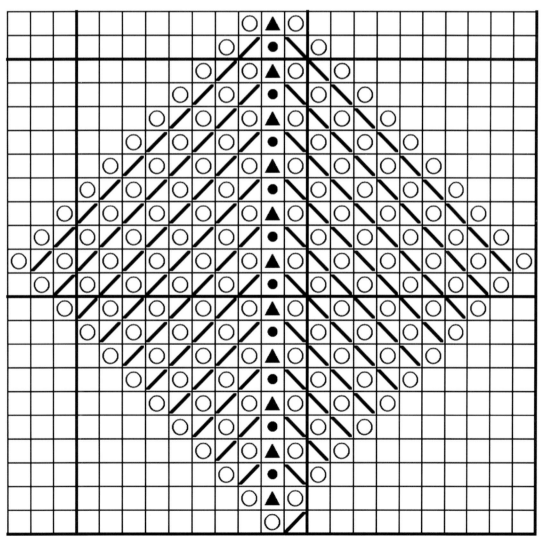

Large – 23 sts wide x 22 rows high, as on the Unst Lace Stole Border, Project 7.

Large Tree of Life

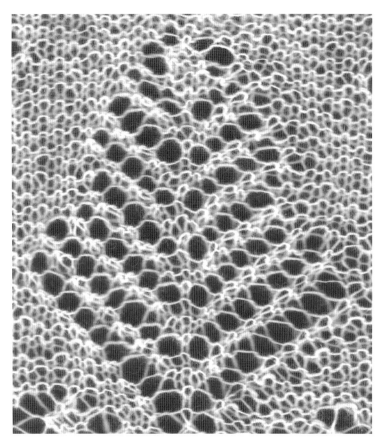

Single Motif – 19 sts wide x 41 rows high

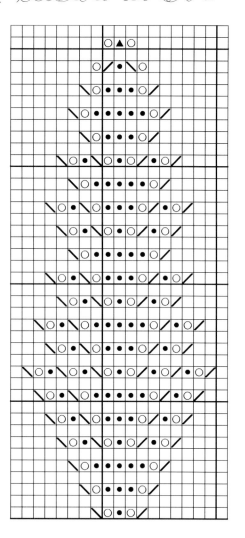

Can be adapted to be larger or smaller, this version is on the Christening Robe, Project 8.

Large Crown

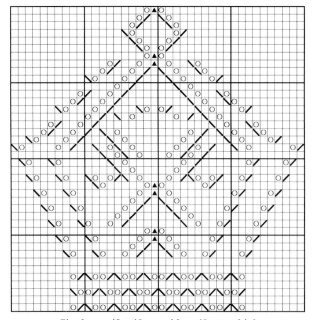

Single motif – 40 sts wide x 40 rows high

Many items knitted for the Royal Family had crowns. This is quite a large version; smaller ones can be created using the basic outline with different "jewel" fillings for centres.

Tree Motifs

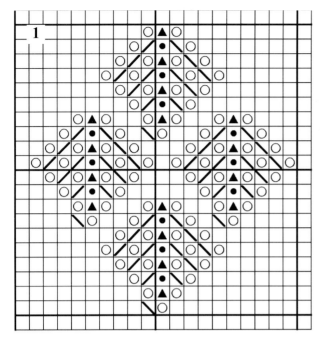

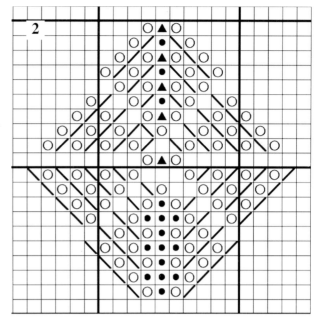

Row repeat block 19 stitches by 20 rows (1); 19 stitches by 19 rows (2) per diamond shape. Size can be altered.
Pictured as border fill-ins on the "Unst Lace Stole, Project 7".

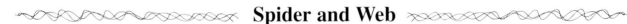

Spider and Web

Web: row repeat block – 14 stitches by 25 rows per web shape. Size can be altered.

A Spider: row repeat block – 7 stitches by 6 rows.

Pictured on page 145.

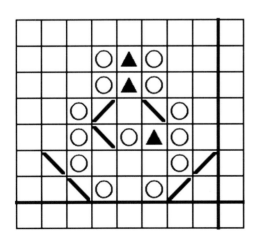

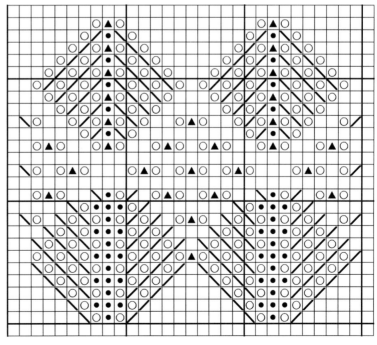

Lace Hole Diamond

Can be made in various sizes, see outlines on chart.

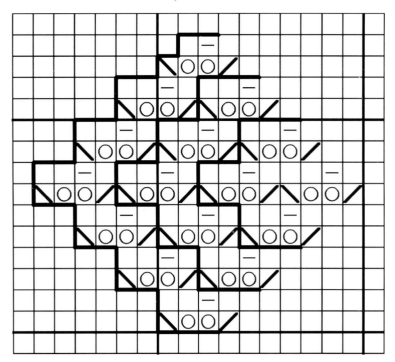

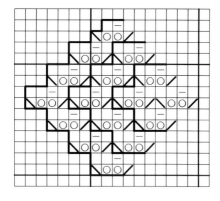

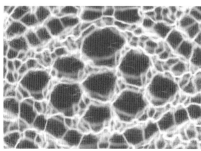

Single – 8 sts wide x 6 rows high   Small – 12 sts wide x 10 rows high
Medium – 16 sts wide x 14 rows high   Large – 20 sts wide x 18 rows high (not shown); etc.

Shown on Shetland Twins with Lace Hole Diamonds Pattern page 139.

Lace Hole Diamond in Diamond

Can be made in various sizes.

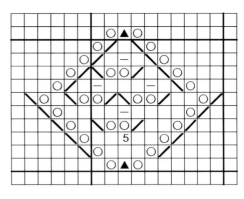

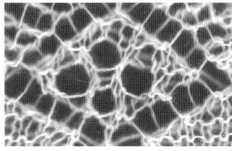

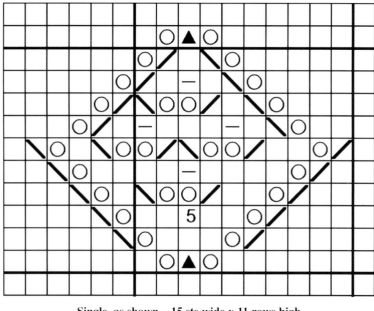

Single, as shown – 15 sts wide x 11 rows high.
Shown as an allover on page 100.

Hexagonal Shield with Spider Filling

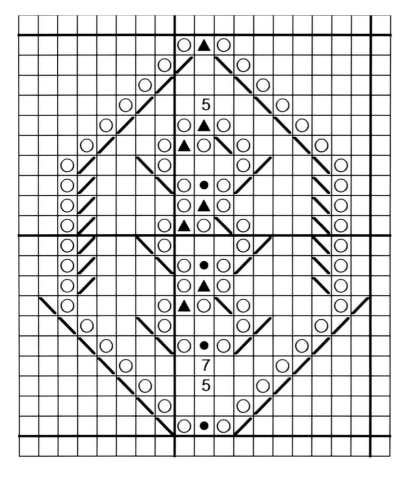

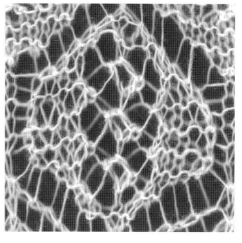

Shown on Spider, Tree and Diamond Lace Pattern, page 141 and in another size on page 85, with a bead filling.

Mesh Diamond

Can be made in various sizes, outlines on chart show examples.

Also known as Roache Diamond. Shown also in Christening Robe Border Lace, Project 8.

Single – 7 sts wide x 5 rows high
Small – 11 sts wide x 9 rows high
Medium – 15 sts wide x 13 rows high
Large – 19 sts wide x 17 rows high; etc.

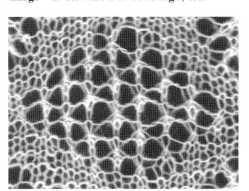

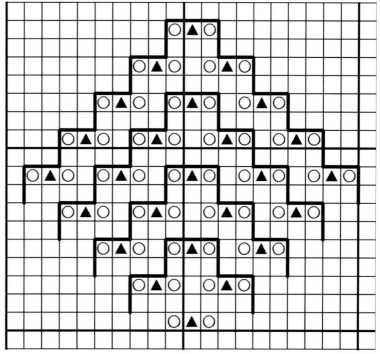

Spider Diamond

Can be made in various sizes, see outlines on chart.

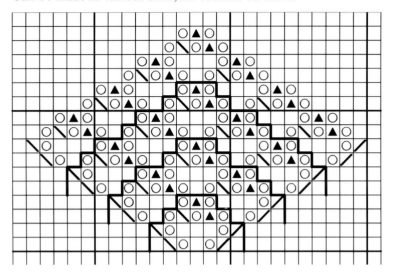

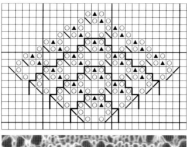

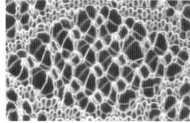

Single – 7 sts wide x 4 rows high   Small – 13 sts wide x 8 rows high
Medium – 19 sts wide x 12 rows high   Large – 25 sts wide x 16 rows high; etc.

Bead Diamond

Can be made in various sizes, see outlines on chart.

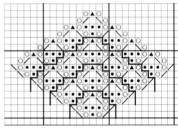

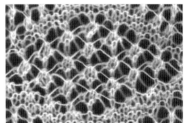

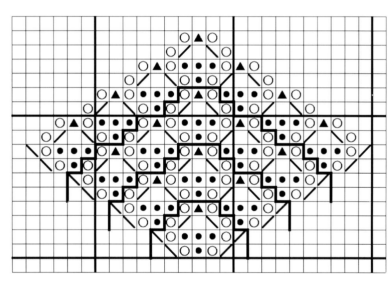

Single – 7 sts wide x 4 rows high   Small – 13 sts wide x 8 rows high
Medium – 19 sts wide x 12 rows high Large – 25 sts wide x 16 rows high; etc.

Also known as Steek Diamond.

Spider Diamond in Hexagonal Shield

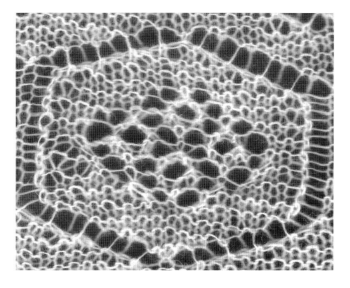

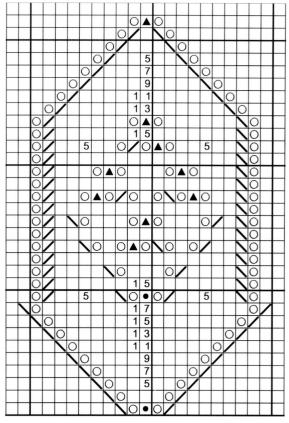

Individual motif size –
21 sts wide x 32 rows high

Strawberry Motif

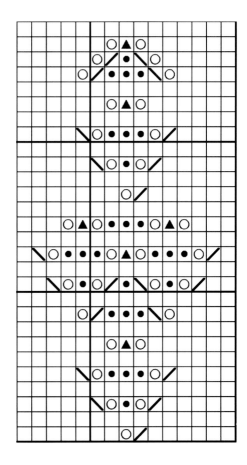

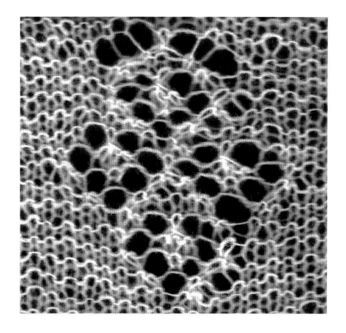

Individual motif size – 13 sts wide x 27 rows high

Used in the skirt of the Lace Christening Robe, Project 8.

Simple Diamond Grid

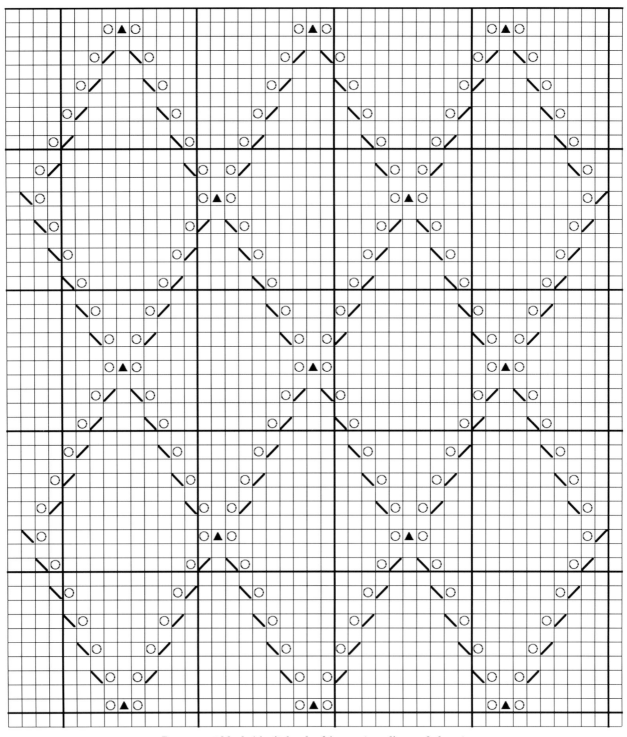

Row repeat block 14 stitches by 24 rows (per diamond shape).

Interlaced Diamond Grid

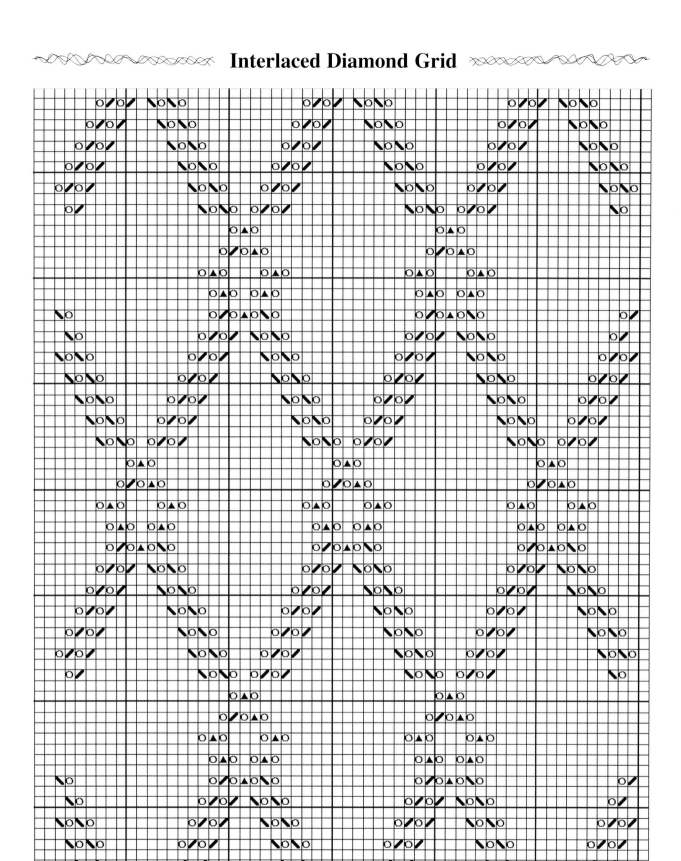

Row repeat block 20 stitches by 44 rows (per diamond shape)

Pictured as background mesh to Rose Lace, page 105. *Close worked*, this is the background mesh to Rose Diamond Lace, page 134.

Diamond Trellis Grid

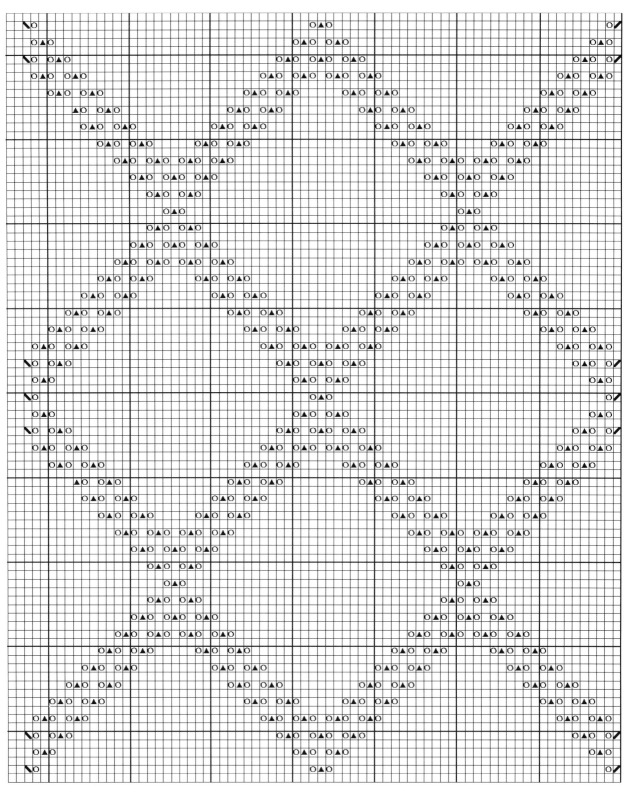

Row repeat block 36 stitches by 44 rows (per diamond shape).

Pictured as background mesh to Unst Lace Stole Border, Project 7.

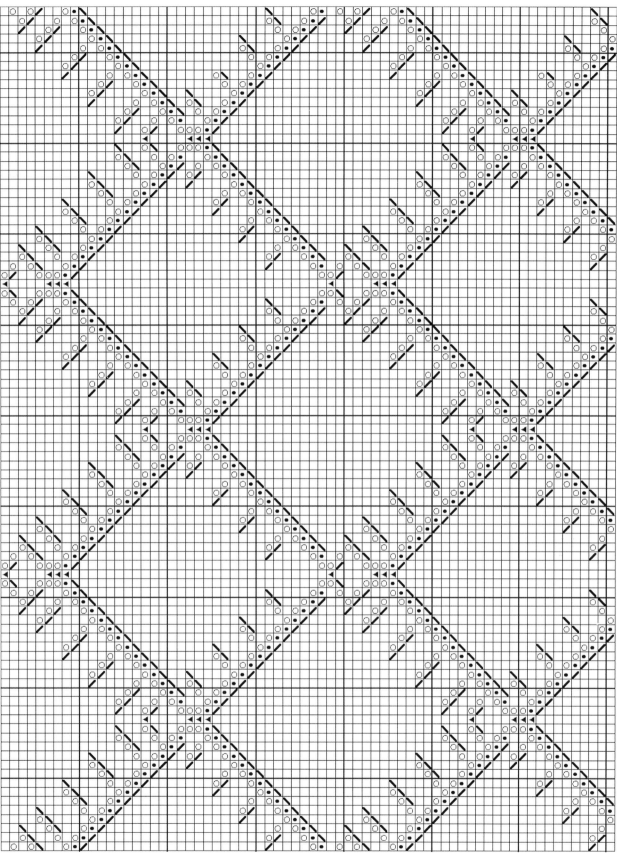

Row repeat block: 32 Stitches By 37 Rows

Pictured as background mesh in Christening Robe Border of Project 8. Could be knitted with plain, alternating rows for a bigger design.

Lace Hole Trellis Grid

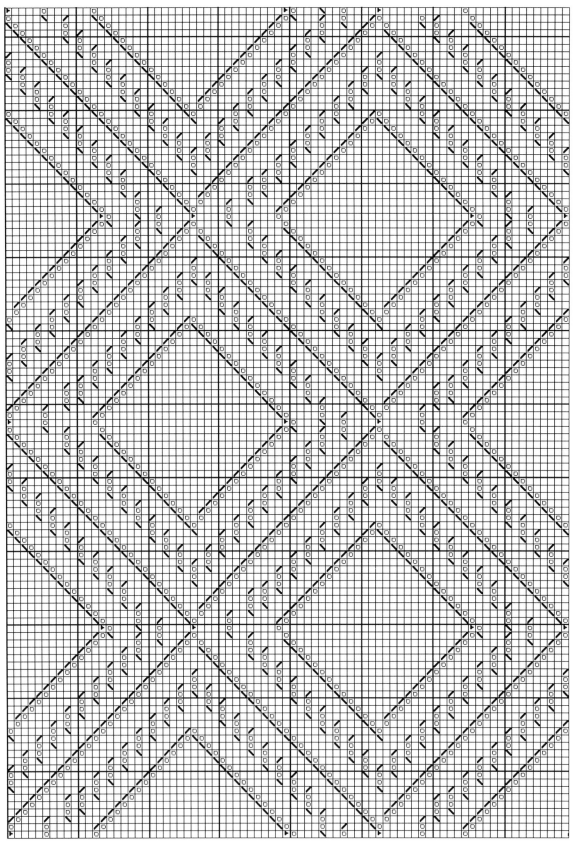

Row repeat block 56 stitches by 52 rows.

Each inner plain diamond can be filled with small motifs selected from the "Design Library". I designed this pattern for fun, but haven't knitted it yet. Note: there is a mistake on the first chart line – there shouldn't be any 'double decreases' (black triangle symbols).

Heirloom Knitting

Section Five – Projects

Level * * Baby's First Jackets and Bootees Project 1

This project makes a traditional jacket to fit a newborn to 3 months old baby and is an ideal way to "fine" down your knitting from ordinary double-knitting to the Shetland 2 and 1 ply (remember, these equate to classic 4 ply and 2 ply respectively). Here, the jacket is shown with a narrow, knitted edging as a final touch; it could just as well be left plain, or a picot crochet finish worked instead. A variation of this jacket with a lace pattern and a picot crochet edging is also given.

Materials

2 x ½ ozs of Shetland Cobweb 1 ply (28g)* or **2 x 1 ozs (56g) of Shetland Lace-weight 2 ply** *; wound into balls ready for knitting – I have used white but both come in several shades. If using the Cobweb 1 ply, you will only need a little from the second ball to finish off the second front. Enough should be left over to make a bonnet or bootees, and there is a bootee pattern with this project.

2.75 mm Circular needle – (British size 12), 40cm long* or equivalent knitting needles

Blunt tapestry needle or similar, for sewing up

Small Button

2.5 mm Crochet hook

Finished Size

When made up and dressed, the jacket is a 20 inch (50cm) chest exactly and the back measures 9 inches (22.5cm) from nape to hem. In practice, the knitting and the wool are most elastic, which together with the button-at-neck style means this jacket easily fits a new baby. This pattern is based on a 1913 baby vest and has a narrow back and overlapping fronts (see Field of Flowers Jacket's chart, following).

* Available from Jamieson and Smith, see "Suppliers' List" in Appendix 6.

234

Tension

My personal working tension is **8 stitches and 16 rows to the square inch/2.5cm**, using above needles and the Shetland 1 ply. This is measured over undressed knitting gently spread – i.e. knitting still on the pin, not washed and stretched. If your tension is near this and you are comfortable, don't worry too much – the finished jacket will fit one baby or another. If your tension is much tighter and you have more stitches and rows to an inch (2.5cm), use a size larger set of knitting needles. Other help with this is in the "Knitting Advice", page 30.

Experience * * Knitters

I find I can usually knit and finish a coat in five evenings and I am a slow knitter. Accuracy is the watchword here, because simple garter stitch is unforgiving with mistakes. If the yarn's fineness is worrying, I find **purling** the entire jacket makes for less mistakes with an identical result; so if you are a "beginner knitter" used to double knitting only, I suggest the following:

1. Make a jacket in the Shetland 2 ply using purl throughout **then**
2. Make a jacket in the Shetland 2 ply using knit throughout **then**
3. Make a jacket in the Shetland 1 ply using purl throughout **then**
4. Make a jacket in the Shetland 1 ply using knit throughout.

More experienced knitters could just do 2 and 4. The baby coats amassed as you gain experience will not be wasted and I find making these coats much more satisfying than knitting tension squares.

N.B. Stretch the knitting over your fingers every 8 – 10 rows and examine for dropped stitches or *misknits*. It's far easier to put right a mistake quickly noticed, see "Knitting Advice".

How To Make The Jacket – see photograph of unsewn-up jacket on page 236.

Cast on 61 stitches using the Knitting Cast On – see "Knitting Advice". Knit the cast on stitches back (do not count this as row 1; doing this gets the casting-on tail* back to the usual "odd" side).

Now plain knit 60 rows.

Row 61:	Knit 1, knit into front and back of second stitch to make an increase. Knit to last 2 stitches. Knit into front and back of next stitch, knit 1. (63sts.)
Row 62:	Plain knit. Repeat these last two rows 11 times, so there are 85 stitches.
Row 85:	Cast on 14 stitches and knit them and the 85 stitches. (**99 sts.**)
Row 86:	Cast on 14 stitches and knit them and the 99 stitches (**113 sts.**) Knit 32 rows plain.
Row 119:	Knit 44 stitches. You have now finished knitting the back of the sleeves and are about to work on these first 44 stitches till this side is completed. (Just leave the other side's 44 + 25 neck stitches on the needle). Knit 3 more rows of plain knitting on the 44 stitches.
Row 123:	Knit to end, Cast on 20 stitches at neck (**64 sts.**). Knit 33 more plain knitted rows.
Row 157:	Cast off 14 stitches. (**50 sts.**) Knit to end.
Row 158:	Knit
Row 159:	Knit 2 together, knit to end. (**49 sts.**)
Row 160:	Knit. Repeat last two rows 11 times, until there are 38 stitches. Row 183 knit 57 plain knitted rows and (on Row 240) then cast off loosely from the front edge to the side seam. You have now finished knitting one side. Leave a long thread to use later when sewing up this side and sleeve seam.
Row 1:	Go back to the neck and the other side's stitches; join in the wool at the <u>neck of the</u> <u>finished side</u> and cast off loosely 25 stitches towards the sleeve. Knit to end of the row. (**44 sts.**) Knit 3 more rows plain.
Row 5:	Cast on 20 stitches at the neck, then knit to end. (**64 sts.**)
Row 6 – 37:	Knit.
Row 38:	Cast off 14 stitches from the sleeve end and knit to end. (**50 sts.**)
Row 39:	Knit.
Row 40:	Knit 1, knit 2 together, knit to end. (**49 sts.**)
Row 41:	Knit. Repeat last two rows 11 times, so there are 38 stitches. Now, knit 56 plain rows and cast off loosely – again from the front edge to the side.

* see page 22.

Sew up the seams of the jacket; add the button (it should be fine enough to be able to use one of the other side's stitches as a buttonhole, or you can crochet a button-hole loop on). You can now either leave the jacket plain, or work one of the following edges:

Finishes

Using a 2.5 mm crochet hook, work a line of single crochet around the neck, and then make a **picot edge** around the outside edges of the coat by making 3 chain, 1 single crochet into the knitted edge, into each stitch or into the stitch loops between the rows. **Alternatively**, knit the following **Little Stripe Edging** around the jacket:

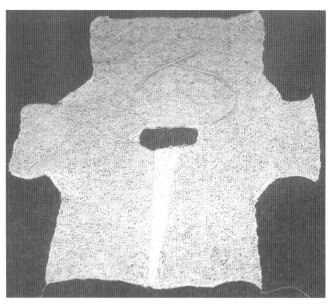

Finished knitting (I have kept the 25 neck stitches on a thread).

Jacket Edging

With right side of knitting facing, cast on 6 stitches and work the lace edging according to the chart round, starting at the centre neck and finishing at the centre back of hem. Pick up 6 stitches from the cast on edge at the neck and work down to centre back again (you have to do this because this little lace edging's points are *directional*). Sew on the button to the chosen side – one of the lace holes on the other side's edge will be the buttonhole.

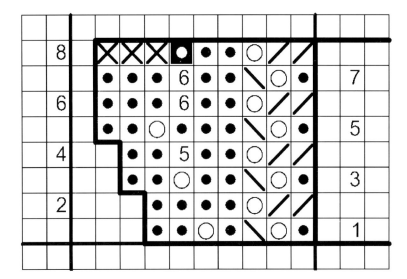

N. B. Little Stripe Edging: The last stitch on each even row is a "knit 2 together" that attaches the edging to one of the jacket's stitches or loops. See "Attaching an Edging", page 38.

Cuff Edgings

Work lace edging if wanted, on the cuffs, starting at the bottom (again, to make sure the points match) each time. Use the wool left over from casting off the fronts to sew the sides and sleeves.

Washing Instructions

Wash the finished jacket in lukewarm water with a suitable wool detergent. Rinse thoroughly in lukewarm water each time, squeeze gently to remove excess water, spread on a clean and colourfast towel and then roll up the towel and jacket together, press gently – this blots more water from the jacket. Stretch gently and spread to shape (it will appear to have shrivelled dreadfully) on another similar towel and leave to dry in a room with an even temperature, **not** in sunlight or with direct heat.

These traditional baby bootees are made with the Bead Faggot Pattern on the leg. Field of Flowers, or any other fine pattern could be used instead; or the bootees could be made in stocking stitch, moss stitch* or garter stitch throughout. This useful bootee pattern is one of the simplest I have come across. To make, you start by casting on the top and finish with the bottom of the foot – see photograph of bootee being knitted on the following page.

Materials

Shetland Cobweb 1 ply wool – oddment of ¼ oz (7g) approx.
3.00 mm Circular needle – (British size 11 3.00mm) or equivalent needles
Blunt tapestry needle for sewing up
Fine ribbon

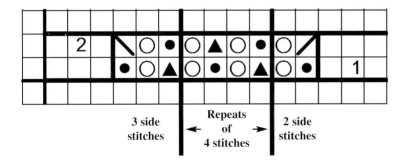

Bead Faggot Pattern

*Moss Stitch

This is a basic form of rib, which makes a lightly textured fabric. Worked on an odd number of stitches, each row is simply:

"knit 1, purl 1, to last stitch – knit 1".

Leg:

Cast on 42 stitches using the Knitting Cast On. Knit 6 rows in "k.1, p.1" rib.

Next row: decrease by "knitting 2 together" once, knit to end. (**41 sts.**) Work in pattern stitch for approximately two inches/5cm (or until desired length).

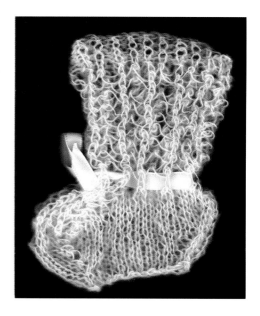

Top of Foot:

(See photograph showing how this and the foot is knitted, below right).

Continue in pattern until last 12 sts., turn*. Next row: continue in pattern until last 12 sts., turn**.

Continue patterning on the centre 17 sts. for 14 more rows.

Plain Heel Finish:

Pick up 8 sts. evenly from down nearest "top of foot" side, then knit across the 12 sts. reserved at * above. (**37 sts.**)

Next row: Purl the 37 sts., then from the other side of the centre panel pick up 8 sts. evenly then knit across the other 12 sts. reserved at** above (**57 sts.**) Knit in stocking stitch for 8 rows.

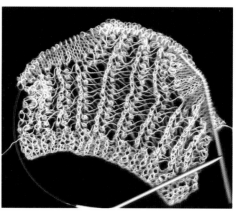

Shaping Toe Row 1:

Knit 1, knit 2 together, knit 16 till above first side "point of toe", knit 3 together, **knit 13** then knit 3 together, knit 16, knit 2 together, knit 1. Purl next row (see toe of bootee – top right).

Shaping Toe Row 3:

Knit 1, knit 2 together, knit 14 till above first side "point of toe", knit 3 together, **knit 11** then knit 3 together, knit 14, knit 2 together, knit 1. Purl next row.

Shaping Toe Row 5:

Knit 1, knit 2 together, knit 12 till above first side "point of toe", knit 3 together, **knit 9** then knit 3 together, knit 12, knit 2 together, knit 1.

Work 10 more rows in stocking stitch then cast off. Sew neatly down back of leg and sole seam.

Thread fine ribbon through ankle as a lace and tie a bow. Make another bootee to match.

Field Of Flowers Baby Jacket 2

The Field of Flowers baby jacket is made in exactly the same way as Baby's First Jacket except that I have worked a slightly modified Field of Flowers Pattern into it. The chart below shows the first 50 of the 60 patterned rows for the back with the initial placing of the motifs, new ones being included and excluded as the increasing and decreasing dictates – see following two charts. This jacket has a picot crochet edging. **Cast on 61 stitches.**

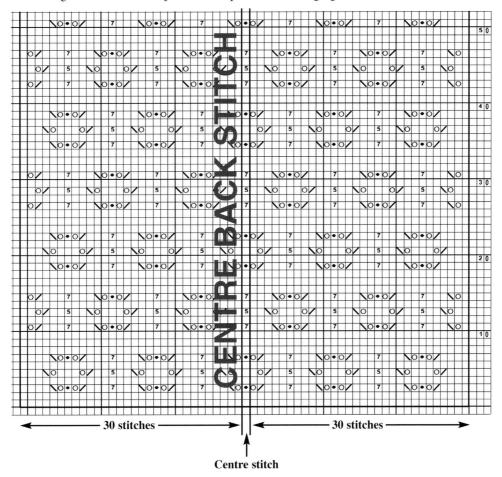

239

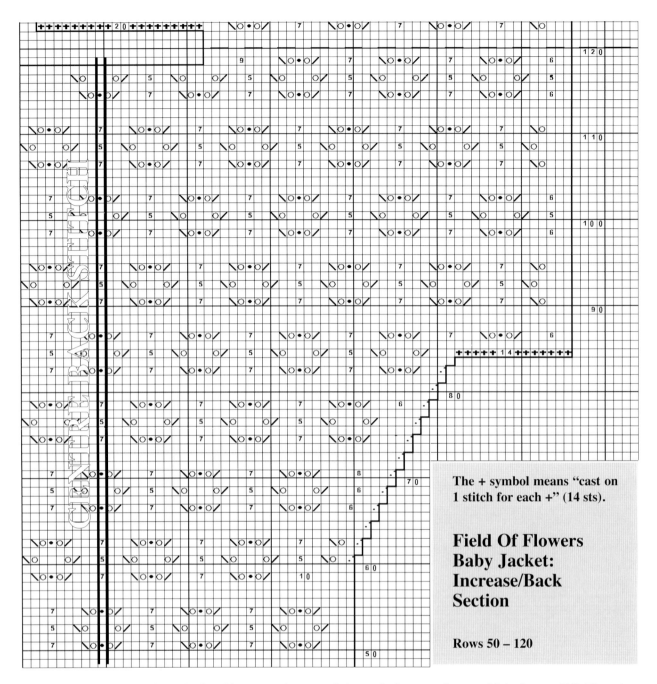

The + symbol means "cast on 1 stitch for each +" (14 sts).

Field Of Flowers Baby Jacket: Increase/Back Section

Rows 50 – 120

This chart continues on from the first 50 patterned rows and shows the increase for one side's sleeve. **N.B.** The other side is an exact mirror image of it, so if an increase is shown at the beginning of the row, work one to mirror it precisely, at the end of the row:

e.g. Row 61: the two dots in the first stitch square mean "knit into front and back of this stitch." So, do this to the last stitch of row 61 as well – there will now be two extra stitches on this row. (61 + 2 = 63 sts.)

The horizontal broken line (across row 120) marks the division between the back and the front.

The **next chart** takes you from this point – row 120, through the decreases to the concluding 60 patterned rows that finish the front. Notice how the increases at the neck (row 123) make the overlapping front. Row 240, remember to cast off stitches loosely from the opening front edge to the side – do an extra row if needed – leave a long casting off thread to use in sewing up.

See directions with the Baby's First Jacket for further row-by-row instruction to complete the other front to match – use these charts to mirror the placing of the motifs each side of the centre-back stitch. If wanted, see instructions with the first jacket for how to do the crochet edging.

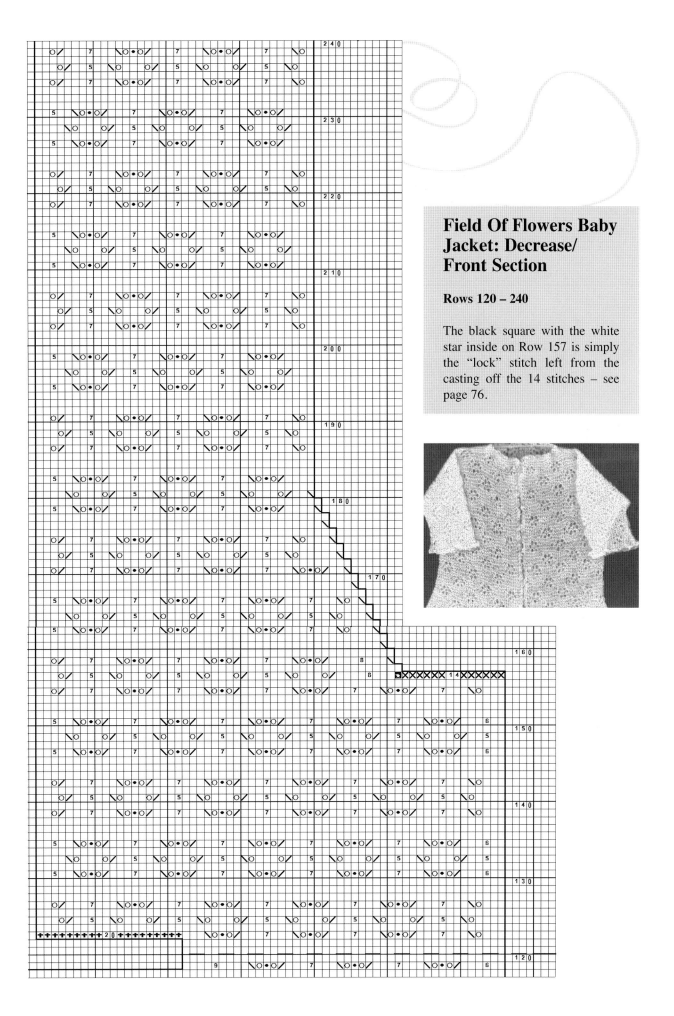

Field Of Flowers Baby Jacket: Decrease/ Front Section

Rows 120 – 240

The black square with the white star inside on Row 157 is simply the "lock" stitch left from the casting off the 14 stitches – see page 76.

This scarf is knitted in the New Shell Pattern, which is a *garter-stitched* variation of a Razor Shell Pattern. It's interesting to see how the arching points created by the central *double decrease* go upwards with the Razor Shell and downwards with the New Shell – compare the pictures – this can only have happened because the even rows are worked differently; purled for the Razor Shell and knitted for New Shell. The beauty of this simple scarf lies in the coloured bands of knitting.

N.B. Leave long "tails" of wool when joining in new colours, to knot and sew in later. If you don't want to do this, knit the scarf in a single colour – it will be easier! Dressed Tension: 28 sts x 36 rows = 4" (10cm) square.

Materials

All wool is Jamieson & Smith Lace-weight 2 Ply*:

1 oz (28g) hank of pink – shade L101

1 oz (28g) hank of dark grey – shade L27

1 oz (28g) hank of light grey – shade L203

2 oz (56g) hanks of charcoal – shade L54

1 oz (28g) hank of white – shade L1

1 oz (28g) hank of mottled blue – shade L40

4.00 mm Circular needle – (British size 8), 60cm long or equivalent knitting needles

Tapestry needle

*see "Suppliers' List", Appendix 6.

242

Using charcoal, cast on **(5 x 10) + 6 + 5 = 61 stitches** using the Knitting Cast On, then work the stitches back. Now, work according to the pattern chart, changing colours as set out below. Use the photograph detail as a colour change reference – the first rows are at the bottom.

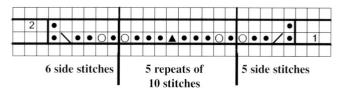

Remember, all even rows are garter stitched.

Rows   1 – 8, charcoal
Rows   9 – 10, light grey
Rows 11 – 14, mottled blue
Rows 15 – 18, white
Rows 19 – 20, light grey
Rows 21 – 22, pink
Rows 23 – 24, light grey
Rows 25 – 26, pink
Rows 27 – 28, light grey
Rows 29 – 30, pink
Rows 31 – 32, light grey
Rows 33 – 40, charcoal
Rows 41 – 44, pink
Rows 45 – 46, white
Rows 47 – 48, dark grey
Rows 49 – 50, white
Rows 51 – 52, dark grey
Rows 53 – 54, white
Rows 55 – 56, dark grey
Rows 57 – 58, white
Rows 59 – 66, mottled blue
Rows 67 – 68, pink
Rows 69 – 76, white
Rows 77 – 78, charcoal
Rows 79 – 80, white
Rows 81 – 82, charcoal
Rows 83 – 84, pink
Rows 85 – 92, light grey
Rows 93 – 94, white
Rows 95 – 96, light grey
Rows 97 – 98, white

Repeat rows 1 – 98 again. Now, knit rows 1 – 4, then leave all the stitches on a stitch holder; this finishes the first half of the scarf. Make another exactly the same – to match; and then graft the two matching halves together. Sew in all the ends invisibly, then *dress* the scarf.

This beautiful and striking shawl is knitted in jumper weight 2 ply Shetland wool, predominantly in natural shades. This demonstrates the characteristics of a *hap* or shoulder shawl but in a circular form, with traditionally inspired colour changes. It would be equally dramatic if it were all black or any other single colour; certainly it would be simpler to knit! The finished size is 72 inches (180cm) in diameter – it could be 48 inches (120cm) instead. It is made by starting with a few centre stitches and knitted outwards; when finished, there is one seam to sew up from the edge to the centre.

Materials

All wool is Jamieson & Smith Jumper-weight 2 ply*:

10 x 1 oz (280g) hanks of charcoal – shade 81 (A)

3 x 1 oz (84g) hanks of dark grey – shade 54 (B)

3 x 1 oz (84g) hanks of mid grey – shade 27 (C)

3 x 1 oz (84g) hanks of light grey – shade 203 (D)

3 x 1 oz (84g) hanks of cream– shade 1A (E)

Tapestry needle

4mm and 5mm Circular needles – (British sizes 8 and 6), respectively 60cm and 90cm long or equivalent knitting needles; the longer size circular needle in the larger size makes knitting this much easier near the end when there is a considerable number of stitches (720sts.) per row. Dressed Tension over garter stitch using smaller needles: 28 sts x 28 rows = 4" (10cm).

*see "Suppliers' List", Appendix 6.

How to Knit the Black Circular Shawl

Remember:

"Make 1" = bring the wool forward purlwise and then take it back over the top of the needle. Otherwise known as an "over".

Work the slash symbols as "knit 2 together", the fanning of this pattern slants their direction.

When breaking off wool and joining in a new colour, leave long "tails" of yarn – at least 6 inches – for sewing in later.

Centre

With the smaller sized needles (i.e. British size 8/4mm) and the Knitting Cast On, use the charcoal yarn and cast on 6 stitches, then knit them back.

Row 1 (make 1, knit 1) to end. **(12 sts.)**

Row 2 and all even rows throughout the centre and border are KNIT.

Row 3 (make 1, knit 2) to end. **(18 sts.)**

Row 5 (make 1, knit 3) to end. **(24 sts.)**

Row 7 (make 1, knit 4) to end. **(30 sts.)**

Continue like this till odd row: "(make 1, knit 59) to end. **(360sts.)**" is worked. Next row : Knit, break off yarn.

Detail of the centre of the shawl when fnished.

Shaded Border

Set up pattern rows: Using **light grey**: knit 3 *(make 1, knit 1) 6 times, knit 6**. Repeat from * to ** to last 9 stitches – (make 1, knit 1) 6 times, knit 3. **(540 sts.)** Next 3 rows – knit. Break off yarn.

Row 1 Using **mid grey**: *(knit 2 together) 3 times, (make 1, knit 1) 6 times, (knit 2 together) 3 times **. Repeat from * to ** to end **(still 540 sts.,** and will remain so till after row 72).

Rows 2 to 4 – Knit, break off yarn.

**See chart 1 below, which gives exactly the same pattern instructions for rows 1 – 4 in charted form.
N. B. The pattern charts referred to change as the border is made.**

Black Shawl Chart 1

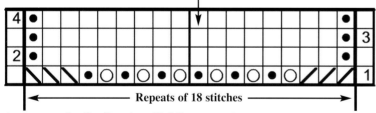

Arrow marks the "centre stitch", see next page.

Tip
Simply knit all decreases as "knit 2 together" – the direction of the slash is taken by the pattern fanning out.

Rows 5 – 8 using **dark grey**: work rows 1 – 4, break yarn.
Rows 9 – 16 using **charcoal**: work rows 1 – 4, twice; break yarn.
Rows 17 – 18 using **light grey**: work rows 1 – 2, do not break yarn.
Rows 19 – 20 using **cream**: work rows 3 – 4, do not break yarn.
Rows 21 – 24 work exactly as for rows 17 – 20, then break yarn.
Rows 25 – 26 using **light grey**: work rows 1 – 2, break yarn.
Rows 27 – 28 using **mid grey**: work rows 3 – 4, break yarn.
Rows 29 – 32 using **dark grey**: work rows 1 – 4, do not break yarn.
Rows 33 – 34 using **charcoal**: work rows 1 – 2, do not break yarn.
Rows 35 – 36 using **dark grey**: work rows 3 – 4, break yarn.
Rows 37 – 44 using **charcoal**: work rows 1 – 4, twice, do not break yarn.

Rows 45 – 46 Still using **charcoal**: work rows 1 – 2, now break yarn.
Change to the larger size needles (British size 6/5mm) and continue using these to the end (still 540 sts.)
Rows 47 – 48 using **cream**: work rows 3 – 4, do not break yarn.
Rows 49 – 50 using **mid grey**: work rows 1 – 2, do not break yarn.
Rows 51 – 52 using **cream**: work rows 3 – 4, do not break yarn.
Rows 53 – 54 using **mid grey**: work rows 1 – 2, break yarn.
Rows 55 – 56 using **cream**: work rows 3 – 4, break yarn.
Rows 57 – 60 using **dark grey**: work rows 1 – 4, do not break yarn.
Rows 61 – 62 Still using **dark grey**: work rows 1 – 2, break yarn.
Rows 63 – 64 using **charcoal**: work rows 3 – 4, do not break yarn.
Rows 65 – 68 Still using **charcoal**: work rows 1 – 4, do not break yarn.
Rows 69 – 70 Still using **charcoal**: work rows 1 – 2, do not break yarn.
Rows 71 – 72 using **light grey**: work rows 3 – 4, do not break yarn.

Detail Of Black Circular Shawl Border

Details of colour changes, starting from the very top, with the charcoal black centre and the light grey band setting up the pattern; and then (the horizontal arrows mark row 1), showing all the colour waves radiating down to the edging. The vertical arrow points to the "centre stitch" of one of the pattern repeats, notice how the overs are balanced equally on either side; on each chart, this centre stitch is marked by a similar arrow.

Increase rows 73 – 74 using **charcoal**: work rows 1 – 2 **as Chart 2**, do not break yarn. **(660sts.)**

Black Shawl Chart 2

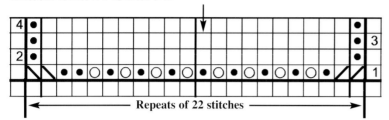

Repeats of 22 stitches

Vertical arrow marks the centre stitch, see previous page.

Rows 75 – 76 using **light grey**: plain knit rows 3 – 4 as chart 2, break yarn.

Increase Rows 77 – 78 using **charcoal**: work rows 1 – 2 **as Chart 3**, do not break yarn. **(720sts.)**

Black Shawl Chart 3

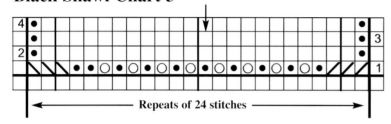

Repeats of 24 stitches

Vertical arrow marks the centre stitch, see previous page.

Rows 79 – 80 Still using **charcoal**: work rows 3 – 4, break yarn.

Rows 81 – 84 using **cream**: work rows 1 – 4 **as chart 4**, break yarn. **(Still 720sts.)**

Black Shawl Chart 4

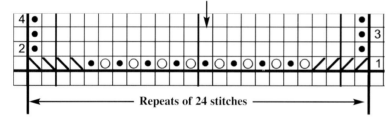

Repeats of 24 stitches

Vertical arrow marks the centre stitch, see previous page.

Continue on these 720 sts. using Chart 4 from now on until you have finished the border

Rows 85 – 86 using **light grey**: work rows 1 – 2, break yarn.

Rows 87 – 88 using **mid grey**: work rows 3 – 4, break yarn.

Rows 89 – 92 using **dark grey**: work rows 1 – 4, do not break yarn.

Rows 93 – 94 still using **dark grey**: work rows 1 – 2, break yarn.

Rows 95 – 96 using **charcoal**: work rows 3 – 4, do not break yarn.

Rows 97 – 104 still using **charcoal**: work rows 1 – 4 twice, do not break yarn.

Rows 105 – 106 still using **charcoal**: work 2 rows knit, do not break yarn.

Hap Triangular Edging

Leave the 720 stitches on the largest size circular needle (or ordinary, long knitting needle) and cast on 10 stitches for the edging.

As you knit the edging round, cast off one of the border's stitches each time you return to them (i.e. every other row) by knitting it "2 together" with the last stitch of the edging's straight side. See "Attaching an Edging", page 38 – the last stitch, a decrease, on the even rows includes one of the border's stitches with the edging as it is cast off.

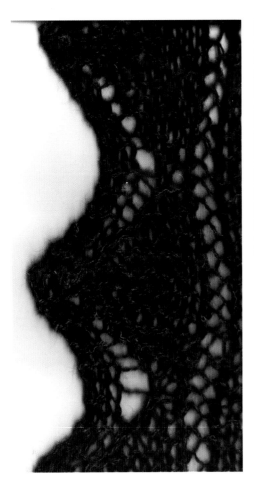

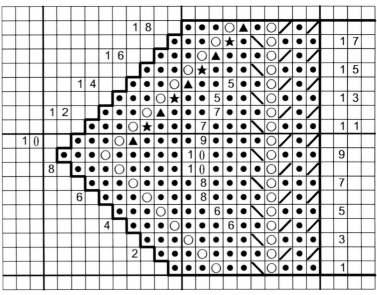

Cast on 10 stitches

N.B. the stars in the edging pattern chart above mean "knit 3 together".

Finally, *graft* the ends of the edging to each other. Spend some time and sew in all the ends invisibly and then sew up the side seam – a reasonably loose backstitch gives the best result.

Dress the shawl by gently washing and pinning to shape, **beware** that the charcoal coloured dye is a little prone to running, so be careful to pin it to a surface that it is unlikely to stain.

This pattern can be used to make a smaller-sized shawl using the above instructions but finishing the centre at "make 1, knit 35" or "make 1, knit 47". The basic rule for this formula is a multiple of 12, -1.

This pattern looks lovely in white 1-ply using British size 11 (3.00mm, American 2) needles, throughout, perhaps switching to larger needles as the pattern grows for a bigger shawl. Or, using increases based on the above charts, the Old Shell Pattern could be expanded to "10 overs", "12 overs" etc.

Try another edging pattern – e.g. Traditional Peaked Shawl Edging or the Cyprus Edging.

Very experienced knitters wil be able to knit this "in the round" using circular needles when the increasing centre's stitch count allows them to link up the start of the next row with the end of the previous one. Then even rows would need to be purled to maintain a garter stitch appearance.

This most attractive square shawl is knitted in Lace-weight 2 ply Shetland wool (which equates with a standard 4 ply yarn). I designed this using a variety of Shetland tree and fern motifs, which are in the centre pattern, border and edging. This is easier to knit than it looks, as it is a pattern-every-other-row design, made on quite large sized needles.

This shawl is not a true Shetland shawl, because the borders are made individually first and then sewn together before the centre pattern is made – and before the edging is knitted round as the final element. The hardest part is *grafting* the final row of the centre square to the last border, but if time is taken, the result is beautiful, and indistinguishable from a knitted row. This would make a striking shawl for an adult if made in black, or in a Cobweb white 1 ply, using British 9/3.50mm – or if using smaller needles, the pattern would need to be enlarged, extra stitches for more repeat panels of the border and centre would need including – only for the very experienced to try.

Finished size is 54 inches (135cm) square approximately. The teddy bear is in the picture to give an idea of scale; he is the size of a ten pounds weight baby – averagely aged two or three months old. Dressed Tension over garter stitch: 20 sts x 36 rows = 4" (10cm).

Materials

11 x 1oz (28g) hanks of Jamieson & Smith Lace-weight 2 ply*, in white, wound into balls

5mm Circular needle – (British size 6), 60 cm long or equivalent knitting needles

Tapestry needle

*See "Suppliers' List", Appendix 6

Detail of Cat's Paw centre square with Fern, Tree and Spider Lace Border. An alternative centre pattern might be Field of Flowers, Mrs Montague's or Madeira Pattern. The edging I used is the Scallop Shell Edging, I really like this edging here because it echoes the tree motifs in the border so nicely – a lovely alternative would be Double Scallop Shell Edging.

How to Knit the Shetland Lace Baby Shawl

Borders – See following two charts giving overview and detail

Cast on 4 multiples of 24 stitches + 85 (42 + 43 extra stitches on each side) = 181 stitches.

Make the 181 stitches using the Knitting Cast On (Tip: leave a long casting on tail to mark the odd rows, this comes in useful when piecing the borders together) knit them back – the casting on tail should be hanging down on the right as it will for all the odd, patterned rows.

Follow the pattern charts as shown, **it is very important to note that only the odd, patterned rows are charted; the even rows are plain knitted throughout** – i.e. the even rows are *garter stitched*. **Also, rows 85 – 96 are starred, because extra stitches have been made in these rows, which are removed in row 97. Knit two or three stitches at those points – as the dots in the squares indicate**. Do not cast off any of the stitches after row 97, knit 4 rows plain on them and leave them on a thread or a stitch holder for use later.

When four borders have been made exactly the same, lay them out so that each border's cast on tail is on the right (this is to make sure that all the right sides are face up). Now, using a blunt tapestry needle and the same wool, *Herring Bone Stitch* the borders to each other so an "empty" square is formed by them.

Overview of a Shetland Lace Baby Shawl Border

(see additional charts, photographs and text for detail)

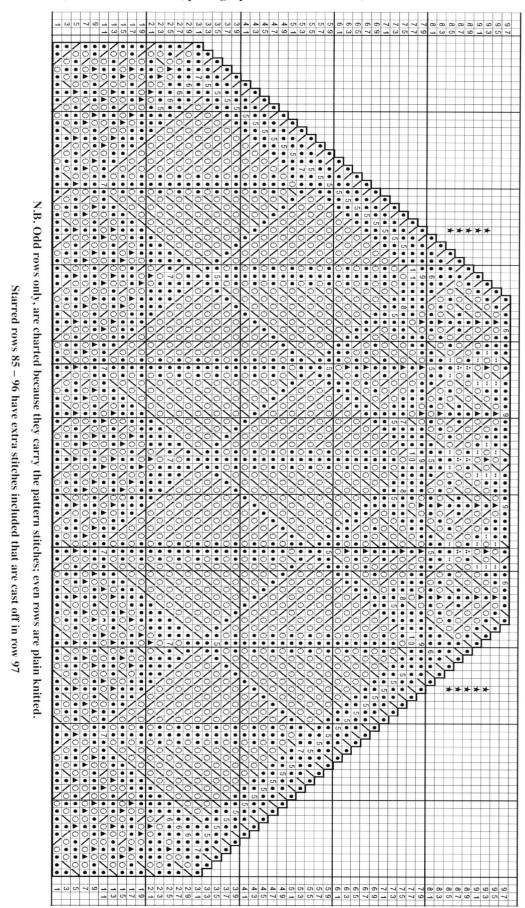

N.B. Odd rows only, are charted because they carry the pattern stitches; even rows are plain knitted.

Starred rows 85 – 96 have extra stitches included that are cast off in row 97

Shetland Lace Baby Shawl Border Details Charts
(see overview as well)

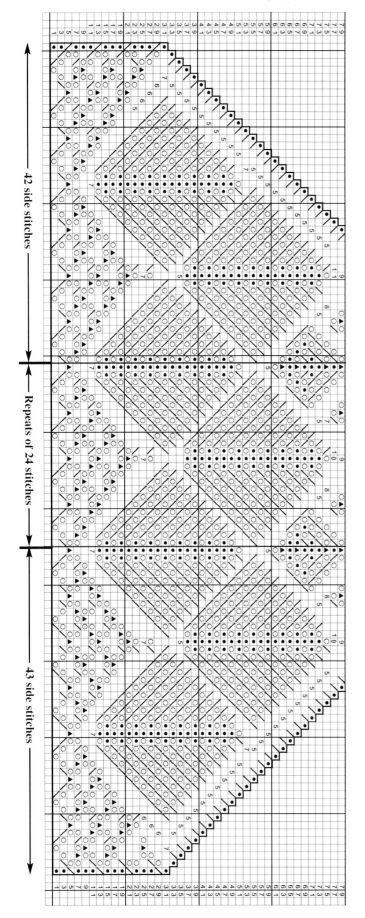

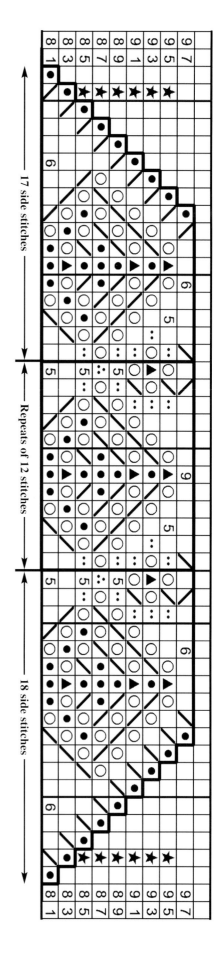

Centre

You are going to use one border's stitches to knit up the centre on, and its two adjacent (L.H. and R.H.) borders will be the growing centre's sides. Because the finish's line of motifs need to balance the start line's, you are going to need to attach the centre pattern's 121 ridges to the sides' 115 stitches, therefore 6 extra ones per side will be needed. So pick up 3 stitches from the Herring Bone seams, left and right, bottom and top as the centre is worked. Look at the photograph on page 250 and you will see that the centre (pictured on its side) shows I did this.

Use the 117 stitches (115 + 2 – one picked up from each side) – from one border to start to knit the centre square as set out below. As you come to the end of each row, take the nearest stitch from that side border's seams and reserved stitches and knit it "2 together" with the last stitch of that centre row – doing this row by row, turn by turn, casts off all the left and right borders' stitches.

Knit 6 rows garter stitch, then follow the chart for the Cat's Paw Pattern below (it differs slightly from the one on page 55 because it has more side stitches). After working the full pattern 11 times, work row 1-10 once more, – just to balance the top and bottom line of motifs of the square. Finally, work 6 more rows of garter stitch, this should have used up both sides reserved stitches but work an extra plain row if you need to. Then graft the last row's stitches to the final border's stitches. See "How to Graft" in the Knitting Advice.

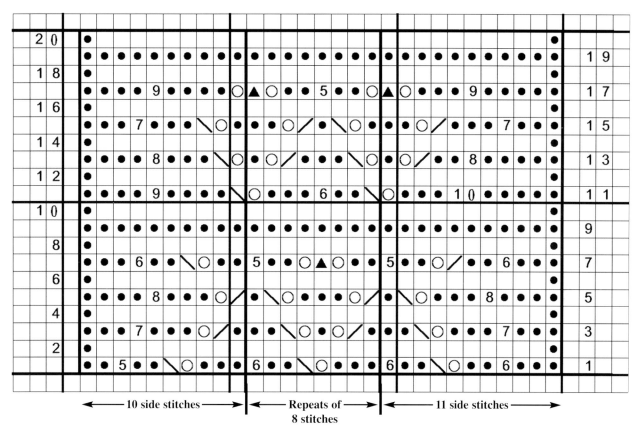

Cat's Paw Pattern for the Shetland Lace Baby Shawl

Pick up 12 multiples of 8 stitches + 21 (10 + 11 side stitches) = 117 stitches.

Edging

Using the Waste Wool Cast On, cast on the 26 stitches for the Scallop Shell Edging and follow the chart on page 77 to work it round* the four borders; 13 points for each side (56 full pattern repeats in all), finish by grafting the two ends together. – See "How To Graft" in the "Knitting Advice". Now, complete by sewing in any ends of wool invisibly and then *dress* the shawl.

* See "Attaching an Edging", page 38 for further help with this.

The finished size of this 1 ply shawl is 48 inches (120cm) square. It is in the tradition of Shetland *Crepe* Shawls and is knitted with a plain garter stitch centre, (but this time, knitted as a diamond, see "Shawl Centres") with an Old Shell patterned border. The edging is Clematis Edging, which is a very early twentieth century European pattern. Experienced knitters could replace this with any other edging of their choice. Again traditionally, this design is knitted without any sewing being necessary (except to *graft* the two ends of the edging) if knitted in the round on a circular needle, but it can be made in other ways if preferred – directions are given. Dressed Tension over garter stitch: 20 sts x 36 rows = 4" (10cm).

N.B. Useful advice is given at various key stages of this pattern that demonstrate some of the alterations to the basic shawl design that can be made. Additionally, helpful advice about working the Old Shell Pattern by identifying the "centre stitch", is given with Project 3. Read the following advice through before working, in order to be clear about what you choose to do.

Materials – for the 48-inch size.

9 x ½ oz (14g) hanks of Jamieson & Smith's Shetland Cobweb 1 ply*– wound into balls

2.75mm Circular needle – (British Size 12), 40 or 60 cm long or equivalent knitting needles

Tapestry needle for final finishing

Row counter optional but recommended

Stitch markers or **contrasting lengths of wool** to mark corner positions if making in the round on the circular needle, ideally three the same colour and one different to mark the start of a round.

*See "Suppliers' List", Appendix 6.

How to Knit the Cobweb Crepe Shawl

The Centre

See the information on shawl centres, page 200 to help you decide which sort of centre square you want to do. If you want to make a larger shawl, read the information box on the next page.

See the information on shawl centres, page 200

For a diamond centre: Cast on 1 stitch, turn. *Put wool around the needle once and knit to end**. **(2sts.)**

Repeat last row from * to ** increasing one stitch each row (see tip above) until the triangle of knitting has **162 stitches**. Now, decrease each row until there is 1 stitch again, by doing the following – *put wool round the needle once and knit 3 together, knit to end** of each row. Repeat this row from * to ** decreasing one stitch each row, until one stitch remains. You should now have a **diamond shape** of garter stitch knitting with loops on each side. – See diagram below, which shows the orientation of the diamond centre in a finished shawl.

For a square centre: Alternatively, the knitter could make a garter stitch square by casting on **81 stitches** invisibly and knitting for **162 rows** – do not cast off the final row's stitches, use them as a foundation row to do the set up pattern row for one of the borders.

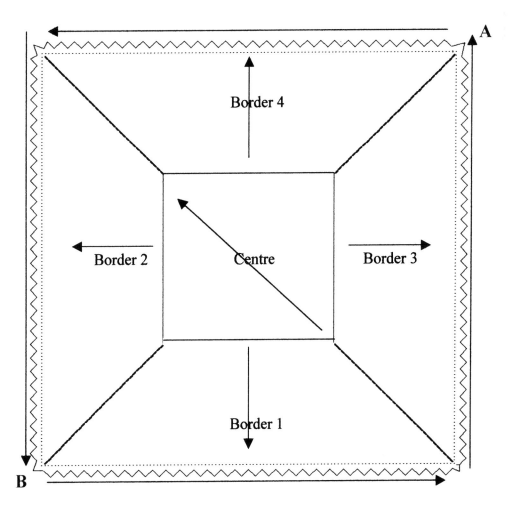

This diagram shows how the shawl has been made with the diamond centre square as its beginning, then the borders picked up from the centre square's sides and knitted outwards – either all at once (methods 1 & 2) or one at a time (method 3). The edging is knitted onto the borders to complete. (Arrows show direction of knitting.) When this shawl is folded across the diagonal A to B, the centre's knitted rows will stay "horizontal".

How to change the size of the Cobweb Crepe Shawl

The overall finished size of this shawl can most easily be adjusted by altering the actual size of the centre; simply keep to the following formula:

Cast on **X** multiples of 12 + (4 + 5 side stitches).

I used **6** "multiples of 12" + (9 side stitches) to get the **cast on 81 (square) or maximum 81 x 2 = 162 (diamond)** stitches I used in my shawl.

8 or **10** "multiples of 12" may be substituted if a larger shawl is wanted:

e.g. Cast on **10** x 12 + (9 side stitches) = 129sts; to be cast on for a **square** centre.

If a larger **diamond** centre is wanted the calculation still applies, but this time the maximum row size of the triangle will be **twice** the total e.g. 129 **x 2** = 258 stitches. So, you would cast on a stitch, increase each row until there are 258 stitches in the triangle, then decrease to a stitch again; following the advice given for the diamond centre on the previous page.

Knitting the Borders

These can be made in any one of the following three methods. Read these through and then decide which one you wish to use and follow it throughout, until it's time to knit the edging.

Method 1 (very experienced knitters): The four borders are made all together on a **circular needle**, but **"knitted in the round"** so that there's no sewing together of separately knitted borders. Even rows are purled to maintain the garter stitch appearance:

From the four sides of the centre, pick up all the (81 x 4) =324 stitches for all four borders at once. Mark each of the 4 corner stitches (see border chart) with coloured thread or with stitch markers, especially the first one that will mark the start of each round with a longer thread or larger/differently coloured marker. Purl one round. Work the set up pattern rows, then follow the Cobweb Crepe Shawl Border Chart as given.

Method 2 (experienced knitters): Again, on a **circular needle** as the first method, but the four borders are *flat knitted* row by row – with the **knitting being turned for each row**; this method needs the sewing up of just one border seam afterwards:

As method 1, from the centre pick up all the (81 x 4) =324 stitches for all the borders at once. Mark each of the 4 corner stitches (see border chart) with coloured thread or with stitch markers. Knit one row. Work the set up pattern rows, then follow the chart. **It's vital to remember that all even rows are to be knitted with this method,** (not purled as charted).

Method 3 (less experienced knitters): On **ordinary needles**, again *flat knitted* as method 2, but this time **knit each border piece separately**, by picking up the 81 stitches from each side of the centre in turn. This needs the sewing together of all the borders' "flaps" before the edging is knitted). **Even rows are knitted** (not purled as the chart – purling would result in a stocking stitch pattern):

*From one side pick up 81 stitches for one of the borders. Knit one row. Now follow the set up pattern instructions below and knit the border through, reserve (save) the finished side's stitches on a thread or stitch holder.** Repeat from * to ** three times, for each side in turn.

When all four borders have been made in the same way, sew them to each other by back-stitching them with a tapestry needle threaded with the yarn. Then, put all the *reserved stitches* together on the knitting needle (4 x 81 = 324 stitches) and follow the directions for knitting the edging.

Set Up Pattern – 4 rows

Increase round/row 1 (for each border/side)

Knit 4, make 1, knit 1. *(make 1 knit 1) 3 times, knit 6, (make 1, knit 1) 3 times**. Repeat from * to ** 5 more times, make 1, knit 4. The chart below gives these instructions in picture form.

Set Up Pattern Row 1

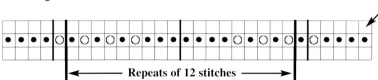

Corner stitch.

N.B. This increase row makes "repeats" of 12 stitches into "repeats" of 18 stitches. Each side increases from 81 to 119 stitches.

← Repeats of 12 stitches →

Round/Row 2

Method 1: Rounds 2**: Purl** all the stitches (as shown on chart) – this produces the garter stitch effect when knitting in the round. **119 x 4 = 476 stitches.**

Method 2: Row 2**: Knit** all the stitches to produce garter stitch when flat knitting. **119 x 4 = 476 stitches.**

Method 3: Row 2**: Knit** all the stitches – this produces garter stitch when flat knitting. **119 stitches per border/side.**

Rounds/Rows 3, 4 and onwards:

Method 1: As border chart exactly, purl all even rows.

Methods 2 and 3: Knit all even rounds/rows.
As shown on the pattern, row 3 and every other odd row from then on is *plain knitted*, whichever method you have chosen.

These four rows or rounds "set up" the pattern and are replaced by the first four rows as given on the border chart. After the first working of row 28, you must work row 29 as a row 5, (as plotted on the Cobweb Crepe Shawl Border Chart), for each subsequent repeat. Experienced knitters will notice that the "knit 6" on this set up pattern row 1, is replaced by "knit 2 together, 6 times" on the border chart's row 1.

Notice from the chart that row 29 repeats row 5, etc. Continue the pattern and increases as shown on the border chart till 96 rounds/rows (or other desired multiple of 4 rows for a larger shawl) are made. Do not cast off. Now, work an edging around the border stitches, see "Attaching an Edging", page 38.

The Edging

I have used the Clematis Edging (page 175) to finish my shawl, but any similarly deep* (or deeper) edging could be used. **Read the following directions all through before starting to knit the edging.**

The photograph is a detail of a corner of the shawl and shows how the edging is *eased* (gathered and spread), around the corners. Attach the edging to a border's stitches as follows:

Keep border stitches on the needle – do not cast them off, but slip them until you are about half way down a border. Using the Loop or Waste Wool Cast On, add the required number of edging stitches to the left hand pin. Knit them back towards the border but at the last edging stitch, knit it as a "knit 2 together" using the next stitch – which will be one left-over from one of the borders.

Now, begin to work the edging's pattern stitches as shown on the Edging Chart along the **side**, but on each return, continue "knitting two together" using the last edging stitch with the next left-over border stitch. Gradually, all the border stitches will be cast off as the edging is worked along.

At the **corners**, this method needs to be modified slightly ("doubling") to allow the edging to open or ease, around the point. When a corner point is approximately twenty stitches away (for this depth of edging), instead of decreasing each

* See note top of page 259.

Cobweb Crepe Shawl Border Chart

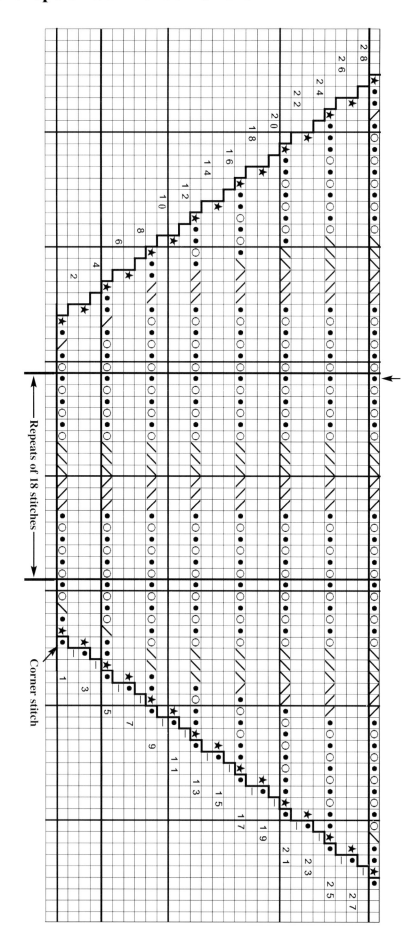

Vertical arrow at the top of the chart marks one of the centre stitches, see page 246.

N.B. The star symbols on the chart mean "knit and purl" into that stitch to make a single increase. Read the text through carefully because this pattern needs a special first row to be worked to establishes the pattern: the set up pattern row charts are given with the text on page 257.

This is a 24 row pattern.

After working row 28, repeat rows 5-28 twice, then row 5 once more, so there are 24 horizontal lines of "holes" counting out from the centre. Then work five plain rows before attaching the edging.

return row, do it every other return, so that the edging is twice as full. Continue doing this till you are an equal distance around the corner on the next side; before working the edging straight again, by decreasing at each return as before. *If a **deeper edging** (i.e. one with more cast on stitches) is wanted, the knitter would have to further change the easing around corners: Again, approaching the corner, work more edging rows before attaching to the border with a "knit 2 together" – see "Attaching an Edging", page 38.

If a slightly **narrower edging** is chosen, the process is easier. "Doubling" the corner edge stitches as described above, may only be required for ten border stitches each side; or may not be necessary at all, if the edging is widely pointed. Once the edging is completed, *graft* the two ends of the edging together, and *dress* the shawl.

Level * * * * *   Handkerchief With Lace Edging Project 6

In the mid-nineteenth century, it was fashionable for ladies to have dainty lawn squares edged with elaborate lace, as handkerchiefs. Sarah McComb Rawson knitted such edgings and three of her exquisitely worked handkerchiefs are in the collection at the American Museum in Bath, Britain. The edging I have worked above is very similar to one Sarah chose, being a very wide Bead Lace *Insertion* coupled to a simple Vandyke and Plain Triangle Edging.

The edging is made using only **one 20 gm reel of DMC Crochet Cotton 70** and the **finest antique needles** I could find. Although this gauge of needle is not readily commercially available now to my knowledge, it is still possible to find them second-hand*, or from specialists.

The Victorian Mauchlinware knitting needle-case shown here, contained two rusty sets of fine **British size 19 double-pointed needles, about seven inches long and with a diameter of 1 mm approximately** (the needles would have been for ladies use in making edgings, purses and other fine laces). After using the finest grade emery paper – also known as "wet and dry paper" – to rub the rust off along the shafts, I made end caps out of map pins (with the pins pulled out), and these needles were again usable. The fine six inch (15cm) square handkerchief was one I found second-hand.

Using the pattern chart A and the Knitting Cast On, I worked 44 complete repeats of the pattern, then carefully *grafted* the edging's two ends together. It really is a matter of trial and error how long to make an edging for an individual item, but I worked here on the principle of eight points (or pattern repeats) for each of the four sides and three points for each of the four corners; giving the sum: (4 x 8) + (4 x 3) = 44 points/pattern repeats.

*you can make a set out of two stitch holders – see page 29, or see "Suppliers' List".

259

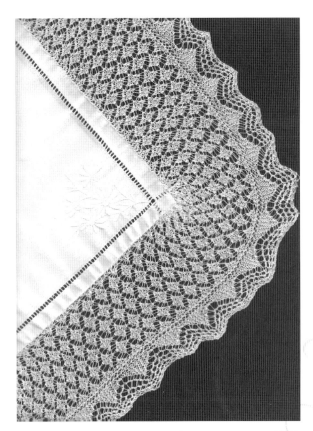

Because this edging is so deep (three inches/7.5cm from straight side to outside point after *dressing*), I had to finely gather the edging around the corners – see the detailed photograph of a corner. A narrower edging could be worked by following pattern chart B should the knitter desire; I think then only 40 pattern repeats would be necessary: – again, eight for each side but this time, only two repeats for each corner. (Remember, a narrower edging needs less gathering to turn around a corner and lie flat – see "Attaching an Edging" for further explanation.)

After first pinning the edging in place, I neatly sewed it to the square with tiny stitches made with fine cotton threaded into a sharp, thin needle.

The finished handkerchief* was lightly starched and dressed to shape. Ironing wasn't needed as the dressing process pulled any wrinkles out. The handkerchief is stored by wrapping it in acid-free tissue paper and then by rolling the package around a suitable cardboard tube. Dressed Tension: 54 sts x 64 rows = 4" (10cm) over pattern.

* 6" (15cm) square of cloth with 3" (7.5cm) edging.

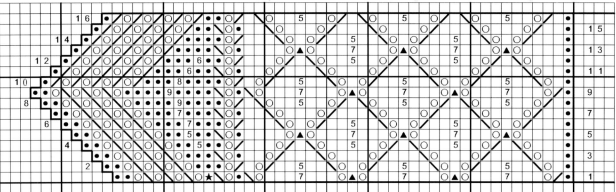

Cast on 46 stitches   **Pattern Chart A**

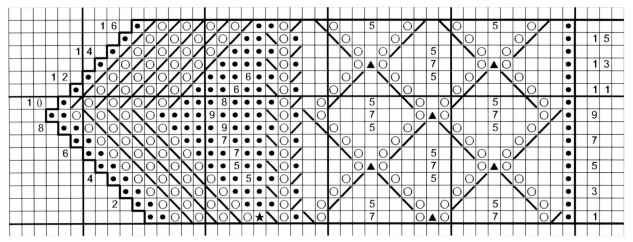

Cast on 36 stitches   **Pattern Chart B**

* N.B. the stitch starred on the first line of each chart is to be treated specially, by being worked as a "knit 3 together" – a double decrease at this point.

The finished size of this beautiful stole is 72 inches by 32 inches (180 x 80cm), the inspiration for it is a traditional Unst shawl knitted approximately 100 years ago. I have recreated this as closely as possible as a stole, using similar patterns. Experienced knitters could re-interpret these directions and produce a shawl again if they should wish to (see advice on how to do this at the end). Dressed Tension: 24 sts x 24 rows = 4" (10cm) over pattern.

Materials

10 x ½ oz (14g) hanks of Jamieson & Smith's Shetland Cobweb 1 ply* – wound into balls

Oddment of contrasting 2 ply Lace-weight wool – for waste wool casting on

2.25mm Circular needle – (British size 13), 40 or 60 cm long – I prefer to use the smaller length but it is up to the knitter to choose. Equivalent knitting needles could be used instead

Tapestry needle for final finishing

Embroidery scissors Sharp pointed, for cutting out the Waste Wool Casting On

Stitch holder

*See "Suppliers' List", Appendix 6.

How to Knit the Unst Lace Stole Centre

Waste Wool Cast On: Using the contrast oddment of wool, cast on 185 stitches and knit 4 rows in garter stitch. Now, **join in the Cobweb 1 ply** and knit 4 more rows in garter stitch.

Break Pattern Row – which makes a row of *eyelets*:

Knit 1, *make 1, knit 2 together **. Repeat from * to ** to the end (**185 stitches**).

Knit four more rows in garter stitch and then follow the Unst Stole Centre pattern chart and knit the centre lace for 10 whole repeats. (**380 rows**).

Knit 4 more rows of garter stitch and then do the break pattern row again.

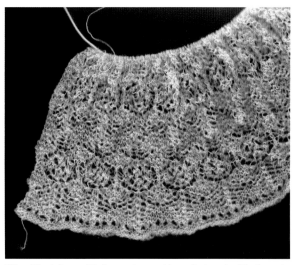

The Unst Lace Stole centre pattern being knitted, note the break pattern row's eyelets at the bottom.

Detail of the finished, dressed Unst Lace Stole centre pattern. Compare this to the centre of the Framed Shawl pictured on page 215, which is a development of this pattern. This is shown "upside down" to the knitting direction.

262

Unst Lace Stole Centre Pattern

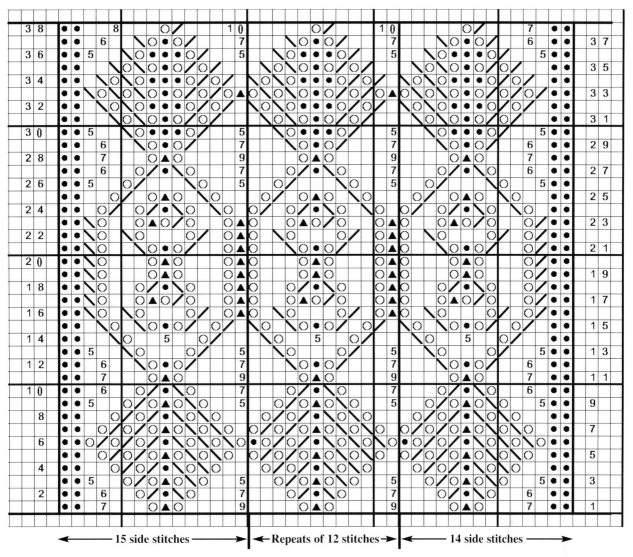

← 15 side stitches → ←Repeats of 12 stitches→ ← 14 side stitches →

Cast on 13 multiples of 12 stitches + 29 (15 + 14 extra stitches on each side)
(12 x 13) + 29 = 185 stitches.

Unst Lace Stole Border Detail

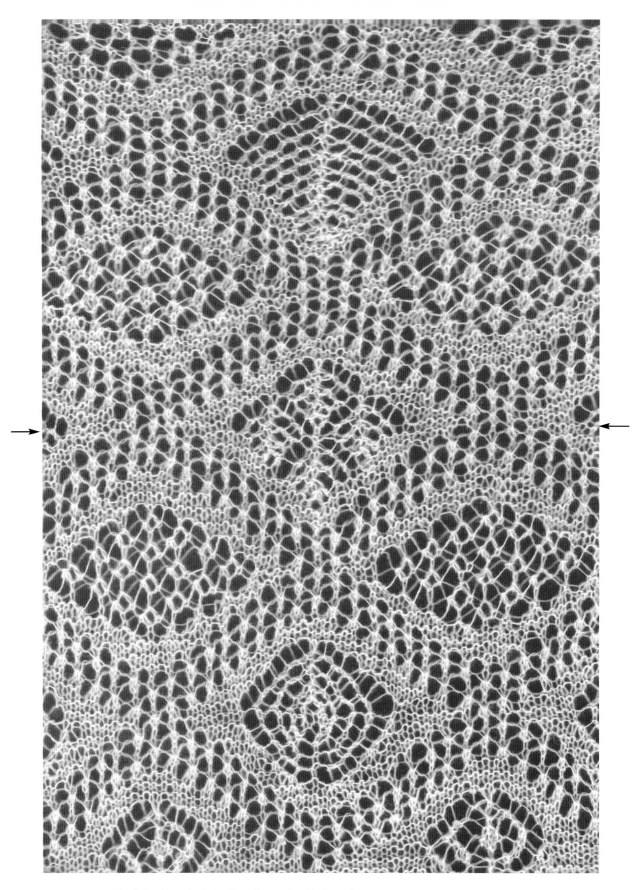

This large photograph of the Unst Stole border gives a detail view of the patterns. The arrows mark the division in the two charts, (these are given on the following pages).

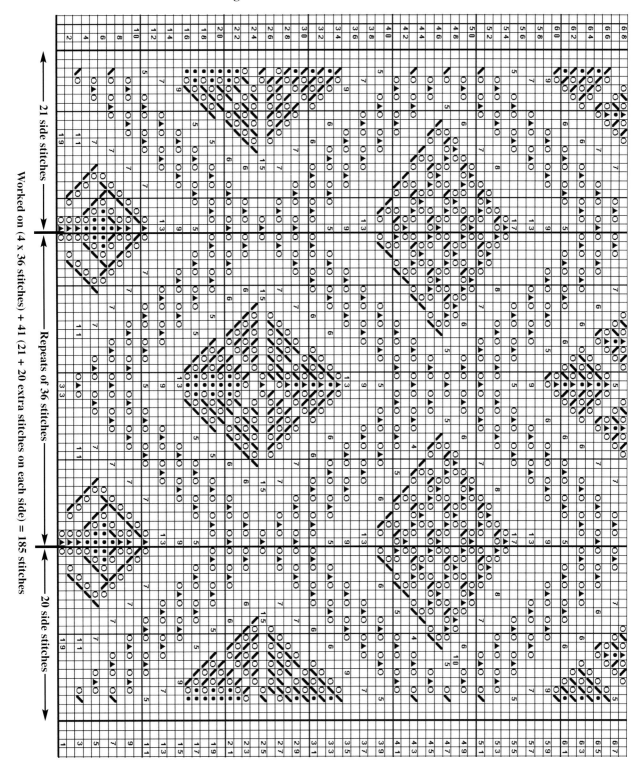

Worked on (4 x 36 stitches) + 41 (21 + 20 extra stitches on each side) = 185 stitches

21 side stitches — Repeats of 36 stitches — 20 side stitches

Knit and purl into '00's on even rows.

Detail of the intersection of the centre, border and edging patterns. The arrow marks the dividing row of eyelets between the centre and border patterns that is made by the break pattern row.

How to Knit the Unst Lace Stole Borders

After the break pattern row, do four rows of garter stitch and then follow the two pattern charts consecutively, starting with chart 1, row 1. When you have knitted the final row – row 136 on chart 2, knit four rows of garter stitch to finish, then transfer these stitches onto a stitch holder to use up later when knitting on the edging. To help knit the next bit, put a contrast marker through the knitting and tie it in a bow on the "front" side of the knitting i.e. with the "odd" side facing you. You can pull this out later.

Turn the work through 180 degrees, so that the cast on is now to hand. Make sure you still have the **front uppermost**. Snip out carefully the waste stitches (as described in the Waste Wool Cast On) and pick up 185 stitches. Rejoin yarn and knit the second border to match the first. Check that the odd rows are still on the same side of the stole; if not, undo the pattern rows and work one more row of garter stitch. When the second border has been completed, keep the stitches on the needle and follow instructions to work the edging.

How to knit the Unst Lace Stole Insertion and Edging

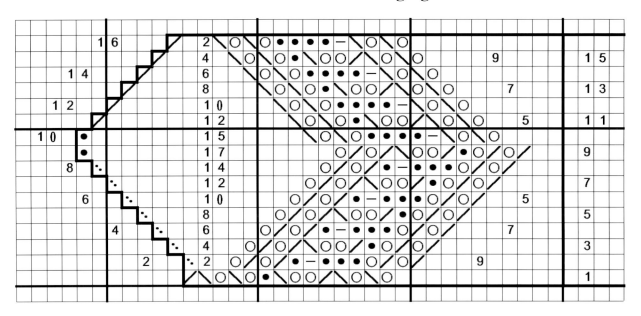

Cast on 9 + 26 stitches for insertion and edging = 35 stitches in all.

Work the *insertion* and edging around the stole:

After finishing the second border, keep its stitches on the needle and cast on 35 stitches with the Loop Cast On. Knit the stitches back to confirm them.

Work the pattern stitches of the first rows as given for the insertion and then the edging. Knit the return row (row 2) of the edging followed by the second row of the insertion. Continue knitting the insertion and edging together, attaching them to the stole on each return or even row (see "Attaching an Edging" in "Knitting Advice").

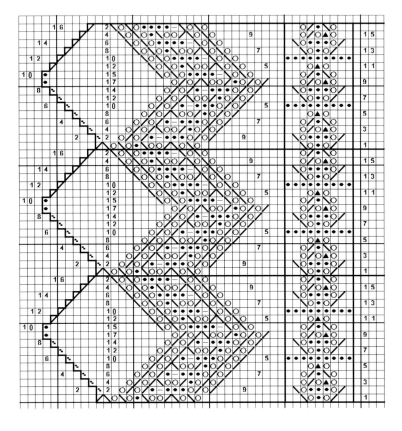

Because the insertion is a 6 row repeat pattern and the edging is a sixteen row repeat, they do not re-coincide until after row 48; i.e. after 3 full repeats of the edging pattern – see chart A. It will be necessary to ease the fullness of this very deep edging around the corners by "doubling" (see pages 39 and 40) for at least 12 returns before and after each corner. *Graft* ends together. Wash and dress carefully.

Chart A

268

Unst Lace Shawl

Experienced knitters will see that the stole border pattern can readily be converted into a trapezoidal or mitred border for a shawl. This is easily done by working a centre on the 221* stitches cast on first, then knitting the borders outwards. The pattern is exactly as given for the stole border but it additionally: increases one stitch **each side** of every odd row – see the chart detail above, which shows the right hand side increases only (obviously, the left hand side is a mirror image of this). The lace pattern stitches are gradually extended outwards to fill in the expanding knitting row by row. This makes a beautiful shawl when finished, I used the All Over Tree and Diamond Pattern as a centre for the shawl photographed here. See page 102, I used 9 repeats of 16 sts + 21 side sts = 165 stitches for the centre.

* I got this figure by multiplying 3 repeats of 36 sts + (2 x 29) side sts. This stitch information is in Border Pattern Chart below.

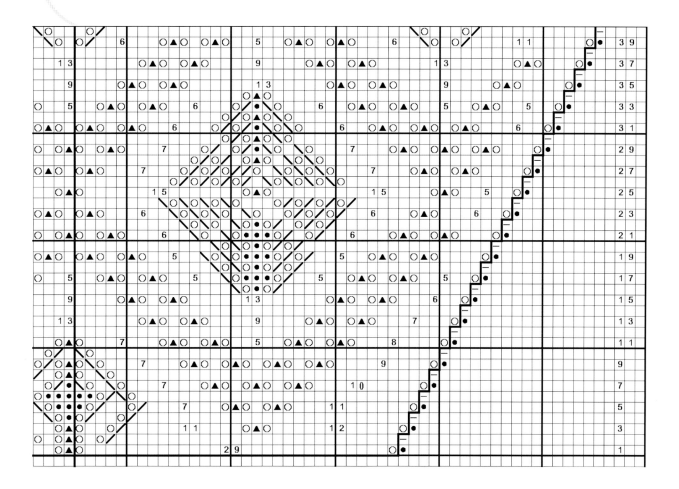

269

As the final "masterpiece" project for this book, I designed this traditional lace christening robe based on existing fine lace patterns from Unst, knitted approximately 100 years ago. I have based this sleeveless, heavily patterned apron-like overdress on original models, but for the sake of completeness, I also designed a separate, plain, sleeved under-dress for the baby to wear underneath – this dress has only a lace edging for ornament. This will fit a four to nine months old baby: the bodice is an elastic 18 – 22 inches (45 – 55cm), the length 36 inches (90cm).

Despite the apparent complexity, the overdress/apron is quite simple in construction, detailed diagrams illustrate the order of working for both dresses, so that knitters can substitute other designs or patterns should they wish. If you are interested in doing this, I give an explanation of what needs to be considered and how I developed this project in the chapter on design. Dressed Tension: 32 sts x 64 rows = 4" (10cm) square.

Materials

10 x ½ oz (14g) hanks of Jamieson & Smith's Shetland Cobweb 1 ply* – wound into balls ready for knitting

Oddment of contrasting 2 ply Lace-weight wool – for Waste Wool Casting On

2.00 mm circular needle – (British Size 14) 40 cm long, or equivalent knitting needles

Tapestry needle for final finishing

Embroidery scissors Sharp pointed, for cutting out the Waste Wool Casting On

5 small buttons

Stitch holder

*See "Suppliers' List", Appendix 6.

Order of knitting the Christening Robe Apron

photograph shows it finished but not sewn up

1. **Edging (with straight insertion) – knitted first**
2. **Bordered skirt – knitted on stitches picked up from the edging (1)**
3. **Waistband insertion (worked along decreased skirt top)**
4. **Bodice, front and back – knitted on stitches picked up from centre of (3)**
5. **Armhole edging – left**
6. **Armhole edging – right**

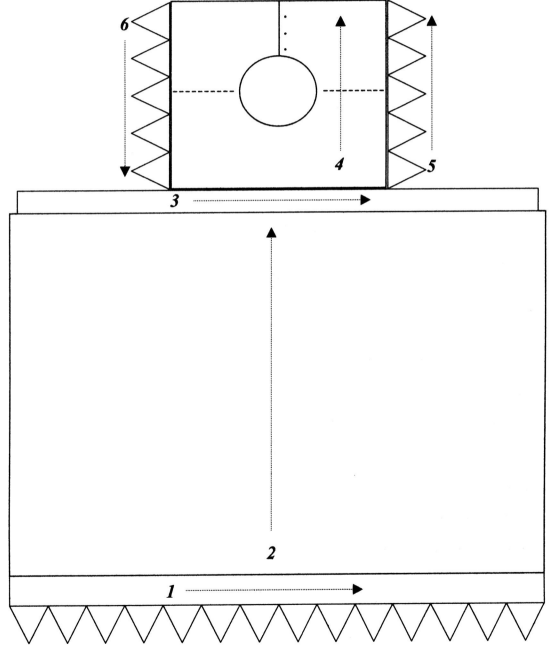

Dashed arrows show the knitting direction.

The Christening Robe Apron

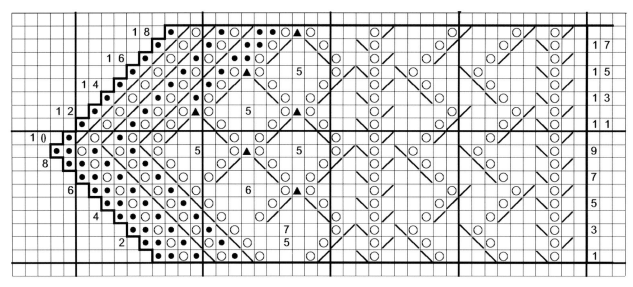

Cast on 33 stitches

Skirt Edging and Insertion Chart

Order of Work

(1) Skirt Edging and Insertion

Using the Waste Wool Cast On, cast on 33 stitches and knit the above edging pattern for 28 full repeats. Leave the 33 stitches on a thread and pick up 259 stitches (1 for each odd row of the edging and 7 extra) evenly from the straight side of the edging strip. Knit four rows garter stitch.

(2) Bordered Skirt

Now, work from the 2 Border Lace and 3 Skirt Lace pattern charts (**Charts 1 – 5**) in sequence, to make the bordered skirt (each row has eight (7 whole + 2 x ½ sides, see charts) full repeats of the pattern panel, and is designed to centre with one of the Tree of Life motifs in the centre-front of the apron – see large photograph of the apron. **Remember to repeat the charted rows 197 – 225, once**. To finish the apron's skirt rectangle, knit four rows in garter stitch (you could work more plain knitted rows here if you want a longer apron).

(3) Waistband Insertion

Decrease Row: Work a row of "knit two together" to end. (128 sts.)
Still with the right wool, cast on 15 stitches (I used the Loop Cast On for this) and after knitting two rows in garter

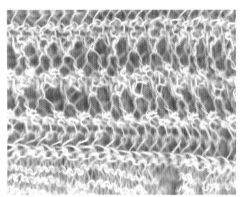

stitch, work the four row waistband insertion pattern (**chart 6,** below right) along the decreased skirt top. For the insertion, I found that it was a good idea to slip the first stitch of each row to get a tight, chain effect. When the 128 stitches of the skirt top have been used up, cast off loosely the waistband's 15 stitches. You should now have a rectangular skirt "gathered" onto a waistband.

Waistband insertion detail – shown as it is on the skirt – at right angles to the pattern chart, right.

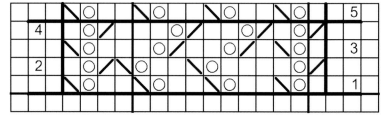

Cast on 15 stitches

Chart 6

272

Overview of the Christening Robe Border Lace Chart

See the two separate Border Lace Charts for detail

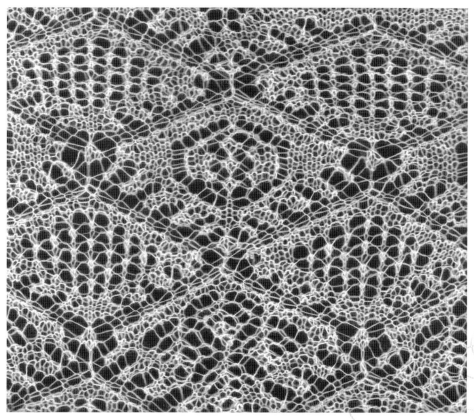

Christening Robe Border Lace – Rows 1 – 45

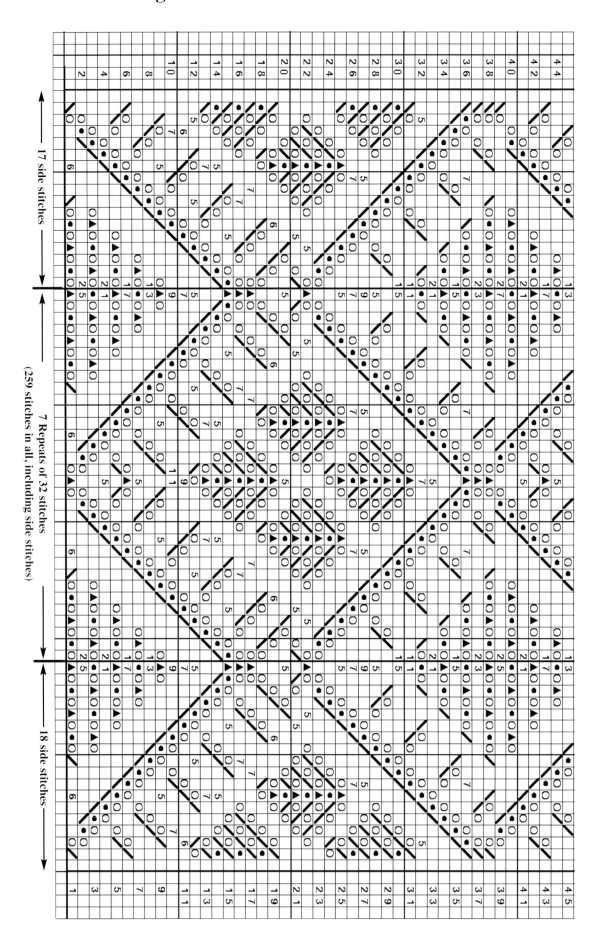

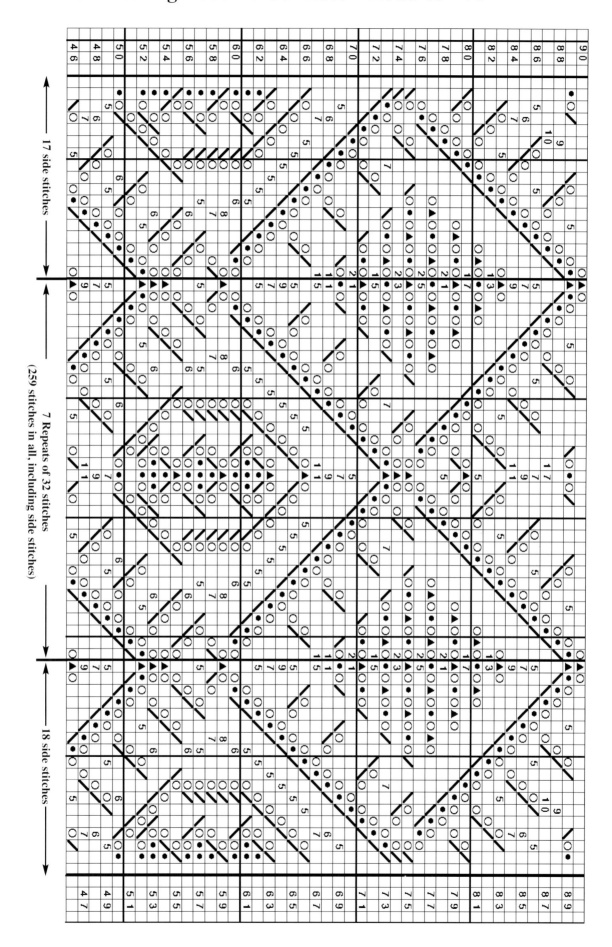

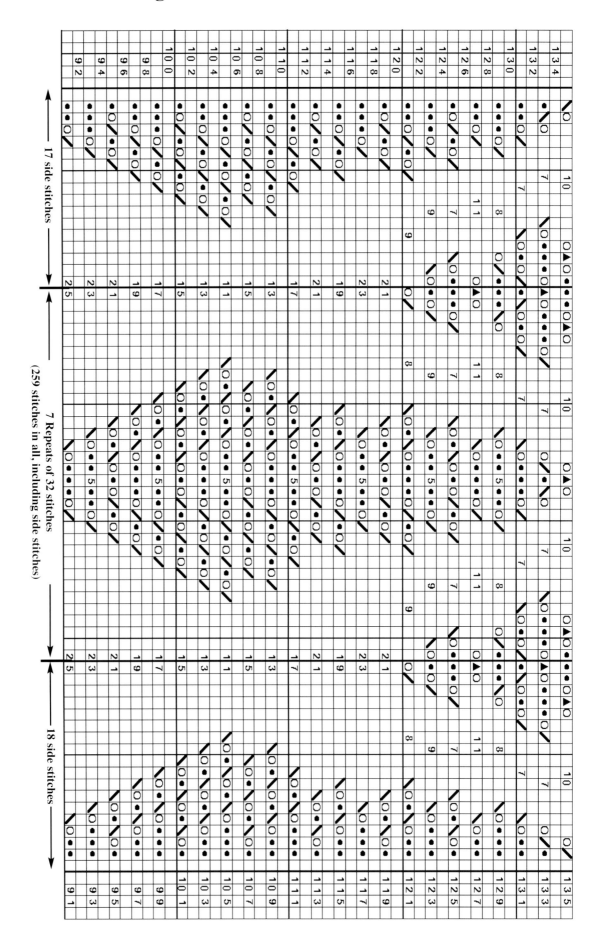

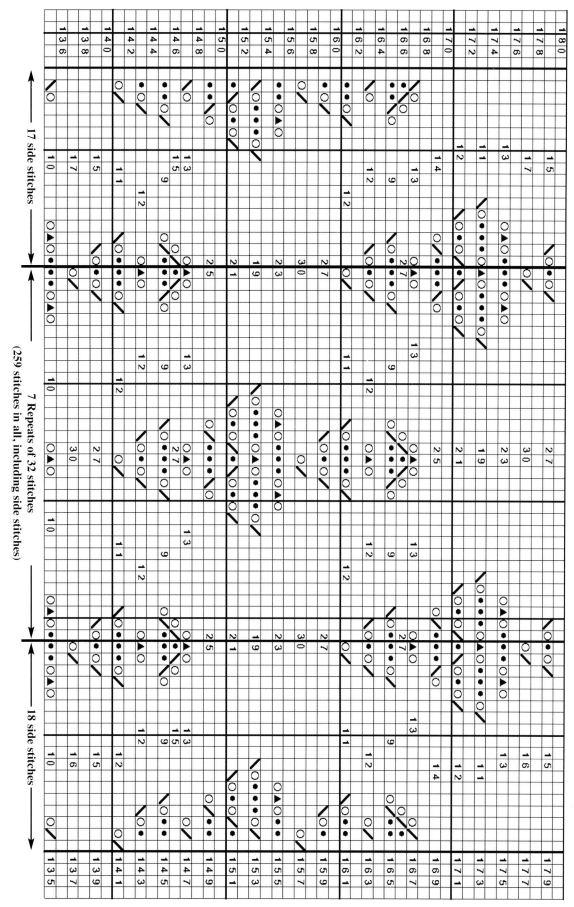

Row 135 given again for reference.

Christening Robe Skirt Lace – Rows 181 – 252*

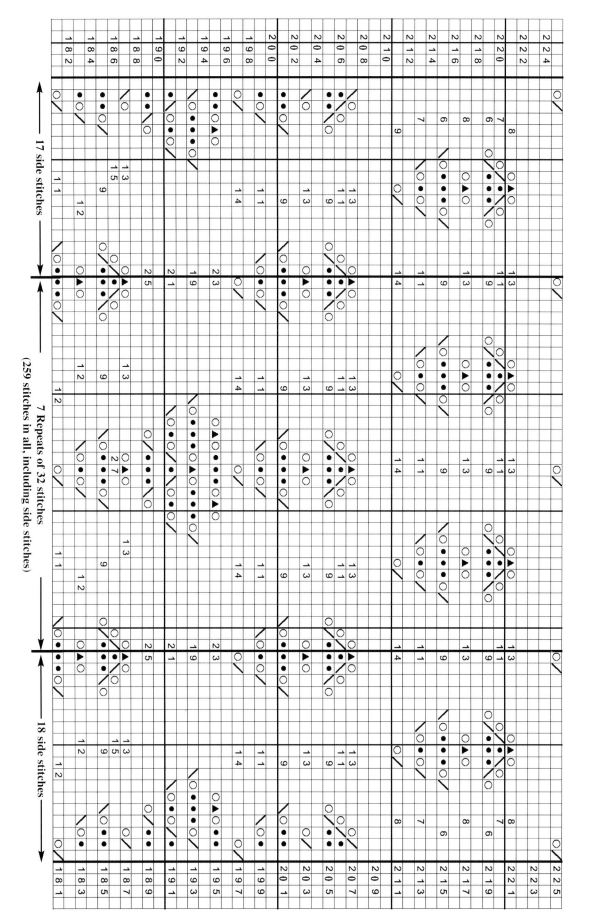

17 side stitches

After row 225, repeat rows 198 – 221 once; then knit 3 rows garter stitch to make 252 rows.

7 Repeats of 32 stitches
(259 stitches in all, including side stitches)

18 side stitches

Chart 7

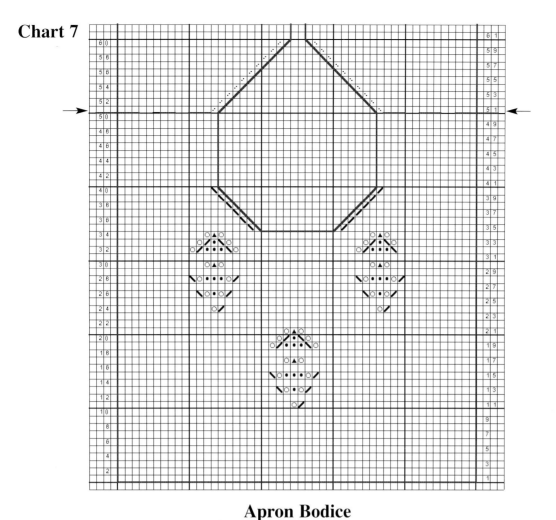

Apron Bodice
Front Chart

Arrows show the fold line that forms the front and back of the bodice (Row 50). Row 35: cast off 10 centre neck stitches.

(4) Bodice

Find the centre of the skirt's waistband and mark it with a pin. Using this as a guide, pick up 50 stitches (25 for each side of the pin) for the bodice – remove marker pin. Now knit the bodice – which as you can see from the diagram above, is like a square with a hole in it, – according to **chart 7** above. This chart is just to show the placing of the strawberry motifs on the bib front of the bodice and the shaping for the neckline – see picture detail below. The two sides of the back are indicated by row 61 which shows the start rows for the left and right sides and are knitted straight, from row 61 until row 100, then cast off. – In other words, each side is knitted separately and is a simple rectangular flap knitted in garter stitch, i.e. 24 stitches wide, by 40 rows long (counting from row 60).

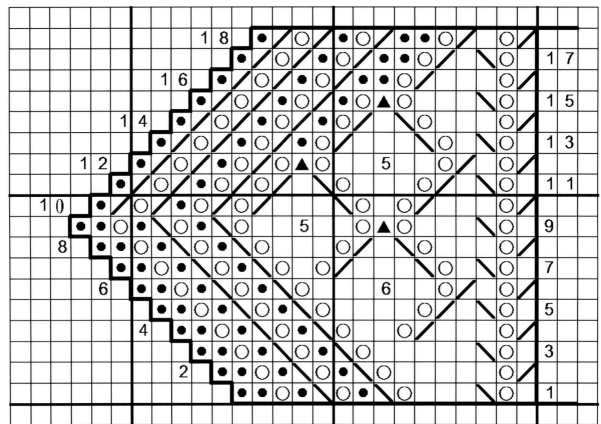

Cast on 14 stitches

(5 and 6) Armhole Edgings

On each side of the square bodice there are 50 side loops to attach the armhole edgings. I had decided that an odd number of edging points per side would look best because the centre point of one would then lie on the top of the shoulder (see photograph). The edging I chose had 18 rows for each pattern repeat which meant that it would naturally use up (18 divided by 2) x 5 = 45 stitches; so to work in the remaining five stitches I cast an extra one off from the *body* at the end of every row 18. It is tricky to knit this on as an edging and get each side's joining chain* of stitches to "mirror" the other; if you are unhappy with the effect you are achieving, knit each edging strip separately and stitch it on afterwards.

*Indicated by the arrow on photograph, right.

To Finish

Sew up back centre seam of skirt. Fold the bodice backs down and sew to waistband. Work a picot chain crochet edging** around the neckline and opening back. Sew three tiny buttons to the desired side – use opposite picot crochet loops as buttonholes. Sew in any remaining ends of wool securely and *dress*. See photograph on page 283.

** See page 236.

Order of knitting the Christening Robe Under Dress

1. Edging (with straight insertion) – knitted first
2. Skirt – knitted on stitches picked up from the edging (1)
3. Ribbing waistband (worked along decreased skirt top)
4. Bodice, front and back – knitted on stitches picked up from centre of (3)
5. Sleeve – left
6. Sleeve – right

Compare this to the apron diagram and notice the following differences: sleeves, ribbed waistband and longer skirt. Other than these, and that both sleeves and neck-line have a crocheted picot edging, this dress is completely plain.

Photograph shows the top half of the finished dress.

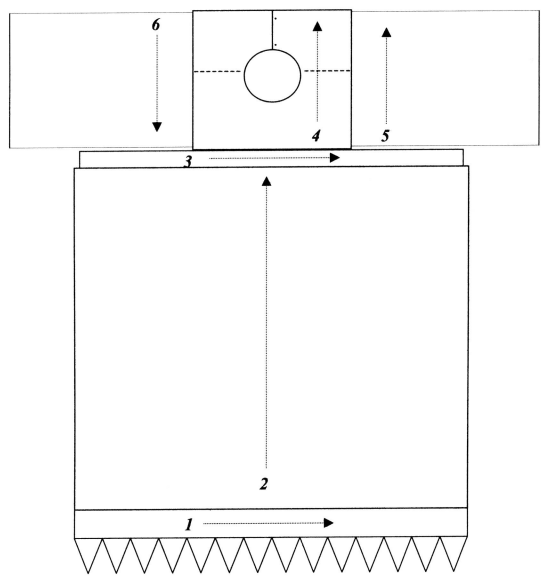

Dashed arrows show the knitting direction.

The Christening Robe Apron

The Christening Robe Dress

Order of Work

(1) Skirt Edging and Insertion

As for the apron exactly.

(2) Skirt

With the 259 stitches picked up from the edging, (and transferred to a size 10/3.25mm needle if preferred for quicker knitting, for the skirt only) start knitting in stocking stitch until the length of the skirt is approximately four inches (10cm) longer than the Christening Robe's apron.

(3) Waistband

Decrease row: Again with the smaller needle, work a row of "knit two together" to end. (128 sts.)

Now, work "knit 1, purl 1"* *ribbing* to make an elasticised waist-band of about two inches (5cm) in height. Cast off 39 stitches in rib at the beginning of the next two rows. (50sts.)

*I found it best to do all the "knit 1"s for this as "knit 1 through the back of the loop" so that each actual knit stitch is twisted; this gives a tighter, and therefore more elastic, ribbing.

(4) Bodice

Now knit the bodice (which as before, is like a square with a hole in it) according to the directions given for the apron, but this time, do not knit the strawberry motifs.

(5 and 6) Sleeves

On each side of the bodice square there are 50 side loops to attach the sleeves. From each of these sides in turn, pick up 60 stitches evenly and knit garter stitch for 100 rows (for approximately six inches/15cm). Cast off loosely.

To Finish

Sew up back centre seam of skirt to just above the ribbing waistband. Fold the bodice backs down and sew to waistband. Sew up sleeve seams and attach under-arms to waistband cast off. Work a picot chain crochet edging around each of the cuffs, the neckline and opening back. Sew two tiny buttons to the desired side – again, use opposite picot loops as buttonholes. Sew in any remaining ends of wool securely and *dress*.

Heirloom Knitting

Section Six – Miscellany

READY RECKONER

A Ready Reckoner is a table that helps with multiplying large numbers, e.g. for 17 x 43 – find 17 on the black top line and 43 on the black left column. Where these two lines meet is the answer: 17 x 43 = 731.

	2	3	4	5	6	7	8	9	10	11	12	13	14	15	16	17	18	19	20
11	22	33	44	55	66	77	88	99	110	121	132	143	154	165	176	187	198	209	220
12	24	36	48	60	72	84	96	108	120	132	144	156	168	180	192	204	216	228	240
13	26	39	52	65	78	91	106	117	130	143	156	169	182	195	208	221	234	248	260
14	28	42	56	70	84	98	112	126	140	154	168	182	196	210	224	238	252	266	280
15	30	45	60	75	90	105	120	135	150	165	180	195	210	225	260	255	170	185	300
16	32	48	64	80	96	112	128	144	160	176	192	208	224	240	256	272	288	304	320
17	34	51	68	85	102	119	136	153	170	187	204	221	238	256	272	289	306	323	340
18	36	54	72	90	108	126	144	162	180	198	216	234	252	270	288	306	324	342	360
19	38	57	76	95	114	133	152	171	190	209	228	247	266	285	304	323	342	361	380
20	40	60	80	100	120	140	160	180	200	220	240	260	282	300	320	340	360	380	400
21	42	63	84	105	126	147	168	189	210	230	252	273	294	315	336	357	378	399	420
22	44	66	88	110	132	154	176	198	220	242	264	286	308	330	352	374	396	418	440
23	46	69	92	115	138	161	184	207	230	253	276	299	322	345	368	391	414	438	460
24	48	72	96	120	144	168	192	216	240	264	288	312	336	360	384	408	432	456	480
25	50	5	100	125	150	175	200	225	250	275	300	325	350	375	400	425	450	475	500
26	52	78	104	130	156	182	208	234	260	286	312	338	364	390	406	442	468	494	520
27	54	80	108	135	162	189	206	243	270	297	324	351	378	405	432	459	486	513	540
28	56	84	112	140	168	196	224	252	280	308	336	364	392	420	448	476	504	532	560
29	58	87	116	145	174	203	232	261	290	319	348	377	406	435	464	493	522	551	580
30	60	90	120	150	180	210	240	270	300	330	360	390	420	450	480	510	540	570	600
31	62	93	124	255	286	217	248	279	310	340	372	403	434	465	496	518	558	589	620
32	64	96	128	160	192	224	256	2788	320	352	384	416	448	480	512	544	576	608	640
33	66	99	132	165	198	231	264	297	330	363	396	429	462	495	528	561	574	627	660
34	68	102	136	170	204	238	272	306	340	374	408	442	276	510	544	578	612	646	680
35	70	105	140	175	210	245	280	315	350	385	420	455	490	525	560	595	630	335	700
36	72	108	144	180	216	252	288	324	360	396	432	468	504	540	476	612	648	684	720
37	74	111	148	185	222	259	296	333	370	407	444	481	518	555	592	629	666	703	740
38	76	114	152	190	228	266	304	342	380	418	456	494	532	470	608	646	684	722	760
39	78	117	156	195	234	273	312	351	390	429	468	507	546	585	624	663	702	741	780
40	80	120	160	200	240	280	320	360	400	440	480	520	560	600	640	680	720	760	800
41	82	123	164	205	246	287	328	369	410	450	492	33	574	605	656	697	738	779	820
42	84	126	168	210	252	294	336	378	420	462	504	546	588	630	672	714	756	798	840
43	86	129	172	245	258	301	344	387	430	473	516	559	602	645	688	731	774	817	860
44	88	132	176	220	264	308	352	396	440	484	528	572	616	660	704	748	792	836	880
45	90	135	180	225	270	315	360	405	450	495	540	585	630	675	720	765	810	855	900
46	92	138	184	230	276	322	368	414	460	506	552	598	644	690	736	782	828	874	920
47	94	141	188	235	282	329	376	423	470	517	564	611	658	705	752	799	846	893	940
48	96	144	192	240	288	336	384	432	480	528	576	624	672	720	768	816	864	912	960
49	98	147	196	245	294	343	392	441	490	539	588	627	686	735	784	833	882	931	980
50	100	150	200	250	300	350	400	450	500	550	600	650	700	750	800	850	900	950	1000

EUROPEAN/AMERICAN COMPARISON CHARTS

Metric Needle Sizes	British Needle Sizes	American Needle Sizes
1.75mm	15	000/00
2.00mm	14	00/0
2.25mm	13	0/1
2.75mm	12	1/2
3.00mm	11	2
3.25mm	10	3
3.50/3.75mm	9	4/5
4.00mm	8	5/6
4.50mm	7	6/7
5.00mm	6	7/8
5.50mm	5	8/9
6.00mm	4	9/10
6.50mm	3	10/10.5
7.00mm	2	10.5
7.50mm	1	10.5/11
8.50mm/9mm	00	13
9.00mm/10.00mm	000	15

Cms	Inches
0.5	¼
1	½
2	¾
3	1¼
4	1½
5	2
6	2¼
7	2¾
8	3¼
9	3½
10	4
20	7¾
30	11¾
40	15¾
50	19¾
100	39½

Grams	Ounces
28	1
57	2
85	3
113	4
142	5
170	6
198	7
227	8
255	9
283	10
312	11
340	12
369	13
397	14
425	15
454	16

N.B. The conversions are approximate and are for guidance only: e.g. more exactly, 1 ounce = 28.35 grams.

Children's Size Chart

The sizes given in the guidance table below are based on averages for each age range (in other words, give the medium size for that age). Remember, children grow at very different rates, and if you are making for a particular child it would be best to measure him/her first and work from that information. As a rule of thumb, find the child's actual chest measurement* and work from the information given on the line matching that size in the table.

N.B. All metric to imperial equivalents are approximate and are for guidance only.

Age	Height	Weight (up to)	To Fit Actual Chest*	Coat Length**	Dress Length**	Shoulder Seam	Length of Armhole***	Sleeve Seam Length
0 – 6 mths	69cm/27"	8kg/17lbs	43cm/17"	23cm/9"	36cm/14"	5cm/2"	7½cm/3"	15cm/6"
6 – 12 mths	76cm/30"	10kg/22lbs	47cm/18½"	25cm/10"	38cm/15"	5cm/2"	9cm/3"	16cm/6"
18 mths	85cm/33"	–	48cm/19"	28cm/11"	43cm/17"	5½cm/3"	9cm/3½"	18cm/7"
24 mths	91cm/36"	–	51cm/20"	30½cm/12"	46cm/18"	6½cm/2½"	9½cm/3¾"	20cm/8"
2-3 yrs	97cm/38"	–	52cm/20½"	33cm/13"	48cm/19"	6cm/2½"	10cm/4"	23cm/8"
3-4 yrs	104cm/41"	–	55cm/21½"	35½cm/14"	53cm/21"	7cm/2¾"	11½cm/4½"	25½cm/10"
4-5 yrs	109cm/43"	–	56cm/22"	38cm/15"	56cm/22	7cm/2¾"	12cm/4¾"	28cm/11"

*This means unclothed, just under the arms. The finished garment should be 5 cm / 2" larger around the chest. So for a baby with a 17" (43cm) chest, you should make a coat with a 19" (48cm) chest measurement, that has a sleeve seam length of 6" (15cm) and measures 9" (23cm) from collar to hem.

** Measured from collar to hem, unlike the other measurements given, the coat length and dress length are more affected by fashion and individual growth rates. To get the recommended figures quoted here, I divided the given height by 3 to get the coat length, and by 2 to get the dress length. If you are making long dresses (e.g. Christening Robes) you can make these as long as you think practical.

*** From top of shoulder to 2.5cm / 1" below actual armpit. The measurement quoted is for each of the fronts and back, so this means each "top of sleeve" width should be twice the figure quoted, e.g. for the age 0 – 6 ms, the maximum width of the sleeve top would be 6" (15cm) to fit the armhole opening.

Appendix 4
Explications Françaises Des Cartes

●   Une maille à l'endroit.

─   Une maille à l'envers.

○   C'est à dire, faire un jeté simple; jeté à l'endroit, passer la laine devant le travail.

○○   Double jeté à l'endroit.

╲ or ╱   Une diminution: ╱   Une diminution à droite.
                                     ╲   Une diminution à gauche.

▲   Une maille glissée, deux mailles ensemble à l'endroit, rabattre la maille glissée.

⊠   Fermeture des mailles.

◹   Faites comme indiqué mais avec 2 mailles pour cette carre.

＞   Une maille glissée en la prenart à l'endroit.

∴   Augmentation dans une maille.

★   Instruction extraordinary.*

"cast on"   monter les mailles.

N.B. Les carrés de vide, y compris ceux-là avec les numeros devraient être jarretière de point. Chaque rang bizarre d'un graphique est travaillé de la droite pour partir, chaque même rang d'un graphic est travaillé de part à la droite.

* Expliqué dans le texte anglais.

Appendix 5
Strickschrift – Answeisungen in Deutsch
Zeichenerklarung

●   Eine Masche rechts stricken.

—   Eine Masche links stricken.

○   Aufgelegt; Einmal umschlagen. Sind mehrere Umschläge nebeneinander, so werden diese in der folgenden Reihe oder Runde abwechselnd rechts und links abgestrickt.

○○   Doppler Umschlag.

╲ or ╱   Zwei Maschen rechts zusammenstricken: ╱   rechts abnehemen.
                                                     ╲   durch eine Masche überzierhen.

▲   Durch zwei Maschen überzierhen.

⊠   Abketten der Maschen.

╲°   Zwei soche Zeichen bedeuten, dass sich der Anfang der runde um zwei Maschen verschiebt wie oben erklärt.

>   Eine Masche abheben.

∵   Eine Zunahmen; Zwie Maschen recht stricken.

★   Besondere Anweisungen.*

"cast on"   Anschlagen von Maschen.

N.B. Leere Quadrate, derer mit Zahlen sollen in garter stich gestrickt werden. Jede ungewöhnliche Reihe eines Diagramms wird von rechts zu, jede ebene. Reihe eines Diagramms von von links nach rechts gearbeitet verlassen wird gearbeitet.

* Erklärt im englischen Text.

Amedro, Gladys, *Shetland Lace* Shetland Times Ltd., Lerwick, 1993.
Abbey, Barbara, *Barbara Abbey's Knitting Lace,* The Viking Press, London, 1974.
Abbey, Barbara, *The Complete Book of Knitting,* The Viking Press, London, 1971.
Carter, Hazel, *Shetland Lace Knitting From Charts* (booklet, USA) 1987.
Compton, Rae,* *The Complete Book of Traditional Knitting,* B. T. Batsford, London, 1983.
Don, Sarah, *The Art of Shetland Lace, Bell and Hyman*, London, 1980.
Fryer, Linda,* *Knitting by the Fireside and on the Hillside,* Shetland Times Ltd., Lerwick, 1995.
Lorant, Tessa, *The Batsford Book of Hand and Machine Knitted Laces,* B. T. Batsford, London, 1982.
Norbury, James, *Traditional Knitting Patterns,* B. T. Batsford, London, 1962.
Pearson, Michael,* *Traditional Knitting,* William Collins Sons & Co Ltd, London, 1984.
Rutt, Richard,* *A History of Knitting,* B.T. Batsford Ltd 1987 & Interweave Press, Loveland, Colorado, 1987.
Smith, Mary & Bunyan, Chris,* *A Shetland Knitter's Notebook,* Shetland Times Ltd., Lerwick, 1991.
Stove, Margaret,* *Creating Original Hand-knitted Lace,* Hale, London, 1995.
Thomas, Mary,* *Mary Thomas's Knitting Book,* Hodder & Stoughton, Ltd, London, 1938.
Thomas, Mary, *Mary Thomas's Book Of Knitting Patterns,* Hodder & Stoughton Ltd, London, 1943.
Walker, Barbara G, *A Treasury of Knitting Patterns,* Charles Scribner's Sons, New York, 1968.
Walker, Barbara G, *A Second Treasury of Knitting Patterns,* Charles Scribner's Sons, New York, 1970.
Walker, Barbara G, *The Craft of Lace Knitting,* Charles Scribner's Sons, New York, 1971.
Walker, Barbara G, *Charted Knitting Designs,* Charles Scribner's Sons, New York, 1972.
Waterman, Martha, *Traditional Knitted Lace Shawls,* Interweave Press, Loveland, Colorado, 1998.

Suppliers

Shetland Wool
The wool used in this book is supplied by:

Jamieson and Smith
The Wool Brokers
90 North Road, Lerwick,
Shetland ZE1 0PQ
Tel 01595 693579   Fax 01595 695009

Jamieson's Knitwear
93/95 Commercial Street, Lerwick,
Shetland, ZE1 0BD
Tel 01595 693114   Fax 01595 870297

Specialist Knitting Needles
Handmade very fine needles, suitable for knitting ultra fine lace such as handkerchief edgings or doll's clothes are made to order from miniature knitting suppliers such as:

"Minknit" – 14 Woodbank Drive, Brandlesholme, Bury BL8 1DR
Tel 0161 797 7983   www.minknit.freeserve.co.uk

Needles are made from polished steel and are sized British 16 – 24 (not 17s or 23s) Metric 1.6mm – O.55mm

*Reference books that include information about Shetland Lace and/or the history of knitting

Glossary

Allover A Shetland term for a *centre* pattern.

Binding Off The American term for *casting off*.

Bobbling A descriptive term for the yarn balls that form on the surface of a knitted fabric that is rubbed. A yarn that bobbles is normally unsuitable for lace knitting. Another term for this is pilling.

Body My term for the main part of the knitting. In a stole, the body is the centre pattern plus borders.

Border See page 48.

Break Pattern Like punctuation, a small pattern dividing off elements, see page 268.

Cast Up Shetland term for *casting on*.

Centre The main, middle part of a scarf, stole or shawl. A centre pattern was a pattern suitable to use for as centre – also known as an "allover" or "fill in" pattern in Shetland.

Circular Needle An early 20th century invention of a double-ended knitting needle with a flexible middle part. Initially, the flex was made from fine, steel cable linking the two steel pins; now, aluminium pins are linked by a plastic flex. See "Knitting Needles and Tension", Section Two.

Clew An Old English word for a wound ball of thread or wool, possibly derived from "claw" – perhaps because the hand resembles a claw when the ball is wound.

Close Worked My term for a knitted lace pattern made by omitting the plain knitted alternate rows in a known lace knitting pattern, e.g. Madeira and Diamond Pattern, with the plain rows omitted becomes Madeira and Diamond Lace. See Trellis Diamond Pattern II – page 63.

Cloud In this context, a fanciful 19th century word for a lady's lacy, airy, knitted scarf.

Combing A process that prepares wool for spinning. See "Yarn Production" – Section Four.

Course The formal term for a *row* or *round* in knitting – the horizontal element, as distinct from *wale*.

Crepe An 18th century word to describe a thin, *worsted*, gauzy fabric; used in the 19th century to describe the plain knitted centre of a Shetland Shawl. Also known as Crapes. Relating to the word "crisp", crepe *yarns* are more tightly twisted, which makes their finished knitting appear crisper in stitch structure.

Crimp The natural waviness in a wool or fleece. See "Yarn Production", Section Four.

Crochet A method of constructing a fabric of interlocking loops using a single hooked pin. Crocheted edgings can be added to knitted items to finish them – see "Baby Jacket, Project 1", Section Five.

Cut A measurement of *yarn*, a *hank* or *skein*. See "Yarn Production".

Decrease A term used to describe two stitches being knitted together to reduce their number e.g. "Knit 2 together" is a single decrease, because there is now 1 stitch less than there was before. See "Stitch Advice".

Delayed Decrease A method of producing stitches which appear to slant or "lean over" in the finished pattern – produced by making an increase which isn't immediately followed by a *decrease*, e.g. "make 1, knit 2, knit 2 together"; see Print O' the Wave Pattern – page 71.

Directional A pattern is said to be directional if it has a "right way up", or appears "upside down" if turned through 180 degrees, e.g. Print O' the Wave Pattern, page 71; a lot of *Border* designs are directional.

Double Decrease A term used to describe three stitches being knitted together to produce a single stitch – decreasing the number of stitches by two at that point. The commonest double decreases are "knit 3 together" and "slip 1, knit 2 together, pass slipped stitch over".

Double Increase The formal term for making 2 stitches, usually by "two yarns around needle" in lace knitting, making a large *eyelet*.

Dressing The Shetland term for the process of washing and stretching a finished piece of knitting. See "Dressing Instructions", Section Two. Also known as "blocking" in America.

Drops A Shetland name for an e*yelet* pattern, so called because the eyelets resemble dew drops.

Easing A term used to describe how an edging is gathered and spread around a corner so it lies flat when *dressed*; see "Attaching an Edging", Section Two.

Edging One of the three main elements used in making a traditional *Shetland Shawl*, usually made first or last of all. See "Shetland Shawls", Section Four. Known in Shetland as "lace".

Eyelet The formal name for a hole made in knitting by a "make 1", or "yarn over".

Faggot A lacy pattern, usually of zigzags, made by knitting paired *increases* and *decreases*. Taken from the embroidery term, which is believed to be based on the appearance of a bundle of sticks.

Feather Pattern An alternative 19th century name for the Old Shell Pattern.

Fill In See *Centre*. Also the fine small patterns that go inside geometric shapes.

Fingering Originally "fingram" (17th century) probably derived from the French "fin grain" – fine grain. A fine spun, *worsted* yarn; still in use in the 20th century.

Flat Knitting As opposed to "knitting in the round" (a jumper traditionally made on sets of double pointed pins was knitted in the round). "Flat knitting" means the rows were knitted back and forth, with the needles changing hands with each row.

Floss "Shetland Floss" was a loosely spun 2 ply, *worsted* woollen yarn. French in origin.

Fold American equivalent of *ply*.

Garter Stitch The formal name for the fabric which is formed by rows of knitted stitches only – i.e. each row would read "knit to the end". Originally so-called, as this was the commonest way to finish the tops, or garters of stockings. A traditional *centre* pattern in the *Crepe* Shawl.

Gauge The American equivalent of *tension*.

Grafting The invisible sewing together of two pieces of knitting, using a technique that threads the sewing yarn through the sets of stitches so that they appear as if they had been knitted. Earliest known reference in regard to knitting, dates from 1880. This type of grafting from two knitting needles is known as Kitchener Stitch, or "weaving". See "How To Graft", Knitting Advice.

Ground The stocking stitch or garter stitch background the lace pattern stitches are worked on.

Half Staggering This means motifs are not in serried line but are regularly offset. See "How To Adapt A Pattern".

Hand Cards Wooden implements used to prepare wool for spinning. See "Yarn Production" – Section Four.

Hank An Old Norse word dating from the 13th century. Another name for a measure of yarn, synonym of skein. Describes a large coil of wool or thread as supplied by the spinners. Wool supplied in hanks needs to be loosely wound into balls before knitting; see "Yarn", Section Two.

Hap Mediaeval English (obsolete) to wrap up warm. A Shetland name for a small, plainly made, everyday shoulder shawl, usually made in dark colours so it didn't need frequent washing.

Herring Bone Stitch An embroidery stitch used to make elastic joins when sewing together borders in Imitation *Shetland Shawls*.

Hole Another Shetland name for an *eyelet*.

Increase The formal term for a "make 1" or "yarn forward", produces an *eyelet*. A single increase means "make 1"; a *double increase* means "make 2", etc. See "Stitch Advice".

Insertion A "ribbon" of patterned knitting, usually accompanies an edging pattern.

Intake Shetland term for *decreasing*.

Invisible Casting On A method of making an unobtrusive cast on – see "How to Cast On", Knitting Advice, where three suitable castings on are explained.

Kitchener Stitch Another early 20th century term for a form of *Grafting*. See "How To Graft", Section Two.

Knit Old English, derived from North European "cnyttan" for tie in, or knot. Earliest traced reference to the forming of a fabric dates from the 16th century. See "Stitch Advice", Section Two.

Knitting Pins One of the many alternative names for knitting needles.

Knitting Sheath The wooden holder (which was worn on the knitter's belt) into which the unused end of a double pointed needle could be inserted while the other end was being worked. Similar in purpose to the *whisk*; using such an item enabled the knitter to work at speed because one hand was freed from holding a needle. In use since the mid 18th century, early knitting sheaths were often highly carved and were often given as love tokens.

Knitting Whisk Deriving originally from a bunch of straw twisted together, this was applied to a filled and covered pad worn on a belt, into which the sharp end of a double pointed knitting needle was placed while the other end was being used. Similar to a Knitting Sheath in function. A Shetland term, also known as a Whisker or Wisker.

Knitwise To insert a needle into a stitch as if to make a knit stitch, i.e. from the left side of the front strand of a stitch loop.

Lacy Edge Stitch An elastic, fancy, loopy finish to the outside of an edging – see page 118.

Lady Betty Wool A very fine, soft and airy wool, originally available in white only; the finest commercially supplied wool of the early 19th century. Possibly named in commemoration of Lady Elizabeth Germaine (1680 – 1769) whose spinning wheels were at Knole, Kent, England. Lady Betty Wool was still in use in the 20th century.

Lay up The Shetland term for *casting on*.

Left Loop The Shetland term for *purl* stitch.

Loft A description of wool's lightness/texture. See "Yarn Production", Section Four.

Loop 1. The Shetland term for a stitch. 2. Another name for an *over* or "make 1" (19th century).

Loop About The Shetland term for "plain and purl".

Macking The Shetland term for knitting, possibly derived from "making", itself an Old English/North European word.

Madeira The Shetland name for a fan-like pattern made in lace knitting, possibly reflecting the Spanish contribution to the Shetland tradition of knitting.

Make 1 Make 1 - a single *increase*. Make 2 – a *double increase*. Another expression for "yarn over". See "Stitch Advice".

Matinee Coat An early 20th century term for a fancy baby coat or jacket.

Misknits My term for stitches that have been wrongly made in some respect.

Needles Another name for knitting needles or pins.

Niddy Noddy A 19th century term for a hand held "T" shape of wood, used for measuring and winding wool into *hanks*. Known in Shetland as a reel.

Open Stitch An *eyelet*, a mid 19th century term used by Jane Gaugain in the first knitting manuals.

Over The old term for "yarn over needle", "yarn around needle" or "make 1". Also, an obsolete term for "bring wool forward" – as if to *purl*.

Pattern Derived from the word Mediaeval English/Old French "patron", became by the 16th century to mean a model object or design. Today, a knitting pattern is understood to mean the specific written instructions/directions to make a particular knitted item. The first known English knitting pattern is called "the order how to knit a hose" and is printed in a medical directory dated 1655 – "Natura Exenterata – or Nature Unbowelled".

Pattern Stitches/Rows My term for the stitches that are altered in their structure (usually by *increases* and *decreases*) in a row of knitting. As distinct from the ordinary knit stitches that are *plain* or *garter stitched*. Pattern rows are rows with pattern stitches worked in.

Peerie The Shetland word for "small", e.g. "Peerie Flea" page 152 is a small pattern.

Pick up The formal term for adding stitches to a knitting needle by taking them from the edge *loops* of an existing piece of knitting. See "How to Attach an Edging", Section Two. A 17th century term.

Picot From the French "picoter" meaning to mark with pricks or points (18th century). Now used to mean a tiny pointed edging made with a narrow strip of knitting or by crochet.

Pilling See *Bobbling*.

Pin Another term for a knitting needle.

Plain Intake Rare 19th century terms for the following: 1. Plain intake – "knit 2 together". 2. Plain intake taken from behind – "knit 2 together through back of loops".

Plain Knitting A term that describes un-patterned knitting; i.e. all *garter stitched*.

Plain Macking The Shetland term for *Flat Knitting*.

Plain Stitches/Rows My term when referring to ordinary, *garter stitched* or knit stitches. Plain rows are rows without pattern stitches – usually garter stitched throughout.

Ply Describes the number of separately spun "threads" twisted together to form a yarn or wool, such as 1 ply (a single thread) 2 ply (two threads) 3 ply (three threads), etc. The number of a ply doesn't necessarily always equate to the actual thickness of a yarn. See "Substituting Yarn", Section Two.

Pricks The Old English term for knitting needles, dating from the late 16th century.

Pull Over One Rare term for slipping a stitch. "Pull over one – Take in" means "slip 1, knit 1, pass slipped stitch over".

Pull Stitch Over An American term for "pass *slip* stitch over".

Purl Possibly derived from "pearl", the appearance to the knitter of a single purled stitch. First traced usage in the knitting sense dates from the mid 17th century.

Purled Intake Rare 19th century term for "purl 2 together".

Purlwise To insert a needle into a stitch as if to make a purl stitch, i.e. from the right side of the loop.

Receipt An old (obsolete?) term for the written directions for a knitting pattern.

Reef Knot A non-slipping or binding knot used to join threads. Made by taking the left hand strand (white) over the right hand strand (black) and tucking it under. Then, to finish, by taking the right hand strand (now white) and placing it over the left hand strand (now black) and tucking it under. Pull to tighten. Look at the picture, the first part of the knot is at the bottom.

Reggies The Shetland term for *garter stitch*.

Reserved Stitches Stitches that are left over but not cast off.

Ribbing A dense, elastic, two row pattern, made of alternate pairs of "knit and purl stitches to end of first row", "purl and knit stitches to end of second row"; which produces distinct vertical lines in the finished knitting. Usually done for *welts*.

Ridge The Shetland term for the pronounced horizontal line that appears on both sides of the knitting when two rows of *garter stitch* have been worked.

Right Loop The Shetland term for a knit stitch.

Ring Shawl An extremely finely knitted large shawl, usually of intricate lacy design, made from a one ply yarn so finely spun that the whole of the shawl can be pulled through a wedding ring. Also called Wedding Ring Shawls, see "Historical Background".

Roache A type of small Shetland pattern, possibly resembling strawberries, see page 225.

Roo The Shetland term for plucking the fine neck wool from the native sheep. This process enables the maximum length of the softest wool to be drawn for spinning, as it isn't cut. Said to be painless to the sheep! Earliest traced reference dates from the 1600's. See "Historical Background" – Section One.

Round A course in circular or tubular knitting; as distinct from a course or *row* in *flat knitting*.

Row Another term for a *course*, usually in *flat knitting*. The number of stitches on a knitting needle has a direct relationship to the length of the row. Simply speaking, if there are 30 stitches on the needle, once they have all been knitted, that row has been completed. Dating from the early 19th century, this denotes a course in flat knitting that has to be worked. When the flat knitting is turned because all the stitches on a needle have been used up, that row is finished. The next row is ready to be knitted once the knitting needles have changed hands, so that the needle with stitches on is in the left hand and the right hand holds the "empty" needle.

Row Repeat Block My term for the "block" of rows to be regularly repeated in a knitting pattern.

Shell Another name for the popular Shetland pattern Old Shell. See page 51.

Shetland Shawl This specially refers to the shawls that were traditionally knitted in the Shetland Islands, without any casting off. All joins were (and still are) done by grafting, usually the edgings were knitted first, the borders picked up from the edging stitches and then the centre pattern was finally made. Imitation Shetland shawls are easier to knit because some of the elements are sewn together. See "Shetland Shawls" – Section Four.

Shetland Wool First commercially available in the mid 19th century, this was a very soft, fine, naturally coloured, light, two ply *worsted* yarn, finer than *fingering*, originally, but not always, from the Shetland Isles. Mentioned in Mrs Gaskell's novel of domestic gentility, "Cranford" (1853) chapter 2.

Side Loop When picking up stitches from the selvedge (side) of a knitted article, this refers to the single strands at the edge of each *row*. Normally, it is advised to pick up one stitch from between each *ridge* (pair of *rows*).

Single Increase or **Decrease** See *Increase/Decrease*.

Single Macking The Shetland term for *Flat Knitting*.

Skein Unknown origin – possibly French. A loose coil of yarn or thread, synonym of *hank*.

Slip To transfer a stitch from the left hand needle to the right without knitting it – "slipped".

Slip & Bind Rare term for "slip 1, knit 1, pass slipped stitch over".

Slip Knot There are several ways to make slip (or running) knots. This is one of them: Start by making a single knot near the end of a thread from a ball of wool – do not pull it tight, picture 1. Now, take the "free" end and feed it back through the knot, picture 2. Finish by pulling on the pairs of threads on both sides of the knot to tighten, picture 3. This is a good way of making the first of a number of cast on stitches. N.B. Pulling on the free end undoes the knot.

Spacing Rows My term for the plain knitted rows that are inserted between bands of pattern to make the patterns more distinct (see Pattern and Lace Hole Stripe Design, where for example, the four rows 8 – 11 are plain knitted).

Spencer Named after the Earl of Spencer (1758 – 1834), this was a 19th century term for a closely fitting jacket, usually worn by women and children.

Splice Join A method of joining knitting yarn securely. See "Knitting Advice".

Staple The length of a fibre, usually wool. See "Yarn Production" – Section Four.

Steek Diamond A Shetland name for a diamond-shaped pattern with a small bead diamond *fill-in* (see page 226). Often used as an element in a border design

Stitch Dating from the late 16th century, this is the formal term for a single loop on a knitting needle intended to be knitted. The Shetland term is simply "loop".

Stockinette Stitch The American term for *Stocking Stitch*.

Stocking Stitch The two row knitting pattern in which stockings were commonly worked, i.e. in alternating rows of knit and purl. This produces an elastic fabric that has a smooth surface, customarily shown on the outside.

Take In A Shetland term for *decreasing*. "Take In With 3 Stitches" means "slip 1, knit 2 together, pass slipped stitch over"– a *double decrease*.

Tension See "Knitting Needles and Tension", Section Two.

Thread As distinct from *yarn*. I use this to denote a non-elastic spun fibre for knitting, e.g. cotton, linen or silk. See "Yarn Production", Section Four.

Twin Pin An American term for a *Circular Needle*.

Un-bordered My term for a shawl or stole made using only two patterns – a centre pattern and an edging, without any borders in the design. These were commonly made as ladies head squares, scarves and stoles in the 19th century.

Unravelled This means taking the knitting off the pins and completely undoing it. See "Dealing With Mistakes".

Unst Lace A Victorian term for the intricately patterned Shetland laces, usually made on the northern-most of the Shetland Isles where the wool was finer.

Vandyke An edging constructed with pronounced points; now a Shetland term, named after the collars portrayed by Sir Antony Vandyke 1599 – 1641.

Wale A vertical column of loops or stitches in knitting. Mediaeval origin. See also *Course*.

Welt A thicker band of knitting e.g. the *ribbing* around neck, cuffs and bottom of a jersey.

Wheeling An early 19th century coarsely spun 3 ply yarn.

White Knitting As it says, knitting which was worked entirely in white, commonly finely knitted or lacy knitting. A 19th century term.

Wire A Shetland and Old English term for a knitting needle.

Wool Forward A single *increase*, one of the many variations of "make 1".

Woollen Yarn As distinct from *Worsted* yarn. See "Yarn Production", Section Four.

Worsted Also known as Wassit or Worset, derived from Worsted, Norfolk, England; a tightly spun woollen *yarn* originally made there since Mediaeval times. In the 19th century, worsted applied to any knitting yarn broadly equivalent to a modern 4 ply/double knitting. See "Yarn Production", Section Four.

Yard An Imperial measurement – 3 feet/36 inches. Metric equivalent – 91cm approx.

Yardage A measurement in *yards*.

Yarn An elastic, spun fibre for knitting with – usually made from wool. I have made a distinction between yarn and *thread*. See "Yarn Production", Section Four.

Yarn Over A single *increase*, another of the many variations of "make 1". Also known as "yarn forward".

Zephyr In this context, a fanciful 19th century term for a light, finely knitted item, usually an airy shawl. Originally, a gentle breeze from the West.

 # Index of Patterns